COVID-19 COLLABORATIONS

Researching Poverty and Low-Income Family Life during the Pandemic

Edited by
Kayleigh Garthwaite, Ruth Patrick, Maddy Power,
Anna Tarrant, and Rosalie Warnock

With a foreword by
Alison Garnham, Chief Executive,
Child Poverty Action Group, and an afterword by
Cat Fortey, participant in Covid Realities

D1610497

P

First published in Great Britain in 2022 by

Policy Press, an imprint of
Bristol University Press
University of Bristol
1–9 Old Park Hill
Bristol
BS2 8BB
UK
t: +44 (0)117 374 6645
e: bup-info@bristol.ac.uk

Details of international sales and distribution partners are available at
policy.bristoluniversitypress.co.uk

British Library Cataloguing in Publication Data
A catalogue record for this book is available from the British Library

ISBN 978-1-4473-6448-1 paperback
ISBN 978-1-4473-6449-8 ePub
ISBN 978-1-4473-6450-4 ePdf

Cover design: Tom Flannery
Front cover image: Luke Jones/Unsplash
Bristol University Press and Policy Press use environmentally responsible print partners.
Printed in Great Britain by CMP, Poole

Contents

List of figures and tables   v
List of abbreviations   vi
Notes on contributors   vii
Acknowledgements   xviii
Foreword   xix
Alison Garnham

Introduction   1
Kayleigh Garthwaite, Rosalie Warnock, Ruth Patrick,
Maddy Power, and Anna Tarrant

PART I   Social security in the spotlight
1   Bringing up a family and making ends meet: before and   15
        during the COVID-19 crisis
        Ruth Webber and Katherine Hill
2   Welfare at a (Social) Distance: accessing social security and 30
        employment support during COVID-19 and its aftermath
        David Robertshaw, Kate Summers, Lisa Scullion, Daniel Edmiston,
        Ben Baumberg Geiger, Andrea Gibbons, Jo Ingold, Robert de Vries,
        and David Young
3   Families navigating Universal Credit in the COVID-19 pandemic 44
        Rita Griffiths, Marsha Wood, Fran Bennett, and Jane Millar
4   Complex lives: exploring experiences of Universal Credit   56
        claimants in Salford during COVID-19
        Lisa Scullion, Andrea Gibbons, Joe Pardoe, Catherine Connors,
        and Dave Beck

PART II   Intersecting insecurities in action
5   The impact of the COVID-19 pandemic on families living in   73
        the ethnically diverse and deprived city of Bradford: findings
        from the longitudinal Born in Bradford COVID-19
        research programme
        Josie Dickerson, Bridget Lockyer, Claire McIvor, Daniel D. Bingham, Kirsty
        L. Crossley, Charlotte Endacott, Rachael H. Moss, Helen Smith, Kate
        E. Pickett, and Rosie R.C. McEachan, on behalf of the Bradford Institute
        for Health Research Covid-19 Scientific Advisory Group

6   A tale of two cities in London's East End: impacts of   88
        COVID-19 on low- and high-income families with young
        children and pregnant women
        Claire Cameron, Hanan Hauari, Michelle Heys, Katie Hollingworth,
        Margaret O'Brien, Sarah O'Toole, and Lydia Whitaker
7   Size matters: experiences of larger families on a low income   106
        during COVID-19
        Mary Reader and Kate Andersen
8   Caring without Sharing: how single parents worked and   122
        cared during the pandemic
        Elizabeth Clery and Laura Dewar
9   The impacts of the COVID-19 pandemic on young fathers   135
        and the services that support them
        Anna Tarrant, Laura Way, and Linzi Ladlow
10   Social security during COVID-19: the experiences of   149
        military veterans
        Lisa Scullion, Philip Martin, Celia Hynes, and David Young

PART III Innovating in sharing experiences during COVID-19
11   "Together we are making a difference": participatory research   165
        with families living on a low income during the pandemic
        Geoff Page and Katie Pybus
12   Living through a pandemic: researching families on a low   179
        income in Scotland – findings and research reflections
        Beth Cloughton, Fiona McHardy, and Laura Robertson
13   The Commission on Social Security and participatory research   193
        during the pandemic: new context, abiding challenges
        Rosa Morris, Ellen Morrison, Michael Orton, and Kate Summers
14   UC:Us now? Reflections from participatory research with   204
        Universal Credit claimants during COVID-19
        Ruth Patrick, Ciara Fitzpatrick, Mark Simpson, and
        Jamie Redman with UC:Us Members

Conclusion   218
Rosalie Warnock, Kayleigh Garthwaite, Ruth Patrick,
Maddy Power, and Anna Tarrant
Afterword   227
Cat Fortey, participant in Covid Realities

Index   229

List of figures and tables

Figures

1.1	Participants' financial situation over four interviews, 2015–20	19
5.1	The timeline of the Government's response to COVID-19 in England and the corresponding timeline of the longitudinal BiB COVID-19 research	75
7.1	Mean weekly working hours during the pandemic by family type	108
7.2	Proportion of adult respondents who identify as key workers and are able to work from home some or all of the time by family type, April 2020	110
7.3	Average hours reported by parents and family members helping children with home schooling by family type, April 2020	111
7.4	Proportion of adult respondents who have ever been furloughed by family type, April–July 2020	112
7.5	GHQ-12 mental health scores from a pre-pandemic baseline to March 2021 by family type	115
14.1	The domino effect of the five-week wait	206

Tables

4.1	'Our sample', Universal Credit in Salford project	59
6.1	Ethnic diversity in Tower Hamlets and Newham, compared to London	90
6.2	Ethnic diversity in the Tower Hamlets and Newham survey data	91
6.3	Household income of respondents by income band, compared to median	92
6.4	Tower Hamlets, respondent employment status, by household income	93
6.5	Newham, respondent employment status, by household income	94
6.6	Tower Hamlets, benefits claimed, by household income	95
6.7	Newham, benefits claimed, by household income	96
6.8	Tower Hamlets, food bank use in most recent four weeks, by household income	97
6.9	Newham, food bank use in most recent four weeks, by household income	97
6.10	Tower Hamlets, housing circumstances, by household income	99
6.11	Newham, housing circumstances, by household income	100
6.12	Tower Hamlets, relationship quality, by household income	100
6.13	Newham, relationship quality, by household income	100

List of abbreviations

BMJ	British Medical Journal
CAAG	Community Activist Advisory Group
CPAG	Child Poverty Action Group
DfC	Department for Communities Northern Ireland
DfE	Department for Education
DWP	Department for Work and Pensions
ESA	Employment and Support Allowance
ESRC	Economic and Social Research Council
GHS	Get Heard Scotland
IES	Institute for Employment Studies
IFS	Institute for Fiscal Studies
JRF	Joseph Rowntree Foundation
JSA	Jobseeker's Allowance
LCWRA	Limited Capability for Work-Related Activity
LFS	Labour Force Survey
OECD	Organisation for Economic Co-operation and Development
ONS	Office for National Statistics
PHE	Public Health England
PIP	Personal Independence Payment
SEISS	Self-Employment Income Support Scheme
SWF	Scottish Welfare Fund
TUC	Trades Union Congress
UC	Universal Credit
WCA	Work Capability Assessment
WFI	Work-Focused Interview
WHO	World Health Organization
WTC	Working Tax Credit

Notes on contributors

Kate Andersen is Research Associate at the University of York. Her research explores the intended and unintended consequences of new social security policies. Kate is especially interested in investigating how government justifications for welfare reforms compare with the everyday lives of people in receipt of social security benefits. Her research also particularly focuses on how welfare reforms impact women. She has published an article titled 'Universal Credit, gender and unpaid childcare: mothers' accounts of the new welfare conditionality regime' in *Critical Social Policy* (2020).

Ben Baumberg Geiger is Reader at the University of Kent, and co-lead of the Welfare at a (Social) Distance project. He has worked on secondment at the Department for Work and Pensions (DWP) (on disability benefits assessment), and his work also looks at attitudes towards benefits and the experiences of benefits claimants, as well as how to create a better version of the Work Capability Assessment (WCA). You can see his full publications list (including open access versions) at: http://www.benbgeiger.co.uk/

Dave Beck is Lecturer of Social Policy at the University of Salford. He has teaching and research interests in the social security system and its impact on poverty and people's lived experience. He has research interests in understanding poverty reduction methods through social security such as the introduction of Universal Basic Income and how this can be used to end (food) poverty. Recent publications include a chapter in *Social Policy for Welfare Practice in Wales*, edited by C. Williams and H. Gwilym (2021) and an article in the *Journal of Poverty and Social Justice* (2020, with H. Gwilym).

Fran Bennett is Associate Fellow in the Department of Social Policy and Intervention, University of Oxford. She works on poverty, social security, and gender issues in particular, and is a member of the policy advisory group of the Women's Budget Group. She was a member of the ESRC-funded research project 2018–21 Couples Balancing Work, Money and Care: Exploring the Shifting Landscape under Universal Credit (ES/R004811/1).

Daniel D. Bingham, BSc (Hons), MSc, PhD – Bradford Institute for Health research, Born in Bradford. Senior Research Fellow, interests – children and young people's movement behaviours such as physical activity, sedentary behaviour, and sleep, and related outcomes of obesity. https://borninbradford.nhs.uk/about-us/meet-the-team/daniel-bingham/

Claire Cameron is Professor of Social Pedagogy in the Thomas Coram Research Unit, University College London. Her research focuses on children's services and addressing social disadvantage. She is Co-I on UKPRP funded ActEarly: a city collaboratory approach to early promotion of good health and wellbeing (2019–24), and co-leads strands of work on healthy livelihoods and healthy learning in Tower Hamlets. She is PI of *Families in Tower Hamlets* (ESRC, 2020–2021). Recent publications include co-editing *Transforming Early Childhood in England: Towards a Democratic Education* (with Peter Moss, UCL Press, 2020).

Caroline has always worked within the care sector supporting vulnerable adults to live independently and in child care. She has been a single parent for over eight years and has always worked and studied to improve her employment opportunities. Being a single parent meant she has needed support to top up her income. Caroline joined Covid Realities in the middle of the pandemic and has played an active part in highlighting the struggles of living on a low income. She has appeared on many BBC news reports, radio, newspapers, and her own local TV channels.

Elizabeth Clery is a freelance social researcher, with a particular interest in poverty, inequality, and welfare and in ensuring that social research fully informs policy development and evaluation in these areas. She has led research projects on behalf of Gingerbread, Sightsavers, the Joseph Rowntree Foundation, and the Equality and Human Rights Commission. Elizabeth has contributed to the British Social Attitudes survey series as an author and editor for over a decade, with a particular focus on public attitudes to poverty and welfare. She has previously worked for NatCen Social Research, the Government Social Research Service, and in the voluntary sector.

Beth Cloughton is Community Researcher at The Poverty Alliance. She is currently undertaking a PhD at the University of Glasgow. Her research interests are qualitative and creative methods, inequalities, and social justice.

Catherine Connors is Principal Officer of Salford City Council's Welfare Rights and Debt Advice Service, leading an established team of expert welfare rights and debt advisers. Catherine has over 25 years' experience in a range of roles within local government including as a welfare rights practitioner and Commissioning Manager focused on financial inclusion. Over the last three years, as Honorary Research Fellow at the Sustainable Housing and Urban Studies Unit (SHUSU) at the University of Salford, Catherine has worked in partnership with the University on the Salford Anti-Poverty Taskforce.

Kirsty L. Crossley, BSc (Hons), MPsyc, Research Fellow at Bradford Institute for Health Research, Born in Bradford. Research interests include child and maternal health, which includes the prenatal period, maternity services, and now the impact of COVID-19 on pregnancy and the postpartum period. The link to some of her papers: https://borninbradford. nhs.uk/about-us/meet-the-team/kirsty-crossley/

Deirdre was formerly a teacher in England. Unforeseen personal circumstances led her to claiming Universal Credit. Deirdre is currently campaigning on issues around Universal Credit and affordable school uniforms, to improve the lives of low-income families.

Robert de Vries is Senior Lecturer in Quantitative Sociology, University of Kent. His research focuses on social stratification, the sociology of status, and attitudes towards disadvantaged groups.

Laura Dewar is the Policy and Research Lead at the charity Gingerbread. She leads the charity's policy and parliamentary work on welfare reform including Universal Credit, the benefit cap, and employment including flexible work and in-work progression. Laura has led research projects on in-work progression, work conditionality, and most recently two projects focused on the impact of COVID-19 on single parents' employment and caring. Laura is called upon for her expertise in Parliament, within the last year presenting at the All Party Parliamentary Group on Women and Work and giving oral evidence to the COVID-19 and Economic Affairs Committees in the House of Lords.

Josie Dickerson is Research Director for the Better Start Bradford Innovation Hub at Born in Bradford and co-PI of the BiB COVID-19 research programme. Josie's research focuses on reducing health inequalities by integrating research into practice to improve the quality and equity of services. Particular research interests are in perinatal mental health and early childhood interventions. https://borninbradford.nhs.uk/about-us/meet-the-team/josie-dickerson/

Daniel Edmiston is Lecturer in Sociology and Social Policy at the University of Leeds, UK. He has undertaken national and comparative research drawing on mixed methods approaches to critically examine the effects of welfare policy and politics. Daniel's research focuses primarily on poverty and inequality, comparative public policy, and social citizenship.

Charlotte Endacott, BA (Hons), MSc: Research Fellow, Born in Bradford, Bradford Institute for Health Research. Charlotte's research interests lie in exploring the social determinants of health inequalities in societies and the evaluation of interventions in community settings. https://borninbradford.nhs.uk/about-us/meet-the-team/charlotte-endacott/

Ciara Fitzpatrick is Lecturer at Ulster University School of Law. Her research focuses on social security law in the UK. She joined the UC:Us research team in 2020 and has been primarily supporting the group to engage with policymakers and the media and in the creation of a participant-led guide to Universal Credit.

Kayleigh Garthwaite is Associate Professor in the Department of Social Policy, Sociology & Criminology, University of Birmingham. Her research interests focus on poverty and inequality, social security, and health, specifically investigating charitable food provision and food insecurity. She is the author of *Hunger Pains: Life inside Foodbank Britain* (Policy Press, 2016) and *Poverty and Insecurity: Life in Low-Pay, No-Pay Britain* (Policy Press, 2012).

Andrea Gibbons is Lecturer in Social Policy at the University of Salford. With degrees in Urban Planning and Geography, she works on housing, homelessness, health, and social security. Her broader interests are in urban ecosystems, social movement, and the ways that people work to shape their lives and environments at the intersections of race, class, and gender. She is the author of *City of Segregation:100 Years of Struggle for Housing in Los Angeles* (Verso, 2018).

Rita Griffiths is Research Fellow at the Institute for Policy Research, University of Bath. Her research interests include social security, active labour market programmes, and family relationships in the context of mean-tested benefits. Before moving into academia, between 2000 and 2015, as founding partner of a social research consultancy, Rita designed and delivered a series of national research and evaluation studies of government policies designed to help disadvantaged groups and low-income families make the transition from benefits to paid work.

Hanan Hauari is Lecturer in Social Sciences at the Institute of Education, University College London. Her background is in government-funded research on parenting and interventions supporting vulnerable children, young people, and families. More recent research interests include the lived experiences of children and young people living in foster care and their transitions out of care.

Michelle Heys is Associate Professor of Population and Global Child Health, Great Ormond Street Institute of Child Health, UCL and Paediatric

Consultant working in the Community in Newham East London. She has over 25 years' experience in clinical child health in the UK, Australia, and Hong Kong and 15 years' experience in population child health research. Her research uses mixed methods including life course epidemiology, qualitative, implementation science, digital health, and trial methodology to explore inequities in child health outcomes and to develop, implement, and evaluate potential health service and community-focused interventions to address these. She takes a population-based approach as well as focusing on priority groups such as unaccompanied asylum seeking children and young people and those with a neurodisability. See https://iris.ucl.ac.uk/iris/browse/prof ile?upi=MHEYS25 for publications. With Claire Cameron she co-leads the impact of COVID-19 on families in Newham study.

Katherine Hill is Senior Research Associate at the Centre for Research in Social Policy, Loughborough University. Her research, including qualitative longitudinal methods, has centred around low income and disadvantage, the role of social security policy, financial, material, and personal resources in meeting needs and the implications for peoples' lives. She is currently leading a six-year study with families with children, and a project looking at the experiences of families where young adults live with their parents. Publications include an article in *Social Policy and Society* (2020, with D. Hirsch and A. Davis).

Katie Hollingworth is Lecturer in Sociology at the Social Research Institute, University College London. Her research interests concern the lives and wellbeing of children, young people, and families with particular focus on children and young people in and leaving care, early childhood care and education, widening participation, and interventions and policies to support families.

Celia Hynes has over 40 years' experience in the NHS and education. Working with vulnerable groups she has led the programme of transition for military Service personnel and their families formally for the last 18 years as Co-Founder of the initial Centre for Veterans' Wellbeing in the North West of England, and is one of the Founders of the College for Military Veterans and Emergency services (CMVES) at the University of Central Lancashire. She leads the CMVES team at UClan and is a member of key strategic groups such as the Veterans Advisory and Pensions Committee (VAPC) and local Armed Forces Covenant groups. Her knowledge of military service and those making the transition to civilian life from the Armed Forces is extensive and she is able to utilise her background as a health professional to establish good working relationships across a range of partnerships.

Jo Ingold is Associate Professor of Human Resource Management at Deakin Business School, Deakin University. She has a background in central government policy and research and the non-profit sector. Her research focuses on employment programme design, (digital) delivery and workforce, business engagement in labour market policy, and workplace inclusion.

Joanna has recently been undergoing voluntary training as a welfare rights advisor at an independent advice centre. In addition to part-time paid and voluntary work, Joanna has been campaigning on issues around Universal Credit.

Linzi Ladlow is Research Fellow at the University of Lincoln, working on the Following Young Fathers Further project; a qualitative longitudinal, participatory study of the lives and support needs of young fathers. Her research interests include young parenthood, families, housing, and disadvantage. https://followingyoungfathersfurther.org/

Bridget Lockyer is Senior Research Fellow within the ActEarly Collaboratory at Bradford Institute for Health Research. She is an interdisciplinary qualitative researcher with interests in public health, qualitative methodologies, organisations, gender, and inequalities. https://borninbradford.nhs.uk/about-us/meet-the-team/bridget-lockyer/

Philip Martin is Research Fellow in the Sustainable Housing & Urban Studies Unit, School of Health & Society, University of Salford. A central theme of his research is how processes such as work, migration, and welfare intersect with notions of citizenship and community, with a particular focus on Roma. Recent publications include articles in the *International Journal of Roma Studies* (2021) and in *Social Policy and Society* (2021, with L. Scullion, K. Jones, P. Dwyer, and C. Hynes).

Rosie R.C. McEachan is Director of Born in Bradford and a proud (Scottish) Bradfordian. She is an experienced applied health researcher with particular interests in the development and evaluation of complex interventions, environmental determinants of health, green space, air quality, and co-production. Rosie holds honorary chair positions at the University of Bradford and University College London. https://borninbradford.nhs.uk/about-us/meet-the-team/dr-rosie-mceachan/

Fiona McHardy is Research and Information Manager at The Poverty Alliance and responsible for coordinating their 'Evidence' stream influencing policy and practice. Her research interests include families, social security, health inequalities, and utilising participatory and creative methodologies.

Claire McIvor, BSc (Hons), Research Fellow at Bradford Institute for Health Research, Born in Bradford. Research interests include public health, global health, rehabilitation, and the impact of COVID-19 on the health and wellbeing of individuals/communities. https://borninbradford.nhs.uk/ about-us/meet-the-team/claire-mcivor/

Jane Millar is Professor Emeritus at the University of Bath, UK. Her research interests are in the design, implementation, and impact of social policy: comparative research on family policy, social security, and employment policy, with particular reference to gender and changing family patterns.

Rosa Morris is an independent researcher with a particular interest in social security having had long periods where she was unable to work due to ill health which meant she had to claim both Incapacity Benefit and Employment and Support Allowance. This experience led to her completing a PhD which looked at the history of out of work disability benefits and the development of the Work Capability Assessment. Rosa is part of the secretariat for the Commission on Social Security led by Experts by Experience and also works as a welfare rights advisor focused on disability benefits.

Ellen Morrison is a disabled activist. Through her own experiences living on benefits, as well as campaigning with other disabled people in Disabled People Against Cuts and Unite Community, she has seen first-hand how much harm the current benefits system causes. Ellen has been active in the campaign to scrap Universal Credit.

Rachael H. Moss, BSc, MSc, PhD, Research Fellow, Bradford Inequalities Research Unit, Born in Bradford, Bradford Institute for Health Research. Interests: childhood stress, nutrition, the impact of COVID-19 on individual/community health and wellbeing, and other contemporary issues in healthcare. https://borninbradford.nhs.uk/about-us/meet-the-team/ dr-rachael-moss/

Margaret O'Brien is Professor of Child and Family Policy at UCL's Thomas Coram Research Unit. She researches and has published widely on fathers, family life, and work-family policies including the UN's first report on Men in Families and Family Policy in a Changing World Report, 2011; Comparative Perspectives on Work-Life Balance and Gender Equality, 2017 and Eligibility to Parental Leave in EU28, 2020. She has a long-standing interest in researching inequalities in family life in East London as part of the collaboration behind Rising in the East? The regeneration of East London (Lawrence and Wishart, 1996).

Michael Orton is Senior Research Fellow at the University of Warwick. His primary focus is social security (welfare benefits), using approaches that are solutions-focused, participatory, and based on consensus building. He is Secretary to the Commission on Social Security led by Experts by Experience.

Sarah O'Toole is a developmental psychologist. Sarah is Research Fellow at UCL and her field of research involves supporting the development of disadvantaged children and families as well as children with special educational needs and disability (SEND). Sarah is currently leading a project funded by the Department for Transport exploring how to effectively support children with SEND to travel independently. She was also the Research Fellow for the Families in Newham project exploring the impact of COVID-19 on families with a child under the age of five.

Geoff Page is Research Fellow in the Department of Social Policy and Social Work, University of York. His research centres on marginalised populations, with a particular focus on drug users within the criminal justice system. The role of social capital in supporting the (very few) heroin users who achieve abstinence, and the need for a clear prioritisation of harm reduction within policy, comprise key parts of several current projects.

Joe Pardoe is a PhD candidate at the University of Salford; his thesis concerns the mental health experiences of people who claim Universal Credit. Working within the Sustainable Housing and Urban Studies Unit (SHUSU) at the University of Salford, Joe has taken part in several research projects in collaboration with Salford City Council and the Salford Anti-Poverty Taskforce. Joe's research interests concern marginalised populations, especially those who have experienced mental health adversities. Joe's research output includes: Transgender youths who self-harm: perspectives from those seeking support. *Mental Health Today*, 2017.

Ruth Patrick is Senior Lecturer in Social Policy at the University of York. She leads the Covid Realities research programme and is the author of *For Whose Benefit: The Everyday Realities of Welfare Reform* (2017, Policy Press).

Kate E. Pickett is Professor of Epidemiology and Deputy Director of the Centre for Future Health, University of York. She is a member of the Born in Bradford Executive and her research focuses on the social determinants of child and family wellbeing.

Maddy Power is Research Fellow in the Department of Health Sciences, University of York. She currently holds a Welcome Fellowship. Her research interests centre around food aid and food insecurity in multi-faith, multi-ethnic contexts, including further research and publications on ethnic and religious variations in food insecurity. Her monograph *Hunger, Racism and Religion in Neoliberal Britain* will be published in 2022 (Policy Press). She is founder and former Chair of the York Food Justice Alliance, a cross-sector partnership addressing food insecurity at the local level, and Co-Chair of the Independent Food Aid Network.

Katie Pybus is Research Fellow in the Department of Health Sciences, University of York. Her research focuses primarily on social security and mental health. She has a clinical background in mental health nursing and research training in the social sciences and public health. Katie currently holds a Centre for Future Health/Wellcome Trust fellowship and is working on several research programmes relating to socio-economic inequalities and mental health.

Mary Reader is Research Officer at the Centre for Analysis of Social Exclusion (CASE), The London School of Economics and Political Science. Her research interests include the causal impact of income, poverty, and social security on families, with a particular focus on health inequalities, early childhood, and larger families.

Jamie Redman is currently ESRC post-doctoral Fellow at the University of Sheffield. His current research is focused around the history of UK welfare reform and the delivery of employment services.

David Robertshaw is currently Research Fellow at the Centre for Employment Relations, Innovation and Change, Leeds University Business School. His current research interests include active labour market policies, welfare reform during COVID-19, and the digitalisation of employment services.

Laura Robertson is Senior Research Officer at The Poverty Alliance in Scotland. She conducts research on experiences of poverty and inequality in Scotland, working with a range of partners locally and nationally. Her current research interests include participatory and peer-led research, social security reform in Scotland, and education inequalities.

Lisa Scullion is Professor of Social Policy and Co-Director of the Sustainable Housing & Urban Studies Unit (SHUSU). Lisa joined the University of Salford in 2006 and since then has delivered over 60 externally funded research projects. Lisa is currently leading a significant national ESRC project focusing on social security and employment support during COVID-19 and its aftermath, funded as part of UK Research and Innovation's rapid response to COVID-19. Lisa is also leading the UK's first substantive research focusing on the experiences of military veterans within the social security system, funded by the Forces in Mind Trust (FiMT). Lisa is a founder member and academic lead of the Salford Anti-Poverty Taskforce, an innovative research/knowledge exchange partnership with Salford City Council.

Mark Simpson is Senior Lecturer in Law at Ulster University, Derry-Londonderry. He carried out interdisciplinary research with a focus on the social rights of citizenship, taking in social security, poverty, and social and economic rights. Mark is particularly interested in how devolution is changing the UK welfare state and the social union.

Helen Smith is Senior Research Fellow in the NIHR Applied Research Collaboration Yorkshire and Humber (ARC Y&H), Bradford Institute for Health Research. Helen works within the Improvement Science theme, supporting applied qualitative research across the ARC. Helen is trained in applied population research and human geography and has worked in international public health since 1998. Her research interests include the social and behavioural aspects of the provision, use and quality of care, especially maternal and new-born health care. https://yqsr.org/dr-helen-smith/

Kate Summers is Fellow in the Department of Methodology, London School of Economics. Kate's research is concerned with experiences and perceptions of poverty, economic inequality, and related social policies with a particular focus on social security policy, in the UK context.

Anna Tarrant is Associate Professor in Sociology, University of Lincoln and is a UKRI Future Leaders Fellow. Her research interests broadly include men and masculinities, family life, the lifecourse, and methods of qualitative secondary analysis and co-creation. Her current funded study, Following Young Fathers Further, is a qualitative longitudinal, participatory study of the lives and support needs of young fathers. She is co-editor of Qualitative Secondary Analysis with Dr Kahryn Hughes and also the sole author of the monograph *Fathering and Poverty*, published by Policy Press in August 2021. https://followingyoungfathersfurther.org/

Rosalie Warnock is Research Associate in the Department of Social Policy and Social Work, University of York. She works on the Covid Realities and Benefit Changes and Larger Families projects. Her research interests include: austerity, welfare bureaucracies, special educational needs and disability (SEND) support services, family life, care, and emotional geographies.

Laura Way is Research Fellow at the University of Lincoln, working on the Following Young Fathers Further project; a qualitative longitudinal, participatory study of the lives and support needs of young fathers. Her research interests are in ageing, gender and the lifecourse, youth culture, creative methods, and punk pedagogies. Laura is the author of *Punk, Gender and Ageing. Just Typical Girls?* (Emerald, 2020). https://followingyoungfathersfurther.org/

Ruth Webber is Research Associate at the Centre for Research in Social Policy, Loughborough University. During her time at CRSP, she has worked with colleague Katherine Hill on two projects, a longitudinal study on bringing up a family on a low income, funded by the Joseph Rowntree Foundation, and a study about the financial and relational experiences and implications of low- to middle-income young adults living with their parents, funded by Standard Life Foundation. Her wider research looks at the impact of inequalities on experiences of home.

Lydia Whitaker is Research Fellow at the Institute of Education, University College London as well as on the Editorial board of Children and Society. Her research area focuses on social and emotional competencies in childhood and adolescence as well as gender parity.

Marsha Wood is Researcher at the Institute for Policy Research, University of Bath. Marsha's research interests include poverty, social security, childcare, and disadvantaged children and young people. Marsha was a researcher on the ESRC-funded research project 2018–21 Couples Balancing Work, Money and Care: Exploring the Shifting Landscape under Universal Credit (ES/R004811/1). Marsha recently published an article: Childcare costs and Universal Credit: awareness, affordability and the challenge of an embedded system. *Journal of Poverty and Social Justice* (2021).

David Young is Research Fellow at the Sustainable Housing and Urban Studies Unit (SHUSU), University of Salford. David's research focuses on social security policy and the experience of income change and insecurity. Wider research interests include precarious work, welfare reform, and the health and wellbeing impacts of advice services. In 2020, he co-authored (with Kate Summers) the article: Universal simplicity? The alleged simplicity of Universal Credit from administrative and claimant perspectives. *Journal of Poverty and Social Justice.*

Acknowledgements

Firstly, we want to say thank you to all of the authors in this collection who contributed to the 'COVID-19 and low-income families: Researching together' Special Interest Group (SIG) collective, who we have been collaborating with since April 2020. Working together has taken a lot of time, effort, and thought, but has been a thoroughly worthwhile, refreshing, and rewarding way of working at such a difficult time.

Thanks also to the supportive and flexible funding from The Nuffield Foundation, and in particular support from Alex Beer, which meant we were able to carry out the Covid Realities research programme as a whole.

Sincere thanks must also go to all of the participants across our 14 projects who gave up their time to take part in the research, especially when COVID-19 placed additional and increasing pressures on people's lives.

Many thanks to Alison Garnham, Chief Executive of Child Poverty Action Group, and Cat Fortey from Covid Realities who provided the insightful, powerful, and important Foreword and Afterword to the collection, for which we are hugely grateful.

Finally, we would also like to thank the brilliant team at Policy Press for their assistance with the commissioning and production process, and in particular Laura Vickers-Rendall for her enthusiasm and support.

Foreword

Alison Garnham, Chief Executive, Child Poverty Action Group

The book represents a unique account of family life during the pandemic. It is the first of what will become a series of collaborations between researchers and people with direct experience of living in poverty in order to elevate both to the position of expert.

As well as the voices of Experts by Experience, this account shows how researchers were forced to reinvent research methods overnight in order to deal with the fact that face-to-face interviews, focus groups, and the other regular research methods in the toolkit were no longer feasible.

It is worth considering what came before the pandemic. According to the Office for Budget Responsibility analysis, in 2020, when we entered the pandemic we were already spending £36bn a year less on social security than in 2010.[1] Back in 2010, in order to reduce the deficit, some £80 billion of cuts to benefits and services were announced, with over £20 billion benefit cuts and a further £15 billion more in the July 2015 Budget – including the two-child policy and renewed benefit cap. A total of over 50 different cuts and restrictions to working-age benefits, chipping away at the support available to struggling families and their children were made. It was claimed at the time that 'those with the broadest shoulders' would bear the biggest burden and that 'we are all in it together'. Evidently, some were 'in it' far more than others. By 2020, we had more food banks in the UK than we had branches of McDonald's, with teachers warning of children arriving at school hungry, and rough sleepers returning to streets up and down the country. Child poverty had risen by 700,000 to 4.3 million, with 75 per cent of them living with low-paid working parents.

What the pandemic exposed therefore should really come as no surprise to anybody. We saw children going hungry, plus parents facing new costs, such as school equipment and extra heat, food, and lighting to manage children being off school. Parents were charged with home educating and lost hours at work or paid jobs, faced rising debt, and battled poor mental health. That living in poverty leads many children to fall behind in education, to have worse health and low self-esteem is well understood. But to have the strange isolation and hardship caused by the pandemic on top was overwhelming for many. Efforts to support families through food vouchers and government schemes to provide digital devices, though gratefully received, were not received by all and could often be hard to access or difficult to manage compared to what was really needed – more cash.

There have of course been significant increases since 2010 in the national minimum wage (NMW) reducing the number of people on low pay. Significant amounts have also been spent on raising the personal tax allowance. Although this latter, expensive, policy was not well targeted, with around 80 per cent going to the richest half of the income distribution.[2] And, the reality is that for low-income families, net income is most commonly determined by the level of means-tested benefits such as tax credits and Universal Credit. Increasing the NMW does not lead directly to big income improvements as most is clawed back through the relevant means-test – commonly known as the poverty trap.

In 2021, a similar argument to the one put forward ten years ago has been made by the Chancellor that raising the NMW and making improvements to childcare provision is somehow a substitute for improving family incomes. But, in October 2021, the £20 uplift to UC and tax credits was removed, leaving families on Universal Credit to face the cost of living crisis of rising inflation, fuel bills, and NI increases without any additional protection. The decision in the Budget to reduce the rate at which UC is withdrawn for low-income, working families was very welcome but early analysis suggests it still leaves three quarters of UC claimants worse off.[3][4] The evidence presented across this edited collection is that the adequacy of benefits and reform of social security are still outstanding issues that need our urgent attention, and we must listen hard to those most affected.

The Child Poverty Action Group has been part of the Covid Realities project, contributing evidence from our Early Warning System which collects evidence from frontline advisers about the problems that face benefit claimants. Our combined efforts open up new possibilities to bring about policy change.

Cat, one of the Covid Realities participants, points out in the Afterword that those of us with access to policymakers need to share our power and build a bridge that uplifts and supports the human faces and voices with lived experience of the realities of poverty. They are not just data sources, but collaborators who give us a deeper and richer understanding of what it is like to live on a low income, and an insider perspective that many researchers don't have.

If we are to create a social security system that really works for the people who need to use it, we must listen to their voices.

Notes

1   Waters T (2018) Presentation: personal tax and benefit measures, *Slide 26: Still more social security cuts to come*, Table: forecast saving from social security measures announced since June 2010, Source: OBR, Policy Measures Database, various Economic and Fiscal Outlook, IFS calculations www.ifs.org.uk/uploads/budgets/budget2018/tw_budget2018.pdf
2   CPAG calculations using UKMOD version A1.0+.
3   www.resolutionfoundation.org/app/uploads/2021/10/The-Boris-Budget.pdf
4   See Resolution Foundation Budget analysis.

Introduction

*Kayleigh Garthwaite, Rosalie Warnock, Ruth Patrick,
Maddy Power, and Anna Tarrant*

Back in April 2020, several weeks into the first of several lockdowns in the UK to curb the spread of COVID-19, Prime Minister Boris Johnson described the virus as 'the great leveller' that would impact people across the socio-economic spectrum equally. However, to social scientists, it was immediately evident that the differential impact and experience of this unique crisis would need to be documented and explored. This was apparent and of great importance at the beginning of the pandemic, but is particularly vital as we more fully understand the extent to which the crisis has reinforced and exacerbated inequalities across a number of indicators, including socio-economic status (Paremoer et al, 2021), ethnicity (British Medical Journal [BMJ] 2020; Power et al, 2020), and gender (Ruxton and Burrell, 2020; Wenham et al, 2020).

The pandemic and associated lockdowns have also changed the way we work as social researchers, not only in terms of how we conduct our fieldwork, but also in terms of collaboration. As Howlett (2020: 1) observes, 'the Covid-19 pandemic has forced us to re-think our approaches to research'. Due to social distancing measures, and the ongoing uncertainty and risks presented by the pandemic, conducting in-person research was no longer possible. Instead, as researchers we needed to find new ways of documenting and understanding experiences during the pandemic. Researchers had to adapt their fieldwork quickly to adhere to social distancing measures, sometimes in ways that fell outside of existing training and expertise (Howlett, 2020). Tried and tested ways of researching, and of engaging with policymakers and stakeholders, became unsustainable almost overnight. We had to act quickly to embark on new research where needed (and appropriate), but we recognised that it was also important for the research community to collectively think through this new context, ensuring that research responses were appropriate, ethical, and effective in providing policy-relevant findings in a timely manner. Working together alongside other social researchers as we navigated these decisions felt important in helping ensure our research practices remained fit for purpose in the new social conditions brought about by the pandemic context, but also in order to avoid the duplication of efforts and unnecessary burdens on those taking part in research projects.

When devising the project in March 2020, we recognised that within the COVID-19 context, it was vital to document and understand the lived experiences of families living through poverty during the pandemic, while also increasing the policy reach and potential impact of the resultant data through processes of synthesis. A central element of the Covid Realities research programme was to work closely with research teams already undertaking fieldwork across the UK with families in poverty, to support the generation of data specifically on COVID-19 and its impacts, and to disseminate resultant findings.

This introductory chapter begins by presenting the unique collaborative approach taken by the '*COVID-19 and families on a low income: Researching together*' collective, whose work features across the 14 chapters of this book. We highlight the novel interdisciplinary, holistic, mixed methods approaches that have been adopted to produce a complex and cohesive evidence base with a substantive focus on families living on a low income. A brief background literature relating to austerity as the foundational context to the COVID-19 crisis is outlined to illustrate how and why the crisis has impacted in distinctive ways on families on a low income in the UK. Finally, an overview of the key overarching themes and connections across projects and their corresponding chapters is outlined to provide a roadmap of the text. Several key thematic areas are foregrounded, including the (in)adequacy of the social security system response; getting by in hard times; and the importance (and often lack of) support networks for families on a low income.

It is important to note that many of the chapters in this collection make reference to experiences that some readers may find upsetting. This includes the impact of poverty on individuals' lives; domestic abuse; suicide; and food insecurity. Specific chapters in the collection have content warnings to flag this to the reader.

Covid Realities and the '*COVID-19 and families on a low income: Researching together*' collective

Covid Realities is a major research programme funded by The Nuffield Foundation that has documented the everyday experiences of families with children on a low income during the pandemic across the UK. The project involved a collaboration including parents and carers with dependent children, researchers from the Universities of York and Birmingham, and the Child Poverty Action Group (CPAG). A central focus of the project was families' experiences of social security, but also their everyday lives, including how families have been navigating this new and challenging world. There is a strong emphasis on policy engagement and on the development and sharing of co-produced recommendations for change. Chapter 11 in this collection discusses the Covid Realities research in more detail, documenting the participatory online methods that comprise another central part of the research programme.

This edited collection focuses on a discrete element of the Covid Realities research programme, the '*COVID-19 and families on a low income: Researching together*' collective, which is a collaboration between 14 different research projects, including academics and researchers from the voluntary sector, researching with over 4,000 parents and carers across the UK. In this book, we showcase the ways we have collectively examined the impacts of the COVID-19 pandemic on families on a low income in the UK between April 2020 and December 2021. Our collective body of work comprises evidence and insights generated with a major UK cohort of families living on a low income, through which we examine the impacts of the pandemic, and implications for social policy.

An underpinning vision for our collective is that impact is best achieved on behalf of families living on a low income when we work together. The projects committed to working ethically, robustly, and effectively to ensure that evidence was available about the particular needs of families in poverty, and that this evidence would be communicated to policymakers and other beneficiaries in a timely and accessible way. The Covid Realities team were aware of the sensitivities of approaching researchers about taking part in this project, given the ethical considerations and sensitive nature of what was evolving as an incredibly challenging and rapidly changing situation – after all, the pandemic has been universally experienced with impacts on the professional and personal lives of both researchers and participants. We did not want the research to add to any of these pressures. Like Markham et al (2020: 1), we were guided by a 'feminist perspective and an ethic of care to engage in open ended collaboration during times of globally-felt trauma'. This was important in terms of participant wellbeing, but also with regards to our fellow researchers.

We aimed to involve 10–15 research projects in the collaborative process; too many projects could become unmanageable, and too few risked our efforts being unsuccessful (see Garthwaite et al, forthcoming, for further details). Between March and June 2020, we identified 13 existing projects being conducted by academic and non-academic researchers who agreed to participate alongside Covid Realities. The resultant '*COVID-19 and families on a low income: Researching together*' collective have been working together as a Special Interest Group (SIG) to support the generation of data specifically on COVID-19 and families on a low income, and then synthesise and disseminate relevant findings to policymakers and other key audiences.

Despite restrictions on face-to-face fieldwork, our projects have employed a diverse range of methodological approaches, including quantitative, qualitative, longitudinal, participatory, and arts-based approaches. Conducted predominantly online and via digitally mediated forms of communication, methods include online interviews (using Zoom/Skype); telephone interviews; diaries; national surveys, both postal and online; asset mapping;

Zoom discussion groups with parents and carers living in poverty; and zine-making workshops. Many of the projects have also worked closely with community stakeholders and practitioners from support organisations to understand the impacts of lockdown on national support infrastructures. Bringing emergent insights and findings from our projects into conversation with one another at regular SIG meetings was enabled by digital platforms and tools. These allowed researchers from multiple national institutions and organisations to collaborate effectively and efficiently. Flexibility, understanding, and communication were key to ensuring that we worked in the most meaningfully collaborative way possible (see Garthwaite et al, forthcoming). This has been achieved through developing a collaborative framework from the outset, openly exploring the ethics of collaboration, and taking time to establish effective research relationships, while creating space for reflection and iteration of our approach. The solidarity and sense of community engendered through the collective has been particularly welcomed as we all navigated the difficulties brought about by COVID-19. Working collaboratively has had significant advantages in terms of communicating messages and disseminating knowledge to diverse audiences from our strong co-produced evidence base, enabling us to offer timely and much-needed insights into the key issues facing families on a low income during the pandemic.

Austerity and pre-existing inequalities

To understand the impacts, fallout, and policy response to the COVID-19 pandemic, we need to briefly situate it within the context of the last decade of austerity politics and policy in the UK. Since 2010, the UK has experienced a programme of sweeping welfare and policy reforms which not only constitute the biggest shake-up of the welfare state since its inception in 1945 (Hamnett, 2014) but have also, perhaps irreversibly, embedded a philosophy of 'anti-welfare commonsense' at the political and popular levels (Jensen and Tyler, 2015). As poverty levels continue to rise across the UK (Joseph Rowntree Foundation [JRF], 2021; McNeil et al, 2021), the consequences of a decade of cuts and a discursive reframing of poverty as a personal failing and choice has fundamentally altered the lived experiences and life courses of families on a low income.

To say reforms have severely impacted families on a low income would be a gross understatement. The shift to a monthly payment schedule to families through Universal Credit (UC) disregards the ways that much low-paid and casual employment is paid weekly or fortnightly, creating additional challenges for families around budgeting for a low income. Furthermore, advance payment deductions – on top of UC payments which have often already been capped – mean monthly benefit income is often considerably lower than what has already been calculated as the bare minimum income needed for survival. This plunges many into a cycle of debt, compounded by further fluctuations in UC as a result of precarious employment, volatile earnings, and the high UC taper rate (63p of every £1 earned in addition to UC). Chapters 2, 3, 4, and 14 in this collection explore issues relating to UC in further detail.

As a direct result of welfare reforms of the last decade, rates of poverty have notably risen across the UK since the 2008 global financial crash. More than one in five people in the UK now live in poverty (JRF, 2021). The two-child benefit cap alone is estimated to have moved 200,000 children into poverty since its inception (CPAG, 2021). Crucially, social security reforms since 2012 have been accompanied not only by steep increases in housing costs (both homeownership and private rental) (McNeil et al, 2021) but by changes in the labour market, under which precarious employment, particularly zero-hours contracts, have mushroomed. As a consequence, more people now experience in-work poverty than out-of-work poverty (Innes, 2020; McNeil et al, 2021). In-work poverty is defined as households experiencing poverty where one or more people are working (McNeil et al, 2021: 3). In the UK, 19 per cent of UK families live in poverty – of which most (17 per cent) experience in-work poverty (JRF, 2021: 57; McNeil et al, 2021: 4). Rates of poverty are higher among households with a disabled member: 26 per cent of households with a disabled child and 40 per cent of households with a disabled adult and disabled child live in poverty (JRF, 2020: 57). With the value of Child Benefit falling by 23 per cent since 2010 (Garnham, 2020a) and for those directly affected by the two-child cap and household cap, rates of in-work poverty among families with three or more children are the highest they've ever been, at 42 per cent of families – up more than two thirds over the past decade (McNeil et al, 2021: 4).

Documenting family life on a low income during the pandemic

Going into the COVID-19 pandemic, families on a low income who were already experiencing financial insecurity were most vulnerable to the economic and social fallout of the pandemic as a result of a threadbare welfare state and years of austerity (Hill and Webber, 2021). This section draws out several central themes that tie the chapters together, before providing an overview of the collection.

Existing precarity was exacerbated by the pandemic

A major finding across several of the projects, including those that employed longitudinal methodologies, was how financial precarity and insecurity prior to the pandemic made dealing with the pandemic harder, especially for those families in unstable and/or precarious employment; see Chapters 7, 10, and 14. Our synthesis of evidence shows that for families on a low income, everyday life was made increasingly difficult during the pandemic. Previous tried-and-tested strategies for 'getting by', such as managing already tight budgets, shopping around in several supermarkets, and getting help from family and friends, were no longer possible. Food bank use jumped sharply, alongside wider increases in food insecurity overall – often impacting on families with children more intensely. As illustrated particularly in Chapters 2, 4, and 8, employment precarity was further intensified, and affected certain groups, such as young people and single mothers, particularly acutely. In fact, there were gendered implications that meant women predominantly shouldered the burden of juggling multiple and complex roles, particularly in relation to home schooling. The gendered nature of parenting and care represents a major emergent theme and is explored in Chapters 7 and 9. The social security system entered the pandemic itself in ill-health (Garnham, 2020b) and income received from social security, frequently insufficient to cover living costs before COVID-19, was ill-equipped to meet the additional and rising costs experienced by low-income families.

Not only have many incomes fallen, but the cost of living has, for many families, risen considerably throughout the pandemic. As schools shut to all but children of essential workers or those deemed particularly vulnerable, families' utilities, technology, activity, and food costs all rose dramatically (Power et al, 2020; Brewer and Patrick, 2021; Page et al, 2021). Ninety per cent of families on a low income have reported spending more on essential bills while children have been at home (CPAG, 2020). Families on a low income, who normally shop around to find the best deals across a number of large supermarkets, have been forced to shop locally to avoid public transport to out-of-town shopping centres (Page et al, 2020). Additionally, food shortages forced families to buy more expensive, branded products, both increasing the price of a weekly shop, and limiting the number of non-essential items they could purchase. As a consequence, demand for food aid, including food banks, surged (The Trussell Trust, 2020).

Social security changes

A central focus of our collective was to document and understand how the social security system has responded to the additional challenges brought about, and exacerbated by, the pandemic. Across the 14 projects, we can collectively conclude that there remains an urgent need to provide increased support for families with dependent children living on a low income; a group who have thus far been largely neglected in the policy response. It is clear that social security provision has proved inadequate to meet the rising costs incurred by families as a result of COVID-19 (Griffiths et al, 2020; Power et al, 2020; Summers et al, 2021). While welcome, the £20 uplift to UC has not always (or even often) made a decisive difference to the everyday hardship experienced by families with dependent children living in poverty. As lockdowns across the devolved nations triggered business closures, cancellations of contracts, and a wave of redundancies, a raft of measures (most notably the furlough and Self-Employment Income Support [SEISS] schemes) were introduced to cope with the steep rise in the number of people suddenly exposed to vast drops in income, freshly unemployed, and newly eligible for UC or other social security support (Summers et al, 2021). Yet while these measures have been invaluable for many, there has been a lack of COVID-19 policy responses deliberately targeted at families on a low income. As a consequence, pre-existing disparities between children and families have widened even further.

The Government announced a £20 per week uplift to UC per household (for claimants aged 25 and over) at the end of March 2020, initially for a year, although this was extended until September 2021. In July 2021, it was announced that the uplift would not be kept permanently, with Boris Johnson claiming he wanted to spend money on getting people into work rather than on welfare (Waugh, 2021), reinforcing tropes of welfare for the workless. However, those already at the household cap threshold did not receive the uplift; neither did those still receiving legacy benefits. While some UC deductions were frozen, advance repayments continued, meaning some households did not notice the uplift as it went straight towards UC or other debt repayments (Patrick and Lees, 2021). The (in)adequacies of the social security system and its impacts on families on a low income are explored in more depth in Chapters 5, 6, 8, 9, 11, and 13.

(Lack of) support networks

The availability of different kinds of formal and informal support, and how the support landscape for families changed as professionals pivoted to online offers, was highly important for families on a low-income – see especially Chapters 4, 6, 9, and 12. The accessibility and adequacy of support – financial, practical, emotional, and social – were important in navigating the additional barriers presented by the pandemic (Power et al, 2020). COVID-19 has significantly altered the social fabric of society, affecting personal and family lives, and changing the landscapes of partnering, parenting, and the doing of family and community (Tarrant et al, 2020). Formal support networks have either been scaled down or have disappeared, particularly affecting those who might not have familial support networks. This had a very real effect on families' lives as they often had to seek out additional sources of support, such as charitable assistance, which was not always adequate to meet their needs. Informal (family and kinship) support networks became harder to access during the pandemic, but have nevertheless been essential in getting by.

Associated with this are childcare difficulties, particularly for single parents and cohabiting parents trying to balance shift work around each other – as we see in Chapters 8 and 9. Private childcare is often prohibitively expensive. There are also clear gendered aspects which have been exacerbated by COVID-19 – additional burdens have predominantly fallen on women, who are juggling childcare, work, and caring responsibilities. Across our studies, COVID-19 and the subsequent lockdowns have evidently aggravated existing inequalities, with women taking on more care responsibilities and juggling multiple roles.

Outline of this collection

The collection begins in Part I, by shining a spotlight on how the social security system has responded to the challenges brought about by COVID-19, with the first four chapters documenting the impact for families on a low income; both pre- and during the pandemic. We know that the pandemic has not affected families on a low income equally, with variable impacts associated with family identities and circumstances. In Part II, 'Intersecting insecurities in action', the chapters consider how COVID-19 has impacted people across pre-existing inequalities and multiple layers, such as racially minoritised groups (Chapters 5 and 6), larger families (Chapter 7), single parents (Chapter 8), and young fathers (Chapter 9), producing differential experiences of the pandemic. Part III focuses on innovations in sharing experiences during COVID-19. These four chapters explore how researchers have adapted tried-and-tested ways of working to fit the pandemic context, illustrating the possibilities (and also complexities) of working in creative and participatory ways both during the pandemic, and into the future.

Given the multiple ways the pandemic has impacted virtually every aspect of daily life, the difficulties and widening disparities documented across this collection are unlikely to disappear. It seems inevitable that living through COVID-19 has caused long-term national trauma, and exacerbated an already chronic mental health crisis among both adults and children. This creates an urgent task for social scientists to explore, understand, and suggest responses as we move into a post-pandemic context. The concluding chapter therefore emphasises how our collective understanding of the experiences of families on a low income during COVID-19 has been developed and extended by taking a mixed method, interdisciplinary, collaborative approach – and reflects on why that matters in terms of policy and practice. Finally, we emphasise the significant potential of working collaboratively, and note the necessity of continuing to do so in a post-pandemic context. While there was and continues to be a pressing need to examine and understand the immediate and longer-term implications of the COVID-19 pandemic on families on a low income, it remains essential that this is conducted in the most respectful, ethical, and efficient way possible.

References

Brewer, M. and Patrick, R. (2021) Pandemic pressures: why families on a low income are spending more during Covid-19. Resolution Foundation. 11 January. Available at: www.resolutionfoundation.org/app/uploads/2021/01/Pandemic-pressures.pdf

British Medical Journal (BMJ) (2020) Ethnicity and Covid-19. Available at: https://doi.org/10.1136/bmj.m2282 (Published 11 June).

Child Poverty Action Group (CPAG) (2020) Poverty in the pandemic: an update on the impact of coronavirus on low-income families and children. Available at: https://cpag.org.uk/sites/default/files/files/policypost/Poverty-in-the-pandemic_update.pdf

Child Poverty Action Group (CPAG) (2021) 'It feels as though my third child doesn't matter'. The impact of the two-child limit after four years. Available at: https://mcusercontent.com/4fae14f57a18ee08253ffc251/files/6263772a-ec85-4d84-b56c-89cbffd460c6/It_feels_as_though_my_third_child_doesnt_matter.pdf

Garnham, A. (2020a) Low-income parents relying on child benefit for household basics [press release]. *Child Poverty Action Group*. 31 August 2020. Available at: https://cpag.org.uk/news-blogs/news-listings/low-income-parents-relying-child-benefit-household-basics

Garnham, A. (2020b) After the pandemic. *IPPR Progressive Review*, 27(1), 8.

Garthwaite, K., Patrick, R., Power, M. and Warnock, R. (forthcoming) Lessons from researching together: setting the agenda for collaborative research on poverty and life on a low income in a post-pandemic world. Submitted to: *International Journal of Social Research Methodology*.

Griffiths, R., Wood, M., Bennet, F. and Millar, J. (2020) *Unchartered territory: Universal Credit, couples and money*. Bath: Institute for Policy Research.

Hamnett, C. (2014) Shrinking the welfare state: the structure, geography and impact of British government benefit cuts. *Transactions of the Institute of British Geographers*, 39(4), 490–503.

Hill, K. and Webber, R. (2021) Staying afloat in a crisis: families on low incomes in the pandemic. Joseph Rowntree Foundation. Available at: www.jrf.org.uk/report/staying-afloat-crisis-families-low-incomes-pandemic

Howlett, M. (2020) Looking at the 'field' through a Zoom lens: methodological reflections on conducting online research during a global pandemic. *Qualitative Research*. DOI: 1468794120985691.

Innes, D. (2020) What has driven the rise of in-work poverty? *Joseph Rowntree Foundation*. Available at: https://www.jrf.org.uk/file/54061/download?token=7Onk5EZF&filetype=full-report

Jensen, T. and Tyler, I. (2015) 'Benefits broods': the cultural and political crafting of anti-welfare commonsense. *Critical Social Policy*, 35(4), 470–91.

Joseph Rowntree Foundation (JRF) (2020) UK poverty 2019/20. Available at: www.jrf.org.uk/report/uk-poverty-2019-20

Joseph Rowntree Foundation (JRF) (2021) UK poverty 2020/21. Available at: www.jrf.org.uk/report/uk-poverty-2020-21

Markham, A.N., Harris, A. and Luka, M.E. (2020) Massive and microscopic sensemaking during COVID-19 times. *Qualitative Inquiry*. Available at: https://doi.org/10.1177/1077800420962477.

McNeil, C., Parkes, H., Garthwaite, K., Patrick, R. (2021) No longer 'managing': the rise of working poverty and fixing Britain's broken social settlement, IPPR. Available at: www.ippr.org/files/2021-05/no-longer-managing-may21.pdf

Page, G., Power, M. and Patrick, R. (2021) Uniform mistakes: the costs of going back to school. Available at: https://cdn.sanity.io/files/brhp578m/production/8b7902d11787c4c2c62db85f5b050fe573dda7c4.pdf?dl=

Paremoer, L., Nandi, S., Serag, H. and Baum, F. (2021) Covid-19 pandemic and the social determinants of health. *BMJ*, 372. Available at: www.bmj.com/content/372/bmj.n129

Patrick, R. and Lees, T. (2021) Advance to debt: paying back benefit debt – what happens when deductions are made to benefit payments? 7 January. Available at: https://media.covidrealities.org/COVID%20realities%20-%20Advance%20to%20debt%2022%20Dec.pdf

Power, M., Doherty, B., Pybus, K. and Pickett, K. (2020) How COVID-19 has exposed inequalities in the UK food system: the case of UK food and poverty [version 2; peer review: 5 approved]. Emerald Open Res, 2, 11. Available at: https://doi.org/10.35241/emeraldopenres.13539.2.

Ruxton, S. and Burrell, S. (2020) Masculinities and COVID-19: making the connections. Promundo.

Summers, K., Scullion, L., Baumberg Geiger, B., Robertshaw, D., Edmiston, D., Gibbons, A., Karagiannaki, E., de Vries, R. and Ingold, J. (2021) Claimants' experiences of the social security system during the first wave of COVID-19. Welfare at a (Social) Distance. Available at: www.distantwelfare.co.uk/winter-report

Tarrant, A., Ladlow, L. and Way, L. (2020) From social isolation to local support: relational change and continuities for young fathers in the context of the COVID-19 crisis. Available at: https://followingyoungfathersfurther.org/asset/working-papers/

The Trussell Trust (2020) Food banks report record spike in need as coalition of anti-poverty charities call for strong lifeline to be thrown to anyone who needs it. Available at: www.trusselltrust.org/2020/05/01/coalition-call/

Waugh, P. (2021) Boris Johnson says Universal Credit claimants should rely on their own 'efforts' not welfare. *HuffPost*. 26th August. Available at: https://www.huffingtonpost.co.uk/entry/boris-johnson-universal-credit-cuts_uk_61279c88e4b0231e3699003e

Wenham, C., Smith, J. and Morgan, R. (2020) COVID-19: the gendered impacts of the outbreak. *The Lancet*, 395(10227), 846–8.

PART I

Social security in the spotlight

Bringing up a family and making ends meet: before and during the COVID-19 crisis

Ruth Webber and Katherine Hill

Introduction

This chapter draws on qualitative longitudinal data to discuss the role of the financial circumstances of families on low incomes before the pandemic on their experiences of managing to make ends meet during the pandemic. Parents on low incomes with dependent-age children already facing constraints and instability at the start of 2020 were more vulnerable to the impacts of the COVID-19 pandemic, with fewer resources to fall back on. Circumstances have been growing more challenging for these families over time after a decade of austerity, during which the benefit freeze reduced the value of social security payments for working-age adults (Corlett, 2019), entitlements for families with children were limited by the benefit cap and two-child limit, alongside rising housing costs and increasingly insecure work. At the beginning of 2020, half a million more children were living in poverty than just five years ago (Hirsch and Stone, 2021), with single-parent households, larger families, and those containing someone with a disability or health condition at greater risk (Joseph Rowntree Foundation [JRF], 2020; Department for Work and Pensions, [DWP], 2021a). The fact that 75 per cent of children in poverty live in a household with at least one person in work (DWP, 2021a) highlights that despite the policy focus on getting parents into work, it is not a guaranteed route out of poverty, as other studies in this edited collection also argue (Chapter 11). The pandemic has exacerbated an already challenging situation for many families. Research has shown that families on the lowest incomes have struggled disproportionately throughout the pandemic, facing reduced incomes that have had to stretch further while also facing ever increasing costs associated with the pandemic (Brewer et al, 2020; Edwards et al, 2020; Brewer and Patrick, 2021; McNeil et al, 2021).

Like other studies discussed in this collection (Chapters 2, 3, 4, and 10), this chapter draws on qualitative longitudinal research. The study, funded by Joseph Rowntree Foundation, followed the experiences of families with children living on incomes below the Minimum Income Standard over a period of five years from 2015 through to autumn 2020, around six months after the first lockdown was imposed in the UK in March 2020 (Hill and Webber, 2021a, 2021b). The chapter looks longitudinally at the role of families' financial circumstances before the pandemic on their experiences of the pandemic. The analysis demonstrates the potential of qualitative longitudinal research to illuminate the factors which shaped how families on low incomes managed during the COVID-19 crisis. The chapter shows that the stability or insecurity of income from work and social security, changing health needs, and access to support networks can have profound impacts on the ability of families to make ends meet, both before and during the pandemic when families faced additional challenges and costs. It concludes by outlining the key contributions our study makes to policy, arguing for the necessity of a more holistic approach to the multiple and complex needs and stress factors parents face when bringing up a family on a low income.

Method

The research comprised four waves of in-depth interviews with parents of dependent-age children across England. The initial study involving three (face-to-face) interviews in 2015, 2017, and early 2020 provided a valuable insight into these families' lives over time up to the eve of the pandemic. Given the unprecedented and potentially uneven impact of the pandemic, the study was extended to include a further interview (conducted over the phone) in September and October 2020 to explore the families' experiences in the first six to seven months of the pandemic. Fourteen families took part in all four interviews and included a mixture of housing tenure, single- and couple-parent households, parents in and out of work, and children of different ages, with a small number of children becoming non-dependents by the end of the study.

The first three waves of interviews provided an insight into the sudden changes families on low incomes can face, and the ongoing hard work involved in trying to keep afloat (see also Daly and Kelly, 2015; Millar and Ridge, 2017; and O'Brien and Kyprianou, 2017). They shed light on the contrast between participants' deep value of stability and their experiences of sometimes profound precarity (Hill and Webber, 2021b). The aims of the fourth wave of interviews were firstly, to explore the wide-ranging impact of the pandemic on living standards, in the light of families' situations and experiences over the previous five years. Secondly, to identify the impacts of policy interventions taken because of the crisis, assessing the extent to which they helped families to respond to any sudden changes.

A qualitative longitudinal approach allowed us to capture the 'dynamic process' (Neale, 2020) of the impact of change over time, the 'complex causality' of the life events (Neale, 2021) of these families, and interactions *between* multiple factors and stressors that may occur and affect one another simultaneously (Hickman, 2018). Thus, the discussion in this chapter goes some way to addressing the 'growing chasm between empirical evidence and policy-making' (Neale, 2021: 12), by attempting to draw attention to the various, changeable, and interwoven components that shaped the 14 families' experiences of the pandemic. Such an approach moves us beyond a mere 'snapshot' of people's lives within the framework of a global crisis (Smith and Middleton, 2007; McLeod and Thompson, 2009), instead attending to the interaction between economic, structural, and personal factors preceding the pandemic itself.

Key findings

There were several key issues facing families in our study, which often interacted to make managing the effects of the pandemic on a low income more or less challenging. These were: the adequacy and stability of income from work and social security, support networks, and physical and mental health. The longitudinal data points to the deep ties between these factors, illustrating the implications of (in)security and (in)stability within each of these areas. For example, parents' work opportunities over the five years were often intertwined with changes in health or changing childcare needs. This in turn had implications for their finances, which were often more severe for single-parent households (see also Chapter 8). We look at each issue in turn, before presenting two contrasting case studies which further illuminate the ways these key themes interacted with one another before and during the pandemic.

The extent of change over time

Drawing on participant's accounts from all four interviews, Figure 1.1 captures the extent of fluctuation the families in our study experienced in their financial circumstances over the five-year period leading up to and in the six months following the announcement of the first lockdown in the UK in March 2020. The four categories represent the different degrees of managing families experienced at different times in the study. At points, some were managing well and 'getting on' with life improving; others 'getting by' and managing to make ends meet with a little leeway; some were finding it 'hard to keep afloat' having to juggle budgets and make sacrifices; and those 'under increasing pressure' risked going without basics, for instance needing to use food banks, and accumulating debt. Looking at how these families managed during the first six months of the pandemic alongside their financial situations over the preceding years allowed us to delve deeper into the protective and precarious factors that shaped their experiences of the crisis. Crucially, all the families had to navigate periods of struggle at some point throughout the research, and the diagram illustrates the extent to which low income and poverty are not simply a transitory phenomenon, but often protracted states of challenge, which continued and in some cases became more difficult in the pandemic. Nonetheless, as Figure 1.1 shows, some families had managed to get by and keep afloat even during the crisis.

We now turn to look in more detail at what made a difference: what helped or made it harder to manage; the interaction between different factors; and the implications of this on families' experiences of making ends meet during the crisis.

Work and income stability, and financial situation

Employment

Job and income stability prior to the pandemic had implications for household finances when the pandemic hit. Various factors interacted with and influenced the degree of work and income stability throughout the research, including childcare responsibilities, partner status, and physical and mental health. In the initial six months of the crisis, stable work and a supportive employer helped protect some parents' incomes, with jobs continuing or resuming after a short period of furlough, options to work from home, and flexibility around hours which helped to accommodate childcare, particularly given that formal and informal childcare provision became more limited due to restrictions. Indeed, some couple-households where both parents were working saw an improvement in their financial situation over the five years, and stable work and steady earnings were key to keeping families afloat.

However, sudden changes in work circumstances had already catalysed periods of struggle for several households. Families who experienced adverse effects to their work and income due to job loss or reduced hours during the COVID-19 crisis were often already in insecure employment such as temporary, agency, or zero-hours work. Many of these were also jobs that they were not able to do at home. Hopes of temporary or zero-hours contracts being extended or leading to more secure work did not come to fruition for some households. Instead, some parents were made redundant at the end of a period of furlough, or when contracts ended. Having faced periods without work or income drops in the past, these parents' experiences highlight the negative effects of insecure work over time, resulting in added precarity when the crisis hit employment

Figure 1.1: Participants' financial situation over four interviews, 2015–20

Participants' financial situation over four interviews, 2015–20

Each graph represents one case. W1, W2, and so on show interview waves
Some cases include additional changes between waves, as reported by participants

a) In three cases, participants found it hard to keep afloat throughout this five-year period; two of these faced increasing pressure in the pandemic

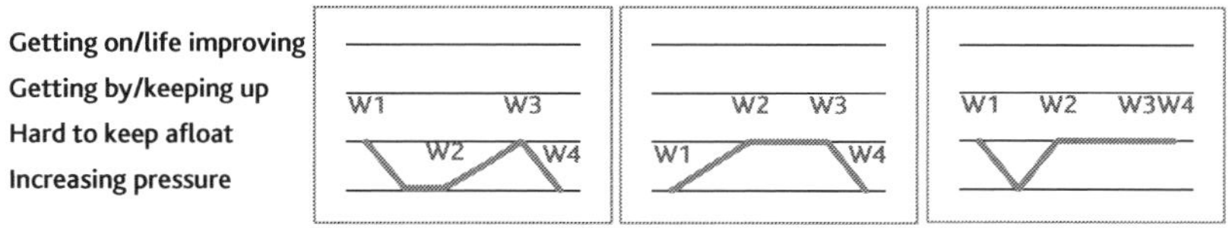

Getting on/life improving
Getting by/keeping up
Hard to keep afloat
Increasing pressure

b) Five had sometimes coped and sometimes found it hard to keep afloat, but had never been under the most severe pressure

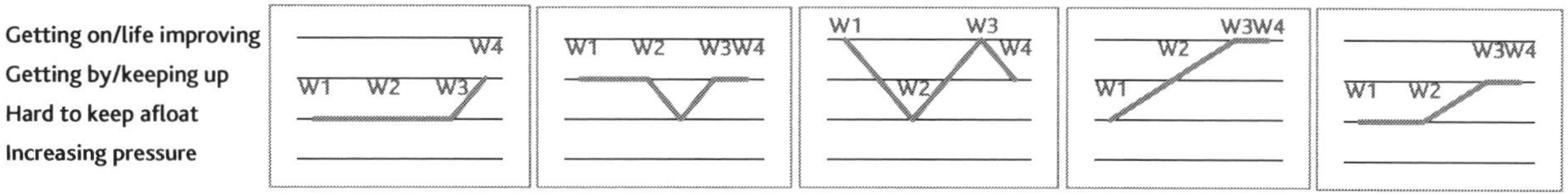

Getting on/life improving
Getting by/keeping up
Hard to keep afloat
Increasing pressure

c) The remaining six had sometimes faced very severe pressures but at other times had managed to get by
Of these, two were at least coping in the pandemic but for three of the other four, things got tougher in the pandemic

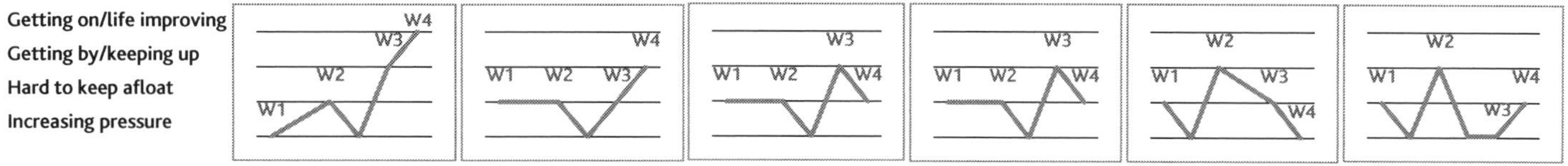

Getting on/life improving
Getting by/keeping up
Hard to keep afloat
Increasing pressure

(Brewer et al, 2020). This varied by sector and kind of employment, as shown by Clery et al in Chapter 8 of this collection. Families affected by high levels of precarity in their employment and income because of the pandemic struggled to improve their financial circumstances and consequently, family living standards. Even participants in long-term or more secure jobs articulated the underlying risks of job loss that although present before, had been exacerbated by the uncertainty and rapid change brought about by the pandemic. Increased precarity of work has raised questions about the extent to which social protection afforded by the social security system is able to be responsive enough to sudden and sometimes short-term changes in work and income (Millar and Whiteford, 2020).

The Government's Coronavirus Job Retention Scheme, or 'furlough', introduced in March 2020 offered some protection, albeit only temporarily in cases where it delayed a loss of work. For other parents and adult children who were in work, it tempered the uncertainty with several participants receiving at least 80 per cent of their wages, and some employers topping up the additional 20 per cent. The furlough scheme could mean the difference between managing and struggling, providing an essential form of continuity at what was an intensely disrupted time. However, not all employment was covered under the furlough scheme, and for one lone parent, the loss of £40 a week income from a casual cleaning job meant she struggled to manage: "We're literally living hand to mouth, and not even getting hand to mouth at certain times. It might only be £40 but it makes a huge difference." Several parents referred to the lack of availability of work altogether: "There's lots of people going for the same job at the moment, with people losing their jobs with the pandemic." An issue for lone parents was lack of work that fitted around children, especially if childcare options were more limited (see also Chapter 8).

Some parents also found themselves unable to rely financially on others whose work or income had been hit during the crisis. Households with older children were affected as the pandemic had the most significant impact on sectors disproportionately employing young adults. In several families, young adults had struggled to find work and were no longer able to contribute to household costs, which put additional pressure on parents' finances: "There's not a lot out there … It's quite challenging and I feel really sorry for her because she is trying. But it doesn't help me and her mum because we are having to subsidise whatever she was earning." Some lone parents in our study lost financial support from ex-partners whose work or health circumstances meant they stopped or reduced financial contributions. Having previously been a crucial source of income, for some parents becoming steadier or increasing over the five years prior to the pandemic, this drop in cross-household income catalysed financial uncertainty during an already very uncertain time.

Social security issues and adequacy

Two key issues related to social security support emerged from our research. Firstly, the inadequacy of income from social security, particularly where families were relying solely on benefits during the pandemic if work had been affected. The figures for Universal Credit (UC) claimants doubled in the pandemic (DWP, 2021b). The £20 a week uplift was a welcome policy change. For one mother in the study it helped to balance a reduction in child support payments. However, parents in several families said they had not noticed an increase to their income where they were claiming UC. The uplift was obscured where awards were affected by deductions such as arrears, or fluctuations in income from work, and more noticeable to those with regular, unchanging incomes. This highlights the extent that UC left families with limited financial flexibility to manage when costs rose at the peak of the crisis, a finding that chimes with other research (Edwards et al, 2020). One lone mother explained that even after the uplift: "I was struggling with most of the debts, because like I said what they pay me on Universal Credit, literally only just covers my bills." Furthermore, one of the major critiques of this significant policy has been that families on 'legacy benefits' were not entitled to this uplift yet faced the same increased costs.

Secondly, families often had to make budgets stretch further in cases where there was a non-dependent child living at home who was delaying claiming out-of-work benefits they were entitled to in the hope of finding work, for fear that claiming would impact on their parents' social security payments. There is a clear need to address young adults' hesitancy around claiming, particularly given that the number of single young adults aged 20–34 living with parents has increased by a third in the last two decades (Hill et al, 2020), which will have consequences for the household's financial circumstances.

Managing increased costs

Food and household bills rose in the early stages of the pandemic with more people at home in lockdown. In particular, parents cited increased demand on electricity with more devices being used for home schooling and entertainment, and greater bandwidth requirements to accommodate increased family needs including where parents were working from home (see also Chapters 9, 11, and 12 in this collection). Some parents explained that their food costs had risen dramatically – those with more children and older children felt the impact of increased food costs particularly keenly, especially at the height of the lockdown when children were off school. While the extension of the Free School Meal vouchers throughout the holidays acted as a buffer for eligible families, parents whose incomes were already under severe pressure and/or had dropped due to unemployment or reduced hours experienced greater precarity: "I thought things had been tight before but this has pushed us to our limits."

Families whose work continued, income increased, or whose outgoings decreased for example through no longer having to commute, had more room in their budget. These families were more able to navigate the increased costs of the pandemic with less financial strain.

Support networks

Access to a range of support networks formed a crucial part of how families managed to make ends meet. This includes informal support from families, communities, and friends, as well as more formal support from services and other agencies.

Hill et al (2021) have written elsewhere of the vital importance of informal support for families – to help get by or improve lives, and crucially in times of economic uncertainty. Throughout this study, this included practical help such as childcare, emotional support, as well as financial support in the form of gifts and loans ensuring some families were able to manage during particularly challenging periods, or if faced with sudden costs such as energy bills, or the repair of household goods. Our research draws out the critical point that often those within families' support networks were experiencing insecurity and instability themselves, in work, health, and income. During the pandemic, job and income insecurity affected those on whom some of our participants depended, including ex-partners as mentioned earlier, and family and friends (see also Chapter 11). Thus, while previously parents had been able to draw on informal support – for example grandparents' help with childcare when working, or going around to family or friends' houses for meals at times of intense financial difficulty – this was curtailed due to lockdown restrictions.

Formal support was another crucial area that was affected by the pandemic; this is also shown clearly in Chapters 2 and 9 in this collection. Families on low incomes rely more heavily on public services than those who are financially able to access private healthcare. The consequences are that families with greater financial constraints often face longer waiting times, which several participants reported were significantly increased during the pandemic. Over time, being able to access support services had helped families in our study increase incomes through support with social security claims, reduce costs through support with debts and use of food banks, and help families with their physical and mental health. Some parents found accessing support more problematic during lockdown with the greatest challenge being support with physical and mental health. Difficulties were encountered where NHS services were reduced to manage the vast numbers of COVID-19 patients, and services moved from face-to-face appointments to online or telephone services which did not always address their needs.

Physical and mental health: 'the second, silent pandemic'

Physical and mental health challenges preceded the pandemic, having implications for work opportunities and income over time (Hill and Webber, 2021b). Lockdown restrictions could compound these with several participants reporting increases in anxiety and depression. Financial pressures linked with the pandemic intensified these issues, echoing findings from Child Poverty Action Group (CPAG) that health problems and financial stress were closely connected in low-income families' experiences of the crisis (Edwards et al, 2020).

Our research drew stark attention to the impact that insufficient support in this area can have on families. One parent even referred to mental health as the "second, silent pandemic". Coping with the additional stresses of the pandemic alongside reduced access to support networks could be particularly hard for parents managing this on their own. One mother emphasised the isolation that could come with being a lone parent throughout the lockdown, saying: "I have never wished I had a partner until now." Although more likely to need more regular contact with health services particularly where conditions worsened, several parents emphasised the difficulties they had faced at times when accessing formal support for physical and mental health both prior to and during the pandemic. Some parents spoke of a lack of support from school for children with anxiety and depression, which compounded the challenges of several months of home schooling and the uncertainty triggered by the lockdown.

A comparative look

While all the families in our study were on a low income throughout the research, the themes explored earlier interacted in different ways for each family, resulting in unique trajectories, with some faring better than others at different times. Looking at two contrasting cases allows an insight into *how* these factors intersect and result in managing or finding things more challenging when the pandemic hit.

Before the pandemic, both Cassie and Lisa[1] were managing health issues alongside work and three school-aged children. However, while Cassie, a lone parent, had to move from two part-time jobs to a zero-hours contract to manage fluctuations in her health, Lisa and her husband were a two-income household, with both working full-time. Thus, while each household faced similar issues, the factors at play interacted differently for each, meaning that while Cassie felt she was 'sinking' during the pandemic, Lisa felt they had 'breezed through' it.

Cassie

Cassie was a lone parent, living in social rented housing with her three children, one secondary-aged and two in primary school. Having had to leave her two jobs due to a deterioration in her physical health, Cassie had been employed on a zero-hours contract at a nearby hospitality venue since the end of 2019. Work was sporadic and while she was receiving UC, her income had dropped. Having struggled with debt in the past, she felt she was just about managing everyday costs before the pandemic hit. Cassie stressed that there was a lot of instability around her work, both with regards to her health and the hours available, and highlighted just how quickly things could change, saying: "You never know what life throws at you."

The lockdown restrictions affected Cassie in several ways. Firstly, a period of furlough from the start of lockdown to the end of June helped as she was receiving a regular amount which she would not necessarily have done, given her contract was zero hours. When she was made redundant at the end of June, she had struggled to find another job for a couple of months, eventually only being able to find work for seven hours a week. While working less was better for her physical health, it did not provide her with adequate income. Furthermore, she had not felt the impact of the £20 a week uplift to her UC amid fluctuations in her claim, and her income from this only covered her bills, leaving her with little left over. She needed work which could fit around childcare and health needs, but this proved elusive.

Secondly, because of the drop in income, Cassie's credit card bills had crept up again to manage increased household costs, and she had fallen behind with loan repayments as well as some household bills. Without the Free School Meal vouchers over the holidays, she felt she would have struggled even more, although she already felt as though she was 'sinking' because of the pandemic. Thirdly, alongside dealing with the additional challenges brought about by the pandemic, such as home schooling and increased food costs, her ex-partner, who had been a 'lifeline' in the past became less able to help as he had also faced a drop in income. Having to manage without this additional financial and emotional support was extremely challenging for Cassie, who felt that she could not cope with another six months of lockdown.

Lisa

Lisa lived in her home which she paid a mortgage on with her husband, with their three children, one secondary-aged and two in primary school.

Her family's situation had improved over the five years, moving from 'finding it hard to keep afloat' in the first interview to 'getting on' both before and during the pandemic. This was due to paying off significant debts by the third interview with a loan from her mother-in-law, and Lisa transitioning from not working in the first interview because her children were not yet at school, to full-time employment by the third interview, just before the pandemic hit. Although she was using painkillers to manage her health condition, this transition into full-time work had a huge impact on her family's finances, relationships, and ability to manage the extra costs associated with the lockdown.

In the six months following the first lockdown, both Lisa and her husband were deemed key workers, so both were working full-time for the first month and a half. Lisa continued to work full-time throughout the pandemic, which provided regular income. Furthermore, although her mother-in-law had to stop helping with childcare when she had to shield, Lisa's husband was offered a four-month period of furlough, and while it was at 80 per cent it was based on the previous year's earnings when he had done lots of overtime. This had three important implications for them. Firstly, it meant that like Lisa, he was able to continue to receive an adequate income at a time when loss of or reduced income could have had significant consequences for their ability to make ends meet. Secondly, he was able to be at home while the children were off school, which meant that Lisa could continue working and bringing in a full-time wage. The financial stability they had during the crisis meant they had not needed to make use of the mortgage holiday, a crucial indicator of the degree to which they felt able to manage without further formal support other than what they were receiving with the furlough. Finally, Lisa felt that her son's additional learning needs and resultant anxieties around school were managed much more easily at home.

Conclusions and contributions to policy

The case studies and findings discussed in this chapter highlight that the families in our study often experienced various 'complex causal' factors and changes concurrently (Neale, 2021) that made managing to make ends meet more challenging or straightforward. As a result, we argue that policy interventions *must* look holistically at families' circumstances, to better understand the complex and interacting factors that shape parents' experiences of bringing up a family on a low income. To conclude, we identify three key policy areas that need further attention to better equip families with dependent children to manage in the context of a crisis like the pandemic, and beyond.

Job and income security

A stable job and income are a crucial foundation for families to cope with sudden shocks like changes in health and income drops in other areas such as child maintenance, as well as bigger crises like the pandemic. It is essential that policy reflects the complex causal relationship (Neale, 2021) between job insecurity, health, and childcare needs. In other words, that policy is developed from the understanding that these factors are all deeply entwined, and as such parents need to feel supported as they navigate challenges with childcare and health needs. With a new Flexible Working Bill being debated in Parliament, this is a salient issue, and one that our research demonstrates has resounding impacts over time, and during times of crisis.

Furthermore, while informal support can act as a 'third source of welfare' (Hill et al, 2021), families should not have to depend on such avenues to make ends meet. Such support networks are themselves vulnerable to insecurity, resulting in varying emotional and financial dependability over time according to the financial situation of those within the network. Ensuring secure employment and income for all, with access to affordable childcare, would reduce the extent to which parents have to rely on others to make ends meet.

The need for an adequate social security safety net

Social security was a vital lifeline for families in our study both in and out of work, before and during the pandemic. As both an in-work and out-of-work benefit, UC has helped working *and* non-working families. At the time of writing the £20 a week uplift to UC was due to end in October 2021, causing much concern about the impact this would have for families. The uplift has been necessary given the long-term freeze and cuts to working-age benefits, bringing the rate more closely in line with inflation rates, hence any reduction would place additional pressure on already thinly spread budgets. Furthermore, although the extension of this uplift to legacy benefits would likely not lift these families out of poverty, it could go some way to buffering against sudden financial change. Encouraging and supporting eligible working-age children to claim UC could also make a real difference to household financial circumstances.

A final key issue with the uplift is that it applies per claim regardless of household size. This means that both smaller and larger families have received the same amount, despite differences in financial need. This must be addressed. One way to do so is to target support through Child Benefit in order that support is distributionally fairer. Additionally, extending this uplift to all those on means-tested benefits would be recognition of the complex and often rapidly changing circumstances that parents bringing up families on low incomes often grapple with.

Access to formal support and services

The availability of support and information relating to key areas such as social security, health, and debt has proved crucial before and during the pandemic, notably given the challenges people faced accessing such support (Williams et al, 2020). Face-to-face services were limited under lockdown restrictions, and some found online support challenging, leading to unmet needs, some of which were exacerbated by the pandemic as we have discussed in this chapter. Ensuring that information and points of access are readily available is therefore of crucial importance going forward.

Living with insecurity is not a new experience brought about by the COVID-19 crisis, but rather a state of being that many people have been having to manage for a long time. This chapter has brought together an analysis of the circumstances of families on low incomes before and during the pandemic. Longitudinal exploration of the interaction between the levels of insecurity these families were already living with when the crisis hit and their experiences of the pandemic, allows a fuller understanding of how such crises deepen pre-existing gulfs between those with the resource to act as a buffer against sudden changes, and those without. Being able to see the impact of having more, fewer, or indeed changing resources over time, and the interaction *between* these different resources, means we can see with greater clarity the areas in which families need more support and stability.

Note
[1]   Names changed for the purposes of anonymity.

References
Brewer, M. and Patrick, R. (2021) Pandemic pressures: why families on low-income are spending more during Covid-19. London: Resolution Foundation.

Brewer, M., Corlett, A., Handscomb, K., McCurdy, C. and Tomlinson, D. (2020) The Living Standards Audit 2020. London: Resolution Foundation.

Corlett, A. (2019) The benefit freeze has ended, but erosion of the social security safety net continues. Briefing Paper. London: Resolution Foundation.

Daly, M. and Kelly, G. (2015) *Families and Poverty: Everyday Life on a Low Income*. Bristol: Policy Press.

Department for Work and Pensions (DWP) (2021a) Households below average income, statistics on the number and percentage of people living in low-income households for financial years 1994/95 to 2019/20. Table 4.3db.

Department for Work and Pensions (DWP) (2021b) Universal Credit statistics. 29 April 2013 to 14 January 2021.

Edwards, Z., Howes, S., Reedy, J. and Sefton, T. (2020) Poverty in the pandemic: an update on the impact of coronavirus on low-income families and children. London: Child Poverty Action Group, The Church of England.

Hickman, P. (2018) A flawed construct? Understanding and unpicking the concept of resilience in the context of economic hardship. *Social Policy and Society*, 17(3), 409–24.

Hill, K. and Webber, R. (2021a) Coping in a crisis: families on low incomes in the pandemic. York: Joseph Rowntree Foundation.

Hill, K. and Webber, R. (2021b) Seeking an anchor in an unstable world: experiences of low-income families over time. York: Joseph Rowntree Foundation.

Hill, K., Hirsch, D. and Davis, A. (2021) The role of social support networks in helping low-income families through uncertain times. *Social Policy and Society*, 20(1), 17–32.

Hill, K., Hirsch, D., Stone, J. and Webber, R. (2020) Home truths: young adults living with their parents in low to middle income families. Edinburgh: Standard Life Foundation.

Hirsch, D. and Stone, J. (2021) Local indicators of child poverty after housing costs. 2019/20. End Child Poverty.

Joseph Rowntree Foundation (2020) UK poverty 2019/20. Report. York: Joseph Rowntree Foundation.

McLeod, J. and Thomson, R. (2009) *Researching Social Change*. London: Sage.

McNeil, C., Parkes, H., Patrick, R. and Garthwaite, K. (2021) No longer 'managing': the rise of working poverty and fixing Britain's broken social settlement. London: Institute for Public Policy Press.

Millar, J. and Ridge, T. (2017) Work and relationships over time in lone-mother families. York: Joseph Rowntree Foundation.

Millar, J. and Whiteford, P. (2020) Timing it right or timing it wrong: how should income-tested benefits deal with changes in circumstances?. *Journal of Poverty and Social Justice*, 28(1), 3–20.

Neale, B. (2020) *Qualitative Longitudinal Research: Research Methods*. London: Bloomsbury Publishing.

Neale, B. (2021) Fluid enquiry, complex causality, policy processes: making a difference with qualitative longitudinal research. *Social Policy and Society*, 653–69.

O'Brien, M. and Kyprianou, P. (2017) *Just Managing? What it Means for the Families of Austerity Britain.* Cambridge: Open Book Publishers.

Smith, N. and Middleton, S. (2007) A review of poverty dynamics research in the UK. York: Joseph Rowntree Foundation.

Williams, S.N., Armitage, C.J., Tampe, T., and Dienes, K. (2020) Public perceptions and experiences of social distancing and social isolation during the COVID-19 pandemic: A UK-based focus group study. *BMJ open*, 10(7), e039334.

2

Welfare at a (Social) Distance: accessing social security and employment support during COVID-19 and its aftermath

David Robertshaw, Kate Summers, Lisa Scullion, Daniel Edmiston, Ben Baumberg Geiger, Andrea Gibbons, Jo Ingold, Robert de Vries, and David Young

Introduction

As the economic disruption of COVID-19 has unfolded, working-age benefits have been an important feature of the national pandemic response. However, after years of successive reforms to social security in the UK, significant concerns have been raised about the accessibility and complexity of the benefits system (Summers and Young, 2020), the regularity and adequacy of its support (Millar and Bennett, 2017; Edmiston, 2021), the challenges of digitalisation (Meers, 2020), and the implications of a more punitive benefits regime (Dwyer et al, 2018; Wright and Patrick, 2019), particularly for 'vulnerable' individuals (Dwyer et al, 2020; Scullion and Curchin, 2021). COVID-19 therefore raises important questions about how the system was experienced both by newcomers and existing benefit claimants, and whether adaptations to social security provision during the pandemic were adequate.

In response to this rapidly changing context, the Welfare at a (Social) Distance[1] project was developed: a major national research project investigating the benefits system during COVID-19 and its aftermath, funded by the Economic and Social Research Council as part of UK Research and Innovation's rapid response to COVID-19. The project started in May 2020 and runs until spring 2022. It is a large-scale mixed methods project comprising three work packages: a three-wave, nationally representative online survey of 7,000 new and existing claimants;[2] case studies of four local ecosystems of support (based upon 32 interviews with support organisations[3]); and qualitative longitudinal research (QLR) with new and existing claimants (74 participants in the first wave). A fourth strand of the project, funded by the Health Foundation, was also added (June 2020–May 2021) and explored the experiences of non-claimants and unsuccessful claimants, again comprising a national survey (2,700 participants) and qualitative interviews (20 interviews) (Geiger et al, 2021a; 2021b).

This chapter reflects on both our key findings and our experiences of undertaking the research during the pandemic. First, we examine the experiences of claimants, focusing specifically on Universal Credit (UC) and those who were engaging with the benefits system for the first time during the pandemic. This chapter draws primarily on our thematic analysis of the first wave of qualitative interviews with claimants (conducted between June and September 2020) and our interviews with support organisations (conducted between June and October 2020). However, we combine this with our quantitative data which enables us to situate people's experiences within a nationally representative picture. Here we focus on three key themes: (i) accessing the benefits system; (ii) understandings of eligibility; and (iii) the use of formal and informal sources of support by claimants. It is argued that insufficient understandings of the social security system have had detrimental impacts for significant numbers of people in the form of delays and non-take-up of benefits. It is also suggested that the 'digital by default' system, although critical to successfully delivering financial support to people during the pandemic, has sometimes compounded uncertainties around eligibility and contributed towards claimant anxieties. In considering the perspectives of support organisations we find an uneven distribution of support for addressing poor benefit knowledge, and risks to vulnerable claimants through increased reliance upon informal sources of support. In the second part of the chapter, we then move on to share our reflections on the practical and methodological issues arising from conducting fieldwork in the context of the pandemic.

Findings

Navigating the benefits system during COVID-19

'When I went online there was millions of people on Universal Credit that same night because everything was taking so long. It kept on pushing me out, and then I think I signed these forms maybe about three or four times, and then it would keep on sending me back to the beginning again.' ('Connie',[4] 20s, in-work UC claimant)

Although many first-time applicants to UC found the application process relatively straightforward, significant numbers experienced difficulties in accessing the system during the first wave of the pandemic. This often reflected the timing of an application and, as seen in the earlier quote, in part related to the sudden nature of the lockdown after which applications for UC initially increased by a factor of ten (Department for Work and Pensions [DWP], 2021a). The DWP took several positive steps in response to the surge in claims including increasing capacity for identity verification; moving staff into benefit-processing roles; calling customers back to finalise their applications; and adopting a principle of 'trust and protect' through the easement of certain checks with a view to facilitating access to the system (Work and Pensions Committee [WPC], 2020: 12–14; DWP, 2021b).

However, although such measures supported the processing of unprecedented numbers of claims, our research found that a range of other factors simultaneously impeded access to UC, including benefits stigma, confusion regarding eligibility, and limited understandings of the system (including changes made since March 2020), all of which sometimes delayed or deterred claims in the early days of the pandemic (Summers et al, 2021). We estimate that between 430,000 and 560,000 people who were eligible for UC did not claim, primarily due to stigma, perceptions of 'hassle', or mistaken assumptions about ineligibility (Geiger et al, 2021a). These issues not only prevented claims, but also delayed them. We estimate that 36 per cent of new claimants delayed their application for between one week and one month, with an additional 14 per cent delaying their applications for over one month (Summers et al, 2021: 11). As with non-take-up of benefits, stigma and perceptions of 'hassle' or ineligibility contributed to delays. In our interviews it was common to hear of claims being initiated only after other options had been exhausted and when the reality of having no money dawned on people. We were also able to investigate people's prior assumptions about their ineligibility. Sometimes this reflected stereotypes about 'who benefits were for', but at other times it could reflect a lack of understanding of the systems' rules (or recent changes to them). For example, income support for self-employed people has been time-limited and based around the notion of 'gainful self-employment' (Caraher and Reuter, 2019). This meant self-employed people could reasonably assume they were ineligible for UC unless they were aware of temporary changes made in response to COVID-19:[5]

> 'I was reading all the stuff and I thought I'm not even going to be eligible for this. I really didn't think I was going to get one pence. I was honest, I put everything in that I had to put in, I declared every last penny. So when it said how much is in this account? I put even down to the last 27p. Did all that and I just thought they're not going to give me anything, but they did. I don't know if it's because the rules changed since COVID.' ('Veronica', 50s, in-work UC claimant)

A lack of understanding and clarity about which benefits to claim could also slow claims down for new applicants (for example confusion around UC and 'New Style' (National Insurance Contribution-based) Jobseekers Allowance). COVID-19-related policies could sometimes also contribute to delays in themselves. For example, the Coronavirus Job Retention Scheme placed the responsibility for applications and decisions about who (and whether) to furlough with employers. As such, some people delayed applications to UC in anticipation of their employer's furlough decisions:

'I was waiting to see if I was furloughed, and as soon as I realised I wasn't going to be furloughed, yes, I had applied. Then with Universal Credit, one thing that I regretted, that I wasn't aware of, is that from the moment you apply for it, your payment will be backdated from the date you apply. Whereas, I wasn't aware, so I applied quite late, so I didn't get that backdated source of income.' ('Helena', 20s, out-of-work UC claimant)

After people had successfully initiated a UC application, it was evident that some had difficulties in understanding aspects of their benefit claim. The most common form of confusion related to understanding how UC payments were calculated, and how much people could expect to receive each month, which had clear implications for household budgeting. The practice of claiming UC as a household was also confusing for some. For example, one interviewee explained that he and his partner had made separate claims only to have them linked afterwards; another explained that her partner had made an application to UC but that this had been delayed for several weeks because she had not understood that she needed to enter information in support of a joint claim. There was also confusion about the meaning of 'household'; for example, one young woman living at her parents' house could not understand the relevance of her parents' income to her claim given that they did not support her financially.

Such ambiguities and misunderstandings could provoke anxieties, which were sometimes compounded by the primarily digital nature of interactions. Responsiveness to the pandemic-induced surge in applications for UC has been associated with a high level of digitalisation, and this worked well for what may be thought of as 'ideal jobseekers' (Scholz and Ingold, 2020). For example, some experienced the process as less embarrassing or stigmatising than anticipated, because they were not required to attend a physical appointment at Jobcentre Plus. The digital interface, however, worked less well for others and although most acknowledged COVID-19 as an unusual operational context, many still articulated a need for in-person reassurance, timely feedback, and a clearer understanding of what was happening at various stages of their claim:

'forms don't really faze me but that's when I'm in sound mind. This just threw me into utter panic because it was like, oh my God, there's no one to ask if I'm doing it right. There's no confirmation of anything. There's no, you've done this wrong, please do it again. You just have to do it and trust you've done it right … I needed, to talk to a human being to either tell me where I'm going wrong or put me on the right path.' ('Tina', 50s, out-of-work UC claimant)

Our research therefore highlighted digital participation and digital exclusion as complex and multifaceted phenomena, and although the digital nature of the system enabled the successful processing of an unprecedented number of claims, some interviewees felt that 'detached' digital interactions had increased their anxieties in the pandemic context. Indeed, many people still required significant amounts of support to navigate the benefits system, initiate applications, or maintain their claims.

Formal and informal sources of support

Official objectives of rationalisation and simplification under UC have been associated with additional complexities for claimants (Summers and Young, 2020). As such, the need for responsiveness to individual circumstances has grown and often been displaced onto external actors (Cheetham et al, 2019) who increasingly 'bridge the claim' with information, advice, advocacy, and material support. COVID-19 effectively presented a high-level 'stress test' for these wider ecosystems of support with claimants still needing and receiving support from people outside of the DWP when applying for working-age benefits during the pandemic. Indeed, a quarter of new UC claimants received help with their applications (Edmiston et al, 2021), and our interviews with support organisations highlighted significant consequences for both those providing and receiving support, which we outline here.

First, levels of awareness, accessibility, and support have varied significantly across the country and between different groups of claimants. Many support organisations observed both increased demand and changes to the composition of support enquiries, reflecting limited general awareness about the benefits system. In response to this, some welfare rights organisations conducted take-up campaigns to raise awareness of eligibility in their communities which, in itself, produced geographical variation in terms of how access to social security was promoted and supported. It was evident that new claimants had also, at least initially, displaced many existing claimants as support clients, raising concerns about whether existing support needs were being met and whether other caseload spikes would emerge in the future (for example for debt support, mental health, or homelessness).

Second, there were significant impacts for people on the periphery of the benefit system. Some organisations noted that demands for support increased not only because of new claimants but also because existing subsistence strategies (for example accessing free food) were disrupted by lockdowns and social distancing measures. As such, COVID-19 exposed additional layers of 'hidden' demand within the system. Simultaneously, some claimants were temporarily trapped between pre-pandemic and pandemic systems; for example, those under sanction at the onset of lockdown and appellants requiring in-person hearings for their case to be fairly and properly considered.

Third, the practical implications of lockdown and social distancing meant that recipients of remote support from organisations had to become more self-reliant (for example in terms of accessing online accounts or forwarding documentation). However, this created a situation where those with the greatest support needs could also experience most difficulties in accessing support. Some organisations were concerned that this situation could push more vulnerable claimants towards informal sources of support, exposing them to risks of fraud and financial abuse. This meant that re-establishing a physical presence became a priority for many organisations.

Despite such risks, informal sources of support have been vital for many low-income households during the pandemic, as we also see in Chapters 1 and 9 in this collection. Our claimant interviews highlighted the centrality of informal support in raising awareness of the benefits system, helping people to understand eligibility and helping people navigate the application process. Friends and family were also key sources of material support, often financially in terms of gifts and loans but also in terms of in-kind support; for example, younger claimants sometimes moved back into parental homes or were relieved of rent contribution obligations by parents they already lived with. This in turn raised significant questions around how those without access to such family resources were coping (see Chapter 10 focusing on veterans' experiences for consideration of this issue). Although access to *material support* from informal sources was a clear asset, *informal advice* presented a more significant risk. As suggested earlier, it could yield both meaningful assistance and poor-quality information:

'My mum told me, "You should look into this because I'm sure you can." None of my other friends even knew about it. I've told them.' ('Jacob', 20s, out-of-work UC claimant)

'I started claiming Universal Credit probably not until April, and the reason for there being probably like a month, I actually was majorly uninformed about the system. I think I mentioned it and my parents were like, "No, you definitely won't be eligible for that," and I thought, oh, okay … I think there's a lot of misinformation around Universal Credit, especially for young people.' ('Henry', 20s, out-of-work UC claimant)

In summary, our research with claimants and support organisations demonstrates that insufficient knowledge of the working-age benefit system has been a pervasive issue during the pandemic. In addition, although presenting a vital channel for accessing financial support during COVID-19, the 'digital by default' system has sometimes prolonged uncertainties around eligibility or exacerbated user anxieties. This has meant that claimants continue to rely on other forms of support and information. However, formal sources of support are unevenly distributed around the country, meaning that claimants often rely heavily upon informal sources of support, but the extent to which these informal networks were able to provide accurate advice and appropriate support is unknown.

Methodological note on interviewing 'at a social distance'

Having discussed some of the key findings from our research, we now reflect on our experiences of conducting research during the pandemic. Like several chapters in this collection (Chapters 1, 3, and 9), we employed QLR 'at a social distance'. At the time of writing, we had conducted 152 remote interviews with people in receipt of a variety of working-age benefits (between June 2020 and July 2021). These interviews were primarily conducted through Zoom video conferencing software, although alternative arrangements were also made in accordance with participants' needs and preferences. Telephone interviews were the main alternative, but in one instance an interview was conducted via email with a participant who was deaf (the interview schedule was broken down into sets of three to five questions to promote a conversational exchange and present opportunities to ask follow-up questions). This section considers how the context for fieldwork changed during the pandemic, the implications of this for researchers and interviewees, and the strategies we deployed for adjusting to that context.

Research in a context of social and temporal disruption

The context for data collection changed significantly during COVID-19 because of lockdown restrictions and social distancing. In broad terms, this can be understood as a destabilisation or disordering of both researcher and research participant experiences. Within this, pertinent issues included the transformation of routines and interactions, new forms of uncertainty, blurred distinctions between home and work, and shifts in people's relationship with time, which presented issues or challenges for at least some of the participants within our sample, as well as members of our research team. For researchers and participants, the pandemic and subsequent lockdowns presented a sudden disruption of daily activities. Most experienced significant changes to their routines and social interactions which exerted pressures upon people in different ways. Social isolation has been increasingly prevalent within the context of social distancing (Holt-Lunstad, 2021), and often compounded by issues such as job loss. The opposite was also common, with many people experiencing 'too much' social contact, in the form of additional burdens upon household relationships, for example additional caring responsibilities, health and financial concerns, and home schooling, all of which could be further compounded by a lack of time to and for oneself (Citizens Advice, 2020; Cheng et al, 2021). Social distancing also presented additional challenges for specific groups; for example lip-readers could be disadvantaged by the practice of face mask wearing and some neurodivergent groups could experience additional stresses from disrupted routines (Armitage and Nellums, 2020; Eshraghi et al, 2020).

In combination, the transformation of daily realities could affect participants' experiences of time. The effect of job loss on experiences of temporality have been observed since the 1930s (Jahoda et al, 1974), and to some extent resonated with aspects of pandemic experiences under lockdown. But while many experienced a repetitive 'Groundhog Day' reality at home, this happened in conjunction with widespread perceptions of epochal transformation (Mitchell, 2021) and uncertainties about the future. In practical terms this could be disorientating, for example in terms of remembering when things had happened within the household, or in terms of feeling anxious or overwhelmed by the pace of external social change. In 2020, COVID-19 also undermined people's existing plans and much of their capacity for future planning. For some participants, this manifested as significant emotional distress, for example, in relation to cancelled or delayed weddings, anniversaries, holidays, and pilgrimages, and others had major life plans disrupted such as planned house moves. Some interviewees lacked clarity about what they could look forward to (if anything) because medium- and long-term horizons were so unclear.

Alongside changed routines and disrupted personal plans, there was also a more fundamental type of disorientation taking place. The sudden and unprecedented nature of COVID-19 was a shock for both researchers and participants (especially when connected to loss of work, health, or relationships). After the initial shock it could also be difficult to re-establish a grounding in the new reality or feel any confidence about it; the pandemic represented a 'rupture of everydayness' (Cover, 2021). A range of phenomena could also be understood as reinforcing those uncertainties, for example sensationalist reporting, inconsistent case/mortality counting, rapidly changing policy responses, polarised debates (for example about vaccines and social distancing), all within an 'infodemic' abundance of information, alongside misinformation and disinformation driven by social media (Marin, 2021). In combination this meant interviews were sometimes conducted with participants who were bored, disappointed, or disorientated, which required adjustments to our ways of working.

It is also worth noting that some of our participants expressed feeling excluded or marginalised under a rapidly emerging, re-stratified social security settlement. For example, it was evident in our interviews that furlough recipients were envied by some participants on mainstream working-age benefits whose employers had made them redundant. Similarly, newly self-employed people (excluded from the Self-Employment Income Support Scheme), 'legacy benefit' claimants (excluded from the £1,000 'uprating' of UC), and 'New Style' benefit claimants (with time-limited protection) were also sometimes upset by the perceived unfairness of the transformed system.[6] Finally, it is also important to reflect upon the fact that the boundaries between home, work, and school disappeared for both researchers and some participants as remote working became the norm. This could potentially impact upon people in a number of ways including work-life balance problems (from unstructured working time), and mental and physical health issues (Ekpanyaskul and Padungtod, 2021). Our experience of fieldwork was therefore mixed, with some participants often more at ease and candid within the home setting, while others – particularly where they were feeling wronged, stressed, or in need of a break – became highly emotionally charged. In such cases, this required adjustments to our approach (see also Chapter 14 for examples of how methodological changes were navigated in the UC:US project).

Adjusting our interviews to this social and temporal disruption

The changes to the interview context outlined earlier had the potential to significantly impact upon people's behaviours and therefore the experience of both the research participants and the researchers. It was evident that some participants were struggling with social isolation, new caring responsibilities, intensified household relationships, the loss of self-esteem from unemployment, or anxieties about the future (for example in terms of an existing job, health, finances and so on). During the pandemic some aspects of life were experienced as more intense and, correspondingly, it seems to make sense that we experienced our research interviews as intensified too. For example, like Howlett (2021) we noted that interviewees appeared less inhibited, with participants sharing personal experiences more readily than in our pre-pandemic research interviews. The team has considered a range of possible explanations for this – were people embracing the limited opportunities for social interaction? Were they more comfortable at home? Perhaps this was the first space that they had used to reflect upon their experiences of the pandemic? We can only speculate as to the reasons behind this.

However, the increased openness could also be offset by an irregular awkwardness to certain interactions. Again, we can only speculate about the reasons behind those but suspect that social isolation may have impacted upon some people's comfort or ease in communicating with strangers, for example in terms of picking up on non-verbal cues (Marra et al, 2020), the use of video-conferencing could also have been new for many. We have further speculated that talking about issues such as benefits stigma or what they anticipated might happen in the future could make some people feel uncomfortable, and potentially even trigger anxieties. However, on balance, our experience was generally that this intensification of interviews had many positive aspects and was beneficial to the research: rapport-building appeared to be quicker, and participants were willing to share detailed, rich information about their lives. As follow-up interviews commenced, we experienced high levels of retention of participants from the first wave (with 80 per cent re-engaged at the time of writing). But, to benefit from these changes, the potential for risks to both participants and interviewers also had to be appreciated, and a number of adjustments were necessary to minimise them.

In acknowledging participant sensitivities, we needed to know the interview schedule well and think ahead to consider whether certain types of questions could be experienced as upsetting. If research participants did experience distress during an interview, a few options were available to us for addressing this. First, (and most often) there was the option of simply allowing more time for the interview – sometimes people gave an impression of just wanting to be listened to and, in a context of emotional distress, we could simply allow the conversation to go on for longer to accommodate this. Less frequently, we opted to omit specific questions from the interview when it was obvious that they would cause significant distress. Finally, the team also had access to a counselling service at the University of Salford to which research participants (and the research team) could be referred or self-refer if they so desired – it was important to have this option available; however, the contact number was only handed out to participants on a couple of occasions.

It was also important for us to reflect on our own experiences within the pandemic context, because as a team, we were similarly exposed to various pressures of social disruption during the lockdowns and social distancing measures. As a research team there were varied caring responsibilities, including childcare and home schooling, alongside team members managing the significant complexities of the shift to home working within that context (sometimes with partners also working at home or undertaking key worker roles). Reflecting on our experiences of delivering research in this context, it was sometimes more demanding to preserve the professional distance as an interviewer – this may have been rooted in the blurring of work/home boundaries under social distancing, or our own similar experiences of social isolation. For example, novel challenges of lockdown life (for example home schooling) provided plenty of content for building affinity and rapport with participants, but in a context of social isolation it was important to take additional care around self-disclosure. Similarly, interviews undertaken via video conferencing (with researchers visible on screen) could reinforce how body language might signal judgements to an interviewee and be experienced as draining in some circumstances. In undertaking fieldwork, it is also important to consider the potential for risks to researchers (Dickson-Swift et al, 2008). In combination, such considerations presented emotionally laden interviews and a more demanding fieldwork experience for researchers, meaning it was necessary to add additional 'decompression time' after interviews. This meant that the number of interviews per day had to be limited (to two per day), and that regular check-ins within the team had to consider emotional loads alongside fieldwork practicalities and emerging findings.

In summary, the experience of QLR at a social distance was found to be one of adjustment to a significantly altered social context. Numerous factors posed challenges for the fieldwork both in terms of participant sensitivities and the resultant emotional labour for us as researchers who worked to respect and accommodate those sensitivities, within a context of our own challenges of balancing various home, care, and work demands during the pandemic. But through adaptations such as interview extension, researcher 'decompression' and regular reviews, we were able to address these various issues, obtain rich and illuminating data, while keeping the wellbeing of participants and ourselves central to our approach. A range of ethical issues, concerns, and compromises arise when researching low-income households under such circumstances, but it is vital that we engage with these sensitively, so that we can properly document people's experiences and support the development of policy and practice in the interests of participants during this unprecedented time.

Notes

[1] www.distantwelfare.co.uk/

[2] 'Existing' claimants are those who were claiming pre-pandemic and continued to claim into the pandemic; 'new' claimants are those who began claims during the pandemic.

[3] For example, welfare rights teams or housing associations. We use the term 'ecosystems' to capture how different actors within this network often depend upon one another in various ways for the overall system to function.

[4] Pseudonyms are used to protect participant anonymity.

[5] For example, relaxed 'minimum income floor' rules under SI2020/371.

[6] The Coronavirus Job Retention scheme was paid at 80 per cent of previous wages but enrolment onto the scheme was exclusively decided by employers. The Self-Employment Income Support Scheme was only paid to people who had completed tax returns for a previous trading period (excluding newly self-employed people). 'Legacy' claimants of (means-tested) Jobseekers Allowance (JSA) and Employment and Support Allowance (ESA), yet to transfer across to Universal Credit (UC), were not provided with the 'uplift'

of an additional £20/week that was added to UC payments. 'New-Style' (contribution-based) claimants for JSA/ESA were also excluded from the 'uplift', and claims were time-limited to six months (Brewer and Gardiner, 2020; Machin, 2021).

References

Armitage, R. and Nellums, L. (2020) The COVID-19 response must be disability inclusive. *The Lancet*, 5(5), E257.

Brewer, M. and Gardiner, L. (2020) The initial impact of COVID-19 and policy responses on household incomes. *Oxford Review of Economic Policy*, 36(S1), S187–99.

Caraher, K. and Reuter, E. (2019) Mind the gaps: Universal Credit and self- employment in the United Kingdom. *Journal of Poverty and Social Justice*, 27(2), 199–217.

Cheetham, M., Moffatt, S., Addison, M. and Wiseman, A. (2019) Impact of Universal Credit in North East England: a qualitative study of claimants and support staff. *BMJ Open*, 9(7).

Cheng, Z., Mendolia, S., Paloyo, A.R., Savage, D. and Tani, M. (2021) Working parents, financial insecurity, and childcare: mental health in the time of COVID-19 in the UK. *Review of Economics of the Household*, 19, 123–44.

Citizens Advice (2020) 3 months of a global pandemic: what Citizens Advice data tells us about the nation's coronavirus concerns. 12 June.

Cover, R. (2021) Identity in the disrupted time of COVID-19: performativity, crisis, mobility and ethics. *Social Sciences & Humanities Open*, 4(1).

Department for Work and Pensions (DWP) (2021a) Universal Credit statistics. 29 April 2013 to 14 January 2021. 23 February.

Department for Work and Pensions (DWP) (2021b) Fraud and error in the benefit system for financial year ending 2021 (appendix 3). 13 May.

Dickson-Swift, V., James, E., Kippen, S. and Liamputtong, P. (2008) Risk to researchers in qualitative research on sensitive topics: issues and strategies. *Qualitative Health Research*, 18, 133–44.

Dwyer, P., Batty, E., Blenkinsopp, J., Fitzpatrick, S., Fletcher, D., Flint, J., Johnsen, S., Jones, K., McNeill, J., Scullion, L., Stewart, A. and Wright, S. (2018) *Final findings report: Welfare Conditionality Project 2013–2018*. York: Welfare Conditionality Project.

Dwyer, P., Scullion, L., Jones, K., McNeill, J. and Stewart, A.B. (2020) Work, welfare, and wellbeing: the impacts of welfare conditionality on people with mental health impairments in the UK. *Social Policy and Administration*, 54(2), 311–26.

Edmiston, D. (2021) Plumbing the depths: the changing (socio-demographic) profile of UK poverty. *Journal of Social Policy*, 1–27.

Edmiston, D., Robertshaw, D., Gibbons, A., Ingold, J., Baumberg Geiger, B., Scullion, L., Summers, K. and Young, D. (2021) *Navigating pandemic social security: benefits, employment and crisis support during COVID-19.* Salford: Welfare at a Social Distance.

Ekpanyaskul, C. and Padungtod, C. (2021) Occupational health problems and lifestyle changes among novice working-from-home workers amid the COVID-19 pandemic. *Safety and Health at Work*, 12(3), 384–9.

Eshraghi, A., Li, C., Alessandri, M., Messinger, D., Eshraghi, R., Mittal, R. and Armstrong, D. (2020) COVID-19: overcoming the challenges faced by individuals with autism and their families. *The Lancet Psychiatry*, 7(6), 481–3.

Geiger, B.B, Scullion, L., Summers, K., Martin, P., Lawler, C., Edmiston, D., Gibbons, A., Ingold, J., Robertshaw, D. and de Vries, R. (2021a) *Non-take-up of benefits at the start of the COVID-19 pandemic.* Salford: Welfare at a Social Distance.

Geiger, B.B., Scullion, L., Summers, K., Martin, P., Lawler, C., Edmiston, D., Gibbons, A., Ingold, J., Robertshaw, D. and de Vries, R. (2021b) *Should social security reach further? Ineligibility for benefits at the start of COVID-19.* Salford: Welfare at a Social Distance.

Holt-Lunstad, J. (2021) A pandemic of social isolation?. *World Psychiatry*, 20, 55–6.

Howlett, M. (2021) Looking at the 'field' through a Zoom lens: methodological reflections on conducting online research during a global pandemic. *Qualitative Research*. January.

Jahoda, M., Lazarsfeld, P. and Zeisel, H. (1974) *Marienthal.* London: Tavistock.

Machin, R. (2021) COVID-19 and the temporary transformation of the UK social security system. *Critical Social Policy*. February.

Marin, L. (2021) Three contextual dimensions of information on social media: lessons learned from the COVID-19 infodemic. *Ethics and Information Technology*, 23, 79–86.

Marra, A., Buonanno, P., Vargas, M., Iaccovazzo, C., Ely, E. and Servillo, G. (2020) How COVID-19 pandemic changed our communication with families: losing nonverbal cues. *Critical Care*, 24, 297.

Meers, J. (2020) 'Fatally upsetting the computer': universal credit, earned income, and the demands of automation. *Journal of Social Welfare and Family Law*, 42(4), 520–3.

Millar, J. and Bennett, F. (2017) Universal Credit: assumptions, contradictions and virtual reality. *Social Policy and Society*, 16(2), 169–82.

Mitchell, W.J.T. (2021) Groundhog Day and the Epoché. *Critical Inquiry*, 47(S2), S95–9.

Scholz, F. and Ingold, J. (2020) Activating the 'ideal jobseeker': experiences of individuals with mental health conditions on the UK Work Programme. *Human Relations.* June.

Scullion, L. and Curchin, K. (2021) Examining veterans' interactions with the UK social security system through a trauma-informed lens. *Journal of Social Policy*, 1–18.

Summers, K. and Young, D. (2020) 'Universal simplicity? The alleged simplicity of Universal Credit from administrative and claimant perspectives. *Journal of Poverty and Social Justice*, 28(2), 169–86.

Summers, K., Scullion, L., Baumberg Geiger, B., Robertshaw, D., Edmiston, D., Gibbons, A., Karagiannaki, E., de Vries, R. and Ingold, J. (2021) *Claimants' experiences of the social security system during the first wave of COVID-19*. Salford: Welfare at A Social Distance.

Work and Pensions Committee (WPC) (2020) 'DWP's response to the coronavirus outbreak, first report of session 2019–2021'. House of Commons. 22 June.

Wright, S. and Patrick, R. (2019) Welfare conditionality in lived experience: aggregating qualitative longitudinal research. *Social Policy and Society*, 18(4), 597–613.

3

Families navigating Universal Credit in the COVID-19 pandemic

Rita Griffiths, Marsha Wood, Fran Bennett, and Jane Millar

Introduction

Long before the COVID-19 pandemic, low-income families in the UK had borne the brunt of the decade-long austerity-driven cuts to social security, with analyses showing rising levels of child poverty and in-work poverty in households with children (Hood and Waters, 2017). Our longitudinal, qualitative research, part of the Economic and Social Research Council (ESRC)-funded project, Couples Balancing Work, Money and Care: Exploring the Shifting Landscape under Universal Credit (ESRC ES/R004811/1), charted the lived experience of couples and families claiming Universal Credit (UC) as they juggled work, money, and care. Two waves of interviews were conducted, two years apart, between 2018/19 and 2020. Wave one comprised 123 individual and joint face-to-face interviews with 90 UC claimants in 53 households, in four areas in England and Scotland. Thirty-nine households had dependent children (30 couples and nine lone parents) and all but one had a child or children under the age of 12. For 28 families, this included at least one pre-school-aged child.

In 2018/19, when we conducted our first wave of interviews, most working-age benefits had not increased in real terms for almost a decade. Child Benefit had been subject to freezes and below inflation uprating since 2011. Over the same period, financial help with housing costs had been decreasing, with many private renters facing a rent shortfall despite qualifying for help (Shelter, 2020). Most benefit recipients are also now expected to contribute towards council tax. After almost a decade of social security cuts, rising living costs, and weak earnings growth, many of the families in our research were struggling to manage (Griffiths et al, 2020). Then came COVID-19.

The wave two interviews with 63 participants[1] took place in September and October 2020. In addition to examining decisions around work and care, interviews explored how well individuals and families were managing in the context of the COVID-19 pandemic, including whether and how UC, and the Government's emergency measures, were helping to support and sustain them through these difficult times. We were also interested to explore whether claimants in Scotland fared any better or felt more supported than those in England. Though UC policy remains largely in the hands of the Westminster Government,[2] Scotland passed a Child Poverty (Scotland) Act in 2017 and additional cash payments and support have been introduced for families. A new Social Security Agency has also been established and a Charter for benefit recipients is grounded on principles of dignity and respect.

Social security support measures during the pandemic

As part of a wider package of emergency measures put in place by the Government to support household incomes,[3] a £20 per week uplift in the standard allowance of UC, alongside a £20 increase in the basic weekly rate of Working Tax Credit (WTC), was announced by the Chancellor, Rishi Sunak, in the Spring 2020 Budget. At the same time, the Government lifted the freeze on working-age benefits, with an uprating of 1.7 per cent, the first since 2015. Financial help with private sector rental costs was also realigned more closely with local rent levels, and funding was provided to local authorities for further discretionary support. The £20 weekly uplift, in addition to the uprating, meant that from April 2020 the UC standard allowance for couples (aged over 25) rose from £498.89 to £594.04 per month, and for single people (aged over 25) rose from £317.82 to £409.89 per month. Taken together, these measures effectively reversed the cuts and freezes to working-age benefits enacted during the previous decade (Brewer and Handscomb, 2020).

But it is not just benefit rates that are important. The regulations, systems, and procedures for determining conditionality in UC, and for assessing and calculating the award, are central to options and decisions about employment, and to the amount of money claimants are entitled to and ultimately get paid each month. For UC claimants, the £20 weekly increase in the standard allowance was accompanied by a suspension of conditionality for claimants in the intensive work search group and a pause in the recovery of benefit over-payments and Social Fund loans deducted from a claimant's UC payment. However, these measures were time-limited. The uplift was scheduled to end in March 2021, while the suspension of certain deductions and work conditionality elements lasted only until the end of June 2020. Nor did the £20 uplift apply to legacy or other benefits. Also notable was the lack of any specific social security help targeted at families with children. The £20 per week uplift to the UC standard allowance was a flat-rate amount given regardless of the presence or number of children in the household (or whether adults were single or in a couple). Moreover, money intended for children is unprotected in UC due to the integrated nature of the payment. No COVID-19-related uplift applied to Child Tax Credit, Child Benefit, or the child element of UC.

In the Spring 2021 Budget, the Government announced that it would extend the uplift in UC by six months, until 30 September 2021. Recipients of WTC would instead receive a one-off lump sum payment of £500. Having reiterated throughout the pandemic that the £20 increase was always intended as a temporary emergency measure, in July 2021 the Government confirmed that the uplift would be phased out from the end of September 2021.

Reducing cash benefits for families with children

The lack of any additional cash benefit provision directed at children during the pandemic reflects a decade-long trend during which financial help for families has gradually been eroded from what some considered to be its high water mark (Bradshaw and Main, 2016), with the enactment of the Child Poverty Act 2010.[4] Successive Labour Governments in office from 1997 to 2010 made child poverty a major focus of concern (Tucker, 2020), resulting in 600,000 children being lifted out of poverty (Department for Work and Pensions [DWP], 2008). With the advent of the Coalition Government in 2010, child poverty reduction targets were abandoned and the cross-departmental Child Poverty Unit was disbanded. The political choices of successive Coalition and Conservative Governments in tackling the financial crisis of 2008 onwards also meant that families became increasingly targeted for cuts.[5] Reflecting the notion that 'work is the best route out of poverty', support for low-income households increasingly moved towards fiscal and employment measures targeted at people in work.

In January 2013, the Government abolished universality in the only solely child-contingent payment in UK social security – Child Benefit – by imposing an additional tax charge where a parent has annual earnings above £50,000. In April 2017, the family element was removed in UC and the two-child limit to UC and Child Tax Credits was introduced. This followed the lowering of the household benefit cap in 2016 (first introduced in 2013). Justified with regard to the need to ensure fairness for working households, the benefit cap imposes a ceiling on the total amount of benefits payable to working-age claimants with no earnings (with certain exceptions).[6] Driven by the unprecedented increase in UC claimants as a result of the COVID-19 pandemic, the number of households affected by the benefit cap hit a record 230,000 households in May 2020, more than four -fifths of whom were families with children (DWP, 2021). The two-child limit removes all means-tested support for a third and any subsequent children born after April 2017 (with a few exceptions). In 2020, 250,000 families were affected by the two-child limit (HMRC and DWP, 2020). However, projections by the Institute for Fiscal Studies (IFS) indicate that, by 2025, the number of families affected by the two-child limit could rise to 500,000 (Joyce and Waters, 2019).

The various freezes and changes to benefit eligibility meant that, between 2010 and 2020, spending on child-contingent benefits fell by £10 billion – or by a quarter for each child – outweighing the positive impact of a higher national minimum wage and increases in personal tax allowances (Cooper and Hills, 2021). Analysis by the Resolution Foundation (before the decision to reduce the taper rate and increase the work allowance) indicated that removal of the £20 uplift could lead to a further 1.2 million people (of whom 400,000 were children) falling into relative poverty,[7] the biggest year-on-year rise in poverty rates since the 1980s, undoing virtually all the work done to reduce child poverty from 1997 to 2010 (Brewer et al, 2021). However, this creeping policy of transferring ever-greater levels of responsibility and risk for raising children onto parents has largely gone unnoticed outside academia and the third sector.

The experience of claiming Universal Credit before and after COVID-19

Against this background, we explore the experiences of two families, one living in England, the other in Scotland; one with two working parents by 2020, and the other with neither in employment. We draw on a total of five interviews conducted with each couple: face-to-face, individual, and joint interviews with the partners in late 2018; and a telephone interview with each partner in September 2020. In 2020, the families had been claiming Universal Credit continuously for about five years. These couples were selected because many of the issues their cases raise reflect those of the wider sample. They tell their stories about their experience of claiming UC before and after the pandemic, largely in their own words. To protect their identities, participants' names and some other details have been changed.

Holly and Ralph

Holly and Ralph, an unemployed married couple in their early 30s, live in a three-bedroomed, rented council house on a Scottish housing estate. In 2018, they have two children aged five and two. Holly suffers from anxiety and depression and rarely leaves the house. As the nominated 'lead carer', Holly is in the 'work preparation' conditionality group for Universal Credit, meaning she must take active steps to prepare for a return to work when her youngest child reaches the age of five. However, a recent attempt at some unpaid work experience seriously dented her confidence when she was investigated for benefit fraud:

'Last year I was helping a friend round at the local hairdressers … If she was busy with a client, I'd answer the phone, didn't get paid anything for it … It was just to get me out the house and get my confidence up, to try and get me to be able to go into work. There was a malicious phone call made to the benefits … saying I was working.' [She sighs] 'I would love to go back to the way it was … in the sixties … you know, the woman brought the kids up … Ideally I would want my husband to be out working full time and I want to be the stay at home parent.'

But Ralph finds regular work hard to come by. His last job, as a warehouse stacker, was almost a year ago. This was the latest in a long line of temporary agency jobs that have never lasted more than a few months, in spite of the promise of being taken on permanently. "What I wanted at the time [was] full-time work [but with agency work] you get a phone call saying … you're not wanted … or there's a text … saying you're not wanted the next week … so you're back to square one again." Working long shifts, he also missed spending time with his children. "You were out at five in the morning … and back for ten o'clock at night … So both were in their bed when I left and both of them were in their beds when I came home." Agency work nevertheless gave the family just enough money to live on. "When I was working … we always had cash, always had food, always had gas and leccy [electricity], we always had clothes on our back … if I had my way, the wee one would be at nursery and I'd be working, but unfortunately it doesn't quite work out that way."

Difficulties in claiming UC, before any help was available, meant that the first payment was delayed longer than it should have been. Holly explained, "I don't have any internet in the house … so you're phoning up, you're waiting in a queue … by the time they've spoke to you they're … saying, we're going to have to scrap it and you need to start again". With no income to live on for almost two months, they were forced to turn to food banks and local welfare charities. "I don't like to admit when I need help but … I was crying all the time … and [the health visitor]… gave me numbers … [for] food banks and there's a charity they'll [top up] your gas and electricity cards." The offer of a UC advance loan, though, was turned down. "We're better off not going down that line because we need to pay it back and it would get us in more debt and we would struggle more than what we are."

When the UC is finally awarded, deductions of £75 per month are taken to repay council tax and rent arrears. Thinking it will help, they opt to change the UC payment to twice monthly, as claimants in Scotland have the option to.[8] But this interferes with their rent payment cycle, so they switch back to a monthly payment. Money struggles are taking their toll on Holly's mental health and on the couple's relationship:

'My depression's got really bad … [the children are] used to going and getting a packet of biscuits at the shop … and we can't do that any more … We have major arguments … over what we're going to get, when we're going to get it … so it has major issues in the relationship.'

Two years later, in 2020, Holly's mental health has not improved and she has been assessed as having limited capability for work, for which the couple receive an extra amount of Universal Credit. Ralph becomes her official carer and is awarded Carer's Allowance. It makes a big difference to the family's finances, which is much needed because there has been a new addition to the family – a third child – for whom the family receive no extra Universal Credit. "It was a shock," Holly says. "I knew that I wouldn't be entitled to [any extra help] … but from my religion, an abortion is out of the question." Ralph says that they are not entitled to Child Benefit for the new baby. This is clearly a misunderstanding, but no one has informed him of this. "I was always told that it was … capped at two." Child Benefit is separate from UC and not subject to the two-child limit, I tell him. "I never knew about that," he says. Yet the couple visited the Jobcentre to present the baby's birth certificate. Did no one mention claiming Child Benefit? "Nobody's said anything about it, no."

With no additional UC money for the new baby, making ends meet is a constant struggle. "It is hard," Holly says. "My other children have had to give up a lot so that we could provide for [baby] … we've had to use a food bank quite often." An unexpected reprieve is that, with a third child, the abolition of the spare room subsidy ('bedroom tax') no longer applies and they are entitled to increased financial help with their housing costs. "My rent got paid – an extra £100 a month … because now we're entitled to three bedrooms." It makes a big difference. Living in Scotland, the family is also entitled to extra help for the new baby:

'We got … £350 and that paid for a cot, pram … I also got the Baby Box, which was a great help … digital thermometer … clothing for zero to three months … three to six months and six to nine months … a comfort blanket … a changing mat … teething rings … nappies … cream … baby books.'

They are also awarded a small discretionary local authority grant on account of Holly's requirement to shield during the COVID-19 pandemic.

By helping to boost their regular household income, the £20 per week uplift in UC has been a lifeline. "Now I've got [third baby], that £20 a week helps towards getting his clothes and food for him." Even so, the extra money is not enough to compensate for the ongoing loss of income due to the two-child limit, or the low level of income on which the family must live. The imminent loss of the £20 UC uplift is an additional source of anxiety. "Once that's away, I'm going to be stuck with what I had before and I think I'd struggle a lot more."

Kate and Pete

Kate and Pete are in their 40s, married, and in 2018 have two children living at home, aged ten and 11. The family lives in a three-bedroomed, socially rented house in the North West of England. Pete is unemployed and has not worked for seven years following a bout of meningitis. He is the nominated lead carer and, with both children at school, he must job search for 20 hours per week. Kate works part time as a cleaner and is studying for a teaching degree. She also manages the household finances. "We've been looking to open a bank account for [Pete]," Kate says, "but he's got no photographic ID." With the responsibility for working, studying, and household budgeting, Kate was feeling the strain.

Two years later, in 2020, Kate has graduated but she is still working part time in the same job. I ask why she is not teaching or working full time. During the lockdown, their youngest child developed mental health issues, she says:

'He's [got] severe behavioural issues and anxiety … so with trying to deal with that as well as everything else, it was just far too much … UCs are so unreliable … I was trying to [work] and study and do everything else in between and it was just far too much … I felt like I was having a breakdown … we didn't know where we stood with UC from one month to the next.'

To help share the load, Pete got a job and is now also employed as a part-time cleaner. Both are employed on zero-hours contracts at the national living wage of £8.72 per hour. Pete typically works 24 hours per week and Kate 15 hours, spread across five weekdays. "[Pete] does part-time hours, I do part-time hours, so one of us are always here with the children when they're at home."

During the first COVID-19 lockdown, the couple were briefly furloughed but, as key workers, resumed working after two weeks of quarantine. Home-schooling has added to Kate's workload:

'It was just a nightmare of juggling! Our boss was really understanding … he changed hours so we could fit the kids in that one of us were here but … [Pete's] … not really up to date with the schooling and … he's not very good on the laptop, so it was me, because … I've done my studies and I'm up to date with everything.'

Though both parents now work, their financial situation has only marginally improved. They are regularly offered additional hours; but earning more on UC is a double-edged sword, giving them extra money in the month it is earned, followed by a drop in income the next. "You're not getting any benefit really … You're working to make your life better but on the other hand, when the UCs come in, you're not really that much better off … It's always a worry the next month … if we've got enough money to live on." The DWP suggests that claimants should put money aside when earnings increase to compensate for the reduced payment of UC the following month. When money is tight, this is difficult enough, but when extra earnings are used to pay for a costly or unexpected item, this strategy does not work. Washing the children's clothes much more frequently than before the pandemic, Kate has been obliged to buy an additional set of school uniforms. "Last month we had to work overtime to pay for the children's school uniforms, and then this month UCs are [only] paying us £300 … We were left with about £700 after we'd paid our rent."

This reduction in UC entitlement as earnings rise has made the couple wary of working any longer than is necessary to meet the family's immediate needs. "We work overtime … to get something we need," Kate explains. "If we're doing overtime, [it's] for a reason … because we need to pay for something, as in, like, uniforms, which are very expensive. [The] council don't provide any help towards uniforms." Not being able to reliably predict by how much the UC payment will vary is an added complication. When their earnings increase, so does the amount taken in deductions. "This month we've only earned £400 more than last month, but we're only getting £300 [from UC] instead of £1,100." Not knowing how much UC they will get until a week before the payment compounds the difficulties. "[They] don't put it up on the computer till, like, a week before how much you're going to get, so we don't know where we stand with that till, like, seven days before."

Working regular extra hours also means they lose out on a budgeting loan they would otherwise have been eligible for. "They do, like, an advance payment for people … struggling with, like, washing machines, uniforms … but because we actually earn over £3,600 between [us] over six months, we're not entitled to that help." Working more hours also reduces eligibility for other means-tested help. "We're not entitled to [help with prescription charges] at the minute because we earned over the amount last month." Kate says:

> 'My glasses are broke, so I'm waiting till next month to be able to go to the optician's because … after we've paid our rent, council tax, food, there's no way I can go and afford a pair of glasses, so I'm waiting till next month when I'll be able to get free prescriptions again to get my glasses.'

Life was a lot easier on tax credits, she says, when entitlement and payments were fixed for a year:

> '[With tax credits] I got an NHS exempt card that I had for the 12 months ... and it never changed from one month to the next ... [With] tax credits ... you were never in this position unless you had a drastic change in circumstances ... You knew what you were getting, you could budget ... Having a fixed monthly payment for a year was much easier to manage ... if you did overtime one month ... it would work out over the year.'

Kate has another bugbear: automated deductions taken without notification. "We had Social Fund loans ... many years ago, and they've taken it direct out of our UC ... but they stopped it during the pandemic ... and then they never contacted us to let us know it was restarting again ... there was nothing, they just started taking it again." She tries, but fails, to stop the deduction:

> 'I did contact UC on my journal and it was two days later I got a message back saying, we can't deal with this, it's debt management. So then I contacted debt management and it took me 50-odd minutes to get through ... He said ... "We can reduce for next month but we can't do anything about this month's payment because it's already gone through" ... He wasn't very sympathetic ... He just said, "No, it's too late, sorry" ... So they've taken £198[9] out ... It's very hard ... We've been to a food bank this month ... it's just a nightmare.'

Are there any aspects of Universal Credit that work well for them? Kate says:

> 'I like the way that they know our earnings ... that is the positive side of it, whereas with tax credits we had to do that annual review ... every year we had to put our earnings in off our P60 ... We never experienced [over-payments] because we always declared it. But whereas UC, they know what we've earned direct by our employer, what he put through to the Inland Revenue ... I think that's the only good thing about UC!'

And the worst thing? Without hesitation, she says, "The inconsistency in payments ... I don't think you can budget properly with UC ... with not knowing what we're going to get from one month to the next." Was she aware that there had been a temporary £20 weekly uplift in the UC standard allowance? No, she replies. It is money they sorely need, but there appears to have been no increase in their payment. Reflecting on why, she says, "I think it might be because they're that inconsistent anyway that I wouldn't know ... We never get the same payment."

I ask what would help to improve their situation. Both would like better-paid jobs but do not have the time or support needed to secure this. Pete tells me that his employer will not commit to giving him more than 24 hours per week. Full-time jobs are scarce and well-paid jobs rarer still. He says, "I'd love a full-time job ... we're bringing home ... just over £1,000 a month ... I'd like to get us out of this rut ... I'd love to be off UC." Work coaches are meant to deliver tailored help that promotes employment, is responsive to local labour markets, and challenges behaviours around work. Already working, Kate and Pete do not need challenging; but their jobs are part time and poorly paid. In the 'light touch' group,[10] they had little or no contact with a work coach even before the pandemic, so the promise of personalised support has a hollow ring. Kate told me, "My husband would like the extra support of courses ... My son, he's [unemployed] ... and they offer him all kinds, whereas because we've gone into light touch, it's like [Pete's] been forgotten."

Before Pete started his job, his work coach mandated him to attend a full-time training course. "They put me on a forklift course ... I [was] out the house for a week and then it [was] quite difficult for [my wife] to go to work ... [The course] was, like, full time ... I'd be out six and a half, seven hours." He got his forklift truck driving licence, but a job failed to materialise. "Because the dole was putting people on forklift licences ... when you went for a forklift job, there was, like, 30 people going for the same job because they've all got forklift licences." His licence had since expired. He says, "They're not very helpful at all ... they never have been, to be honest ... I was out of work for a long time and ... they've never, ever been any help really. [Now] I'm working, they don't ask me for nothing." He swallows hard. This is a man struggling to maintain his dignity. "[Last month] ... we had to go to food bank ... We're working and we shouldn't have to do that." He says:

'It's not fair on the kids ... it's just ongoing, because the kids are at that age now where ... they want money for drinks and bags of crisps ... and sometimes we can't give it them and it makes us feel ... we're failing. I'd like to have a bit of extra money ... to get the kids on holiday once.'

His voice chokes with emotion. "I'm usually the one that doesn't worry, but ... it's been starting getting to me. I'm actually getting quite upset about it now." He's not angry, just worn down; they both are, but there is a sense of resignation.

Policy reflections

Our research suggests that, for both working and non-working claimants, getting UC has done little to address the low level of household income and loss of support many families have experienced over the past decade through swingeing cuts in benefits and child-contingent forms of help. Though the £20 uplift has been a lifeline for the poorest families reliant on UC as their main source of income, its withdrawal in September 2021 means benefit rates will return to their lowest real terms level for three decades (Brewer and Handscomb, 2021). For parents in low-paid, poor-quality, part-time work, through generating income volatility and uncertainty, the design of UC can serve to exacerbate financial insecurity. In this context, it is important to recognise that UC is but one of a number of social security measures with the potential to increase household incomes and reduce poverty. Paid to the main carer and in full for the majority of families, Child Benefit is not subject to the problems associated with monthly means testing in UC, nor affected by the two-child limit or benefit cap. A substantial increase in Child Benefit could therefore be a much more effective way of getting extra money directly into the pockets of more of the poorest families.

Notes

[1] Interviews were conducted by telephone rather than face-to-face due to COVID-19 restrictions.

[2] The devolved nations have some limited flexibilities regarding alternative payment arrangements (APAs). For example, UC claimants in Scotland can choose to have their housing element paid direct to their landlord, and to have the award paid twice a month. In Northern Ireland, direct payments to landlords and twice monthly payments are the default payment arrangement. In England, requests for APAs are assessed on a case-by-case basis and only granted in exceptional circumstances.

[3] These included the Coronavirus Job Retention (furlough) Scheme and the Self-Employment Income Support Scheme (SEISS), and changes to Statutory Sick Pay.

[4] The Child Poverty Act 2010 enshrined child poverty reduction targets in law (Kennedy, 2014).

[5] See Reader and Andersen, Chapter 7 in this collection.

[6] The benefit cap now amounts to £23,000 per annum for couples and single parents who live in Greater London and £20,000 per annum for those who live outside Greater London (or £15,410 and £13,400 respectively for single people).

[7] Relative poverty is defined as those living in a household with less than 60 per cent of median equivalised disposable household income after housing costs.

[8] Claimants in England can request to have UC paid more frequently, but our research showed that most were turned down (Griffiths et al, 2020).

[9] This amount suggests that the UC award was reduced by the maximum deduction permitted at the time: 40 per cent of the standard allowance. The maximum has since been reduced to 25 per cent.

[10] 'Light Touch' claimants are typically working part time with earnings at or close to the national minimum/living wage. They generally have less work conditionality and reduced contact with a work coach.

References

Bradshaw, J. and Main, G. (2016) *The Well-Being of Children in the UK* (4th edition). Bristol: Policy Press.

Brewer, M. and Handscomb, K. (2020) This time is different – Universal Credit's first recession: assessing the welfare system and its effect on living standards during the coronavirus epidemic. London: Resolution Foundation.

Brewer, M. and Handscomb, K. (2021) Half measures: the Chancellor's options for Universal Credit in the Budget. London: Resolution Foundation.

Brewer, M., Corlett, A., Handscomb, K. and Tomlinson, D. (2021) Living standards outlook report for 2021. London: Resolution Foundation.

Cooper, K. and Hills, J. (2021) The Conservative Governments' record on social security: May 2015 to pre-COVID 2020. SPDO Research Summary. London: Centre for Analysis of Social Exclusion. February.

Department for Work and Pensions (DWP) (2008) No one written off: reforming welfare to reward responsibility. London: DWP.

Department for Work and Pensions (DWP) (2021) Benefit cap: number of households capped to May 2020. London: DWP.

Griffiths, R., Wood, M., Bennett, F. and Millar, J. (2020) Uncharted territory: Universal Credit, couples and money. Bath: Institute for Policy Research.

HM Revenue and Customs (HMRC) and Department for Work and Pensions (DWP) (2020) Child Tax Credit and Universal Credit claimants: statistics related to the policy to provide support for a maximum of two children. 2 April.

Hood, A. and Waters, T. (2017) Living standards, poverty and inequality in the UK: 2017–18 to 2021–22. London: Institute for Fiscal Studies.

Joyce, R. and Waters, T. (2019) Benefit changes set to take effect during the next parliament. Briefing Note. Institute for Fiscal Studies.

Kennedy, S. (2014) 'Child Poverty Act, 2010: a short guide'. Standard Note: SN/SP/5585. London: House of Commons Library.

Shelter (2020) 1.7 million renters expect to lose their job in the next three months, press release, 16 April.

Stewart, K. and Reader, M. (2020) The Conservatives' record on early childhood: policies, spending and outcomes from May 2015 to pre-COVID 2020. SPDO Research Summary. London: Centre for Analysis of Social Exclusion.

Tucker, J. (ed) (2020) 2020 Vision: Ending child poverty for good. London: Child Poverty Action Group.

4

Complex lives: exploring experiences of Universal Credit claimants in Salford during COVID-19

*Lisa Scullion, Andrea Gibbons, Joe Pardoe,
Catherine Connors, and Dave Beck*

Introduction

Salford is ranked as the 22nd most deprived local authority in England and the third most deprived area of Greater Manchester, with around 70 per cent of Salford's population reportedly living in areas classed as deprived and disadvantaged (Salford City Partnership, 2017). In response to the challenges experienced in Salford, in 2017 the Salford City Mayor and Salford Youth Mayor launched an anti-poverty strategy[1] aimed at addressing inequality in the city (Salford City Partnership, 2017). Prior to COVID-19, existing research in Salford had begun to highlight intersections between reforms to the social security system and experiences of poverty and inequality, including increased food bank use (McEachern et al, 2019), concerns about the experiences of young people engaging with the benefits system (Jones et al, 2018), and intersections between welfare reform and housing (Scullion et al, 2018; Gibbons, 2019).

The introduction of UC was the flagship of the UK Government's contemporary welfare reforms. However, since its introduction, UC has received criticism in respect of its underlying principles, adequacy of payment levels, and modes of implementation, which have raised concerns around the impact on some benefit recipients (Millar and Bennett, 2017; Wright et al, 2018; Dwyer et al, 2020). For Salford City Council and partners, there was a need to understand the experiences of UC within Salford from the perspective of Salford residents who are claiming UC and also those organisations who are supporting benefit claimants across the City. In response to this, the Exploring Universal Credit in Salford project was developed and began in the summer of 2019. The project forms part of a programme of research delivered by the Salford Anti-Poverty Taskforce; an innovative research and knowledge exchange partnership between the University of Salford and Salford City Council that works collaboratively to support the delivery of Salford's anti-poverty strategy through a model of evidence-based policy making.

This chapter begins with a brief overview of the project and methods. Key issues emerging from the, primarily, pre-COVID-19 baseline interviews are presented next, before moving on to reflections from our UC participants on how specific aspects of their lives had changed following the pandemic. Our findings illustrate the complexity of exploring the impacts of COVID-19, which were simultaneously negative and positive. Although primacy is given to the accounts of our UC claimant participants, we also draw upon data collected during stakeholder consultation, particularly when describing the pre-COVID-19 context. Following the findings, we provide our reflections on the challenges posed when trying to maintain the participation of interviewees who had quite significant and complex needs, before concluding with some policy and practice implications.

The project and methods

Exploring Universal Credit in Salford was designed as an 18-month qualitative longitudinal research (QLR) project, comprising two waves of interviews with UC claimants. QLR has become increasingly important in furthering understandings of the impacts of contemporary welfare reforms (Dwyer et al, 2018; Wright and Patrick, 2019; Griffiths et al, 2020; Scullion et al, 2021), enabling exploration of 'varied and changing fortunes' (Neale and Flowerdew, 2003) over time. A total of 20 people were recruited for the study, and baseline interviews were carried out between November 2019 and April 2020. However, the majority (16) were undertaken pre-COVID-19 (face-to-face), with just four baseline interviews taking place after the onset of the first national lockdown (via telephone). The first interviews focused on claimants' experience of UC, from the process of applying through to their experiences of managing an ongoing claim. The interviews also explored broader issues around managing on a low income, and health and wellbeing. The participants were recruited with the support of a range of organisations in Salford, and efforts were made to ensure that those interviewed reflected the diversity of UC claimant groups (for example, 'jobseekers', 'in work' claimants, disabled people, lone parents). Although diversity was achieved in the sample, recruitment through support organisations meant that there was a high proportion of those who would be considered as having multiple and/or complex needs. In addition to interviewing UC claimaints, we also consulted with 22 stakeholders representing organisations that were providing support to Salford residents in relation to benefit claims but also a broad range of issues (health, housing, and so on). This consultation, which took place prior to COVID-19, primarily occurred through three focus groups (with a small number of indiviudal interviews) with representatives from the local authority, third sector, housing associations, and health care providers.

Towards the halfway point of our study, almost overnight, the pandemic changed people's everyday lives, as many businesses were forced to close, jobs were suspended, schools were closed, and new words and phrases such as 'furlough', 'key workers', 'social distancing', and 'support bubbles' became common parlance. In relation to the benefits system, UC became a central aspect of the national response as an unprecedented number of people submitted new claims for financial support (Summers et al, 2021). The QLR methodology of the Exploring Universal Credit in Salford project proved particularly important within the context of the pandemic, providing vital insights about families' experiences of UC in the pre-COVID-19 world, and the flexibility to adapt and understand post-COVID-19 experiences across this changing landscape. In consultation with Salford City Council, we therefore decided to extend the project timescales and to re-focus our follow-up interviews to explore how the pandemic had impacted on participants.

Recontact was attempted with all of those originally interviewed. However, some participants had changed numbers and had provided no other means of contacting them, while others decided that they would prefer not to be interviewed due to experiencing mental health issues and personal loss. In total, we were able to re-interview nine of the original 20 participants, and these interviews took place in April and May 2021. Eight of the nine interviews were undertaken by telephone, with one participant providing a written response. This individual did not want to be interviewed by telephone and expressed a preference for a face-to-face interview. At that time, the research team was still working remotely, and face-to-face contact required risk assessment and amendment to ethics. Although we began this amendment process, the delay this caused threatened to deter participation. Thus, when the participant made a request to submit a written account instead, we decided that this was the best approach. The sections that follow provide an overview of some key issues that emerged from our research.

Exploring pre-COVID-19 experiences

Before presenting our findings, we provide contextual information about our participants. As described earlier, the high proportion of people who had limited capability for work and work-related activity (LCWRA), were going through a Work Capability Assessment (WCA) or were appealing against the outcome of a WCA reflects the source of referrals for the study from those organisations providing support to claimants. Nonetheless, as illustrated in Table 4.1, our sample was diverse in terms of ages, household types, and types of UC claim.

Table 4.1: 'Our sample', Universal Credit in Salford project

	Age	Gender	Ethnicity	Household type	UC 'status' at first interview	UC 'status' at re-interview
Rowan[2]	60–65	F	White English	Single	LCWRA	LCWRA but applying for work
Rose	50–59	F	White English	Single	Jobseeker	Furloughed from work with UC top-up
Dave	30–39	M	White English	Single, 1 child (9)	Jobseeker	
Chimamanda	50–59	F	Black African	Living with adult granddaughter	Currently on sick note and PIP, waiting for WCA	
Victoria	50–59	F	White English	Single	Jobseeker – appealing against WCA outcome	LCWRA having won appeal and also now on PIP
Daniel	30–39	M	White English	Single	Currently on sick note, appealing against WCA outcome	
George	40–49	M	White English	Single (son visits)	LCWRA	
Phil	30–39	M	White English	Single, living with parents	Jobseeker	
Mo	40–49	F	Kurdish Iranian	Single	Jobseeker	
Betty	40–49	F	White English	Single, 3 children (13, 5, <1)	In work, maternity leave top-up	Returned to work, UC in-work claimant
Melissa	30–39	F	White English	Single, 1 child (4)	LCWRA	LCWRA
Susan	30–39	F	White English	Single, 1 child (4)	Currently on sick note, waiting for WCA	LCWRA following WCA
Jennifer	30–39	F	White English	Single, 1 child (4)	In work	No longer on UC

(continued)

Table 4.1: 'Our sample', Universal Credit in Salford project (continued)

	Age	Gender	Ethnicity	Household type	UC 'status' at first interview	UC 'status' at re-interview
Michelle	20–29	F	White English	Single, 2 children (5, <1)	Currently on sick note, waiting for WCA	LCWRA following WCA
Barbara	40–49	F	White English	Single, 1 child (12)	LCWRA	
Michael	60–65	M	White English	Couple	LCWRA	
Joanna	40–49	F	White English	Couple, 5 children (between 15 weeks and 15 years)	In work but on sick note, two-child limit	
Mark	50–59	M	White English	Single	Jobseeker, once they leave supported housing	
Owen	60–65	M	White English	Single	Sick note, waiting for WCA	Jobseeker (assessed as 'fit for work')
Bob	20–29	M	White English	Single	Furlough top-up	

To explore how participants were experiencing various aspects of claiming UC, the baseline interviews covered a significant range of issues including: understanding eligibility; application process; benefits assessments; benefit levels; the digital system; experiences of employment; interactions with work coaches; and conditionality. Unfortunately, we don't have the space here to present the findings across all these aspects of people's experiences. Although some people had experienced difficulties with elements of the benefits processes, overall the accounts were positive in relation to the process of applying, and interactions with both the digital system and work coaches/Jobcentre Plus (JCP). Where issues had occurred, it was evident that additional advice and support provided, in most cases, by statutory or third sector organisations, but sometimes by JCP, had helped resolve many concerns. Thus, as found in recent research (Summers et al, 2021), it was not benefits *processes* that dominated the narrative in people's interviews; rather, the interviews were illuminating of the difficulties many participants faced in their daily lives as they tried to manage household finances alongside a range of complex circumstances. As such, we focus here specifically on managing on a low income, their health and wellbeing within this context, and the support that they drew upon.

Financial adequacy

The interviews with both UC claimants and key stakeholders (pre-COVID-19) highlighted significant concerns around financial adequacy, with many examples where people described having insufficient money to live sustainably. The account of Barbara illustrates the challenges and compromises that many participants faced when making decisions about how 'best' to budget their limited resources:

> 'When you've got no bus fare … You've got no food in your cupboards, and also if you've got children, "Mum, can I have…? Can I have…? Can I have…? It's half term. Can I have? …" You can't feed your kids and you've got no food parcel … Last Christmas was horrendous … it was the week before Christmas I think they like switched the gas off. "It's freezing." "Go and get in bed," kind of thing. Or I'd ring my dad up and say, "Can you have [daughter] for the day?" and he would. He'd come and pick her up … I think until you've been in that position yourself when you've got absolutely nothing, it is, it's soul destroying. It's really difficult to walk in a food bank and go, "I can't afford to feed my child," … It just strips your dignity right away from you.' (Barbara)

However, as has been highlighted elsewhere (JRF, 2018; McBride et al, 2018; Innes, 2020), entering the paid labour market did not necessarily provide the solution to people's financial insecurity. Indeed, three of our participants were in-work UC claimants (and another had previous experience of this). These participants – who were primarily working zero-hours contracts or undertaking temporary work – described how they could often not earn enough or secure enough hours to meet their household needs. As Rose explained: "For me to actually survive I've got to be earning £300 a week to actually pay everything and be on time with everything … even when I am working … regular shifts and everything, I never earn £300." This was reiterated by many stakeholders who were supporting people with budgeting, and who stated that they worked with many people whose employment didn't pay enough to cover basic bills.

Health and wellbeing

It was evident across our sample that where people had insufficient income to live on, it impacted significantly on people's health and wellbeing, in a number of ways: through an inability to buy or cook healthy food; an inability to keep the home warm; an inability to pay for a bus or taxi to see the GP or pick up food, medication, and other necessities; fear of bailiffs; anxiety over housing costs and fear of homelessness; and depression from the social and physical isolation that often resulted from being unable to afford transport, leisure activities, and so on (see also Chapters 5, 8, and 11). Among those interviewed, turning off the heating was described as a common money-saving strategy, even for those who knew it would exacerbate their health conditions. Indeed, two people described spending much more of the day in bed to keep warm.

Twelve participants had accessed food banks/food pantries, though for most the food was not considered what they would want to eat from a nutritional perspective. It was also evident that some people struggled with the move to the monthly payment schedule that is used in UC, as Phil described: "Under Jobseekers, I'm not saying it was easy, it definitely wasn't, but with it being fortnightly pay that makes a big difference. If you're skint for a fortnight you can live; it's not too long. On Universal Credit, you are literally counting the days." A small number of participants had requested the Alternative Payment Arrangement (APA) to have their payments changed from monthly to twice monthly or to have direct payments to landlords. One of these was a mother of five, who described difficulties affording milk for her baby, so had requested more frequent payments. Her account also illustrated the intersection with other welfare reforms, as her financial difficulties related to budgeting on a monthly payment but also being subject to the two-child limit. Similarly, a lone parent (Michelle) described the relief of having the payment going directly to her housing provider to save her from having to make difficult choices between rent and other necessities:

'It works out easier for me and less stress for me … the money would be going to the rent either way. If it's going straight to them before I even get it, say if there's a month where I'm thinking oh my God, I can't afford to do this or I can't afford to get baby milk or feed my kid, I might think I'll just take money out of it for now.' (Michelle)

Mental ill health was an issue for almost all of those interviewed. Some people described experiencing depression that they related to the isolation they felt when unable to afford to socialise with friends, travel to see friends/family, or even invite people over to their homes. As Rose stated:

'I can't go anywhere because the money that I'm on, I can't travel to the areas where my family live. My family lives in [another area of Greater Manchester]. I can't get away from here. It takes two hours on the bus, and I haven't got the money for the buses. I get stranded here. I get stranded and isolated, and it's not really good for my mental health anyway.' (Rose)

This is within a context of growing rates of mental health issues across the UK, particularly in areas with high levels of deprivation. Indeed, some of the health professionals who took part in the stakeholder consultation described what they were seeing in their patients, particularly where depression and anxiety did not always have a clinical cause, but rather, was a manifestation of adverse experiences:

'I often see different forms of depression. There's one thing that I call a reactive depression, which is probably not actually a depression at all, it's probably, if I was in your situation, and all of these things were happening to me, how would I feel? I say to people, this is a normal feeling because of all the things that are going on in your life, rather than just a chemical imbalance that could be corrected with a pill.' (Health care professional)

One of the most distressing issues highlighted in the research – cutting across both claimant interviews and stakeholder consultation – was the issue of suicide. For some stakeholders there was significant fear for the wellbeing of some of the people they were currently working with across the city, as illustrated in this extract from a focus group of housing professionals:

Housing professional 1: 'Over the summer, I had a case where I would dread opening up my emails because I thought this particular person was going to commit suicide, and I would get an email to tell me she'd ended her life … we've just had the suicide training because it's needed now.'

Housing professional 2: 'Yes, I had somebody that I was supporting and I was ringing up to check to make sure that their payment had gone in, and when I was ringing them, they were actually in the middle of killing themselves. I had to try and keep them on while they were trying to hang up on the phone.'

Within the accounts of our participants, it was also evident that some people had experienced a sense of hopelessness:

'For the part of – God of – I've got [my daughter] and I think nobody else would look after her, and on a number of occasions that has stopped me thinking, I can't do this any more. With all the stuff that's going on at the minute, people with mental health and committing suicide, I get it.' (Rowan)

Although these discussions were less common across our interviews with both stakeholders and UC claimants, they provide a sense of the issues that professionals were responding to with some of their low-income residents. Further, these discussions illustrate how some of our UC participants had reached a crisis point where they had, even if momentarily, (re)considered their future.

Experiences during COVID-19

An overwhelming finding from the pre-COVID-19 interviews was the high level of financial and individual hardship that people were experiencing. The accounts of those who we re-interviewed in April/May 2021 highlighted that despite living through a global pandemic, for the most part, people appeared to be faring better than they had before. This was primarily due to the Department for Work and Pensions (DWP) raising the basic element of UC and Working Tax Credit by £20 per week (aka the £20 uplift) combined with decreased spending due to the various lockdowns and restrictions in place. Many also spoke very positively about the support they had been able to draw upon during the pandemic from family and friends. Indeed, most had family and close friends nearby and had created small support bubbles to care for each other to minimise the negative impacts of the isolation rules they otherwise followed. It would be inaccurate to suggest that there were no negative impacts for our participants and people referred to a range of issues that have been reported elsewhere in this edited collection, relating to the difficulties of home schooling and the impact on children (Chapter 11), and depression and increased anxiety stemming from isolation and the pandemic itself (Chapter 5). Although people often described these as being offset by the increased payments that people had received, it was evident that financial adequacy remained an issue and the increased payment represented a shift from struggling significantly to just about managing; thus people still experienced difficulties managing household budgets. Here we discuss these issues in further detail, drawing upon the accounts of participants.

The '£20 uplift' and financial 'stability'

When asked about the £20 uplift, participants welcomed this increase and reported an improved sense of financial stability. Interestingly, however, none of the participants could recall being told that their payments would increase, and only those closely monitoring their journals realised that their payment had changed. Rowan, for example, who had LCWRA, stated that she did not often check her journal and had been slow to realise she was receiving more, and had contacted her work coach to query it: "I just noticed, because when there was a rise last year – oh, I might have contacted her [work coach] then about that, about the rise, and … She just said, 'Oh, you get' – yes, that was it … about £20 was the rise." Rowan felt that the increase in her payment, despite the lack of communication about it, was "the one thing the government got right". At the same time, although she was more positive about her UC payments, she indicated that she was still dependent on a Discretionary Housing Payment from the council to cover the costs of her housing due to the bedroom tax/under-occupancy charge. Similarly, for Susan, who had not felt able to manage before the pandemic now felt that she was "maybe just" managing, although this varied from month to month: "Yes, it depends what happens in that month. My daughter's growing way too fast and I haven't bought any clothes. My friend bought her a jumper." However, it was evident that for some participants the increase in UC payment had not changed their financial circumstances. One mother of two (Michelle), who was diagnosed with Borderline Personality Disorder in the period between the two interviews and was trying to manage new medications, was experiencing difficulty understanding her payment level and still struggled to 'juggle' her bills. Again, her account illustrates choices and compromises in relation to what the money would be spent on:

> 'at the minute there's been times where I've not been paying certain bills. They're just literally mounting up sometimes because they're through like, direct debits. If they are bouncing then I'm like, right, well, if I need food, I'm going to be buying food over paying my electric if it's not going to go off.' (Michelle)

It was evident that Michelle was reliant on support from her parents, who were regularly bringing food and helping with her children. She also described being in the process of moving onto an electricity meter to help budget; however, this payment method has been problematised given that electricity can cost more using this method (Boardman, 2009), exemplifying the poverty premium that can be experienced by low-income households (Caplovitz 1963; Davies et al, 2016).

Three of those who were re-interviewed were in work and for that reason felt that they were managing better financially. Two of them (Betty and Rose) were newly working (or had found work and then been furloughed). Betty had originally been on maternity leave (and in her first interview described cooking for her three children using a microwave after her cooker had broken and she couldn't afford to replace it). She was now back in work and claiming UC as an in-work claimant. She described being able to afford to replace the cooker and even being able to begin saving a little money again. Rose, despite her frustration at not being able to earn enough either working the 30 hours she was given or with the furlough provision, described still being 'better off' than when fully relying on UC. The third participant, Jennifer, had decided to leave the benefits system altogether after what she described as a 'long battle' to get the housing payment she felt she was eligible for. She had subsequently moved back to her parents' house and with their financial support had been able to recover from the debt that an abusive relationship had left her with: "I'm now back where I was five, six years ago … I'm in a good place, but I'd like to have thought that Universal Credit would have been more willing to help, certainly with the housing cost."

The continuing importance of family and support networks

The account of Jennifer earlier brings us to the importance of family and other support networks. Although, overall people felt more isolated because of the pandemic lockdowns and restrictions, people continued to see and rely on friends and family, especially those with children or long-term health conditions. The role of mothers, in particular, was highlighted by a number of participants. Susan, for example, who experienced pain due to a long-term physical health condition described the importance of her mother as a source of support: "Even though she has two jobs, she'll come up and help me. She'll pick my daughter up from school when she can, as well." Similarly, Jennifer, who is referred to earlier, who had moved back in with her parents described this as a 'lifeline', including her mother helping with home schooling:

'My mum's retired. She retired at Christmas, so that's helped. So she's done a lot of the home schooling, so that's eased a lot of my stress. So it's good being at home with my parents, that it meant that I had that added support to do that. There's no way I would've been able to do it on my own.' (Jennifer)

Likewise, Michelle, referred to earlier, described how central her mother had been for her wellbeing and that of her children:

'Yes, she's started to have to help out quite a lot, like with my kids and having to manage stuff like that as well. When I'm trying to deal with that sort of stuff, especially if I'm off my medication or I'm having a bad day, I can't handle it. I've had to ask her to end up being more involved, so she can know what to do if I am in those states. She knows what medication I'm on and she knows who does what and whatever else.' (Michelle)

Additionally, people referred to receiving support from other family members such as siblings, but also close friendship networks. Participants had therefore created support bubbles to best suit their specific needs. Many also mentioned both the positive and negative aspects of home schooling and/or children being sent home to self-isolate, with the stress of having to provide that support when you are unqualified to do so, alongside the opportunity to grow closer as a family. However, reflecting the findings of other chapters and wider debates about the impact of COVID-19 on gender inequalities (Power, 2020), the gendered nature of care during the pandemic was apparent in many of the accounts of our participants.

Illness, isolation, and mental health

Although those we interviewed described feeling 'better off' financially and talked positively about the support bubbles they had created, the pandemic impacted more broadly on people's physical and mental health, and limited the wider support that they could access. These impacts were felt acutely, for example, by two participants (Jennifer and Susan) who had contracted COVID-19. Reflecting the potential longer-term effects associated with chronic or long COVID (Halpin et al, 2021), Jennifer described the ongoing pain that she was experiencing: "I'm still not 100 per cent right. I'm still very achy ... because my fibro is triggered by infection and stress, it's just never gone away. So, my body's always been in that heightened pain state, just since I've had [COVID-19]." All of those who were re-interviewed described the impact of increased isolation on their mental health (and sometimes that of their close family). Rowan, for example, who had LCWRA, was keen to be able to work in the future. However, during the winter she felt she had been unable to 'shake off' her depression, and additionally described how "it's made – I've even gone more anxious about working". She had waited a year to access support for her depression and post-traumatic stress disorder but had finally been allocated a counsellor. Although the sessions had been undertaken over the phone (due to COVID-19), she felt they had still really helped her. Michelle had managed to access face-to-face support with a specialist in relation to her diagnosis of Borderline Personality Disorder. She had experienced both telephone and face-to-face support during the pandemic and for her, telephone support had not been effective: "That face-to-face appointment that I had, I thought that's more effective than all the telephone appointments that I've had in the last year." She also described that communication between the different members of her support team had sometimes broken down during the pandemic, making it more difficult to get her medication prescriptions.

Policy implications

This chapter provides insights into key findings from our qualitative longitudinal research in Salford. There are key policy implications here, relating to (i) communication with claimants; and (ii) financial adequacy. It was evident that changes to the UC system that occurred during COVID-19 (for example the £20 uplift) were not fully understood or had not been explained to participants. There is therefore a need to ensure that any future changes to the system are communicated clearly and that claimants fully understand what will happen and when.

Although this study is exploring experiences of UC, and so was approached through the lens of the benefits system, the qualitative longitudinal interviews were illuminating in relation to change and continuity across an array of complex needs and circumstances facing the participants, including significant health issues, caring responsibilities, housing insecurity, domestic abuse, and debt. In those situations where UC was described as working for people, this was articulated as one less thing to worry about and related primarily to the process of claiming. Ultimately what appeared to dominate the interviews were the challenges of life on a low income while managing a range of complex circumstances. Although many articulated feeling 'better off' financially during COVID-19 (as payment levels increased and spending decreased), this was often from a starting point of significant financial insecurity or crisis. It is therefore misleading to suggest that people were 'better off'; rather they had moved from 'crisis' to 'just about managing'. Reiterating other research (Summers et al, 2021) and chapters in this edited collection, this signals the need to review the financial adequacy of the benefits system.

Notes

[1] www.salford.gov.uk/media/390192/no-one-left-behind-tackling-poverty-in-salford.pdf
[2] Participants have been given pseudonyms to protect anonymity.

References

Boardman, B. (2009) *Fixing Fuel Poverty: Challenges and Solutions*. London: Routledge.

Caplovitz, D. (1963) *The Poor Pay More: Consumer Practices of Low-Income Families*. New York: Free Press of Glencoe and Collier-Macmillan.

Davies, S., Finney, A. and Hartfree, Y. (2016) *Paying to be Poor: Uncovering the Scale and Nature of the Poverty Premium*. Bristol: University of Bristol.

Dwyer, P., Scullion, L., Jones, K., McNeill, J. and Stewart, A.B. (2020) Work, welfare, and wellbeing: the impacts of welfare conditionality on people with mental health impairments in the UK. *Social Policy & Administration*, 54(2), 311–26.

Dwyer, P., Batty, E., Blenkinsopp, J., Fitzpatrick, S., Fletcher, D., Flint, J., et al (2018) Final findings report: welfare conditionality project 2013–2018. York: Welfare Conditionality Project. Available at: www.welfareconditionality.ac.uk/wp-content/uploads/2018/06/40475_Welfare-Conditionality_Report_complete-v3.pdf

Gibbons, A. (2019) *Living rents and renting in Salford*. Salford: University of Salford.

Griffiths, R., Wood, M., Bennett, F. and Millar, J. (2020) *Uncharted territory: Universal Credit, couples and money*. [Online]. Available at: www.bath.ac.uk/publications/uncharted-territory-universal-credit-couples-and-money/attachments/Uncharted-Territory-Universal-Credit.pdf

Halpin, S., O'Connor, R. and Sivan, M. (2021) Long COVID and chronic COVID syndromes. *Journal of Medical Virology*, 93(3), 1242–3.

Innes, D. (2020) *What has driven the rise of in-work poverty?*. Joseph Rowntree Foundation. [Online]. Available at: www.jrf.org.uk/report/what-has-driven-rise-work-poverty

Jones, K., Martin, P. and Kelly, A. (2018) *Hidden young people in Salford: exploring the experiences of young people not in employment, education or training (NEET) and not claiming benefits*. Salford Anti-Poverty Taskforce. Salford: University of Salford

JRF (2018) *UK Poverty 2018: A comprehensive analysis of poverty trends and figures*. Available at: https://www.jrf.org.uk/report/uk-poverty-2018

McBride, J., Smith, A. and Mbala, M. (2018) 'You end up with nothing': the experience of being a statistic of 'in-work poverty' in the UK. *Work, Employment and Society*, 32(1), 210–18.

McEachern, M., Moraes, C., Gibbons, A. and Scullion, L. (2019) Research brief: Understanding food poverty and the transitional behaviour of vulnerable individuals.

Millar, J. and Bennett, F. (2017) Universal Credit: assumptions, contradictions and virtual reality. *Social Policy and Society*, 16(2), 169–82. Available at: https://doi.org/10.1017/S1474746416000154

Neale, B. and Flowerdew, J. (2003) Time, texture and childhood: the contours of longitudinal qualitative research. *International Journal of Social Research Methodology*, 6(3), 189–99.

Power, K. (2020) The COVID-19 pandemic has increased the care burden of women and families. *Sustainability: Science, Practice and Policy*, 16(1), 67–73. Available at: DOI: 10.1080/15487733.2020.1776561.

Salford City Partnership (2017) *No one left behind: tackling poverty in Salford*. [Online]. Available at: www.salford.gov.uk/media/390192/no-one-left-behind-tackling-poverty-in-salford.pdf

Scullion, L., Gibbons, A. and Martin, P. (2018) *Precarious lives: exploring lived experiences of the private rented sector in Salford*. Salford: University of Salford.

Scullion, L., Jones, K., Dwyer, P., Hynes, C., and Martin, P. (2021) Military veterans and welfare reform: bridging two policy worlds through qualitative longitudinal research. *Social Policy and Society*, 1–14. DOI: 10.1017/S1474746421000166

Summers, K., Scullion, L., Geiger, B.B., Robertshaw, D., Edmiston, D., Gibbons, A., Karagiannaki, E., de Vries, R. and Ingold, J. (2021) *Claimants' experiences of the social security system during the first wave of COVID-19*. The Welfare at a (Social) Distance project.

Wright, S. and Patrick, R. (2019) Welfare conditionality in lived experience: aggregating qualitative longitudinal research. *Social Policy and Society*, 18(4), 597–613.

Wright, S., Dwyer, P., Jones, K., McNeill, J., Scullion, L. and Alasdair, S. (2018) *Final findings: Universal Credit*. York: Welfare Conditionality.

PART II

Intersecting insecurities in action

5

The impact of the COVID-19 pandemic on families living in the ethnically diverse and deprived city of Bradford: findings from the longitudinal Born in Bradford COVID-19 research programme

Josie Dickerson, Bridget Lockyer, Claire McIvor, Daniel D. Bingham, Kirsty L. Crossley, Charlotte Endacott, Rachael H. Moss, Helen Smith, Kate E. Pickett, and Rosie R.C. McEachan, on behalf of the Bradford Institute for Health Research Covid-19 Scientific Advisory Group

Introduction

Situated in the North of England, Bradford is the fifth largest metropolitan district in the country. The city has a young, multi-ethnic population of more than 500,000 people: almost one third of the city's population is aged under 20, nearly half of the births are to women of South Asian (mostly Pakistani) heritage, and there is also a large community of families from Central and Eastern European countries (Office for National Statistics [ONS], 2011). Once a thriving industrial city, Bradford now suffers from high levels of deprivation, with a quarter of children living in poverty, and has some of the worst health and education outcomes in the country (ONS, 2011; Born in Bradford, 2021).

In addition to the deprivation and health concerns in Bradford, there are specific structural characteristics that have made the city particularly vulnerable to the COVID-19 virus, for example, a large proportion of households are multi-generational and many are classed as overcrowded (ONS, 2011). These characteristics also make the communities in Bradford vulnerable to the unintended social and economic impacts of the response to COVID-19, including financial and food insecurity, mental distress, and educational consequences for children (Marmot et al, 2020). There have been a number of large-scale ongoing and new longitudinal studies during the pandemic that have highlighted these issues; however, most of these have included predominantly White participants with a limited range of socio-economic status (for example ONS, 2020; Pierce et al, 2020).

BiB is an internationally recognised applied health research programme comprising health and wellbeing information on more than 30,000 Bradfordians enrolled in three birth cohort studies (McEachan et al, 2020; Born in Bradford, 2021). Participants in the BiB cohorts consent to the use of their routine health and education data for research, and to be contacted for future research studies; participants in the Born in Bradford Family Cohort Study (BiB) and Born in Bradford's Better Start (BiBBS) cohort also complete detailed questionnaires at recruitment and in ongoing waves of data collection (McEachan et al, 2020; Born in Bradford, 2021). Recent pre-pandemic data collection meant that BiB was in a unique position to be able to conduct a longitudinal programme of research comparing pre-pandemic and pandemic outcomes in a highly diverse and deprived population.

BiB prioritises engagement, co-production, and dissemination with communities and stakeholders in the city to ensure that they have a major voice in determining research priorities, and in interpreting and disseminating these findings. This ethos was harnessed in this research programme by establishing a community steering group (comprised of lay members of the Bradford community) and liaison with the Bradford Institute for Health Research COVID-19 Scientific Advisory Group (BIHR C-SAG) (comprised of academic and public health experts) (BIHR C-SAG, 2021). Information to deliver an effective COVID-19 urgent response, and longer-term recovery from the pandemic was shared with the C-SAG which provided a mechanism for feeding back emerging findings quickly to decision makers.

Longitudinal quantitative data collection was conducted with BiB families enrolled in the three cohorts (see Figure 5.1) using domains co-produced with the aforementioned advisory panels. Surveys also included open-ended questions that asked a) adults: the three biggest worries they had; a challenge faced in the past two weeks; and anything that had become easier; b) children: three worries they had and three things that made them feel happy at the moment. Surveys were completed at three time points: Phase 1 March–June 2020; Phase 2 October–December 2020; Phase 3 June–August 2021. Participants were women who were pregnant during the pandemic, parents with children aged 0–13, and children aged 9–13 (McEachan et al, 2020). The study situated in Tower Hamlets in Chapter 6 in this collection by Cameron et al, and BiB shared co-investigators and aligned their data collection where relevant to allow comparisons between populations.

Responsive in-depth qualitative research was completed based on the findings of the surveys and on the priorities set by the community and stakeholders. This included the key topics of: experiences of having a

Figure 5.1: The timeline of the Government's response to COVID-19 in England and the corresponding timeline of the longitudinal BiB COVID-19 research

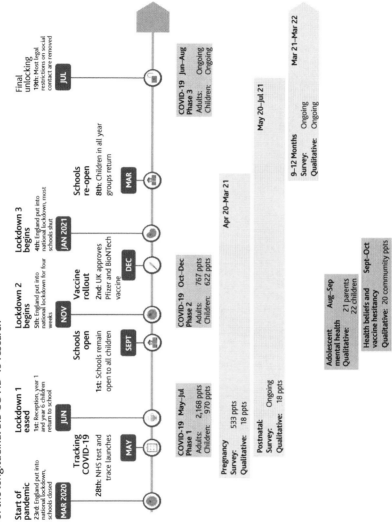

baby in the pandemic, adolescent mental health, and health beliefs and vaccine hesitancy.

In this chapter, we describe the key findings from Phase 1 and 2 of the parent and child surveys and the adolescent mental health qualitative work. Together these data tell a powerful and bleak story of how the COVID-19 pandemic has exacerbated inequalities for the most vulnerable families – making things even harder for those who were already struggling prior to the pandemic, and having far less of an impact on those who were secure and healthy.

Overview of findings

In Phase 1, of 7,652 surveys sent to parents, 2,144 (28 per cent) participated; 2,043 were mothers and 101 partners (Dickerson et al, 2020). Of 5,298 child surveys sent out, 970 (19 per cent) participated. In Phase 2, of 2,288 adult surveys sent out, 767 (34 per cent) participated and for the child survey, of 1,841 sent out, 622 (34 per cent) children took part. Respondents in the adult and child surveys were representative of the ethnicity in the BiB cohorts. For example, in Phase 1, 47 per cent of parents and 44 per cent of children were of Pakistani heritage, 35 per cent and 41 per cent (respectively) were White British, and 46 per cent of adult participants lived in the lowest quintile of deprivation in England.

Three overarching themes were apparent across a large number of participants: (i) high levels of financial insecurity; (ii) increased mental ill health; and (iii) low levels of physical activity. These themes were evident at both survey time points, indicating long-lasting impacts of the pandemic.

Financial insecurity: "sometimes it's eat or heat"

One of the most prominent findings from our surveys was the lack of buffering for families on low pay (Dickerson et al, 2020; BIHR C-SAG, 2021). In our first survey, one in three families said they were worse off than before the pandemic, and just over one in three (37 per cent) were financially insecure.[1] In our second survey, just under one in three (31 per cent) continued to report being financially insecure.

In Phase 1 (the first UK lockdown), a large number of the main earners in families were unable to work, with 15 per cent furloughed and 11 per cent self-employed and unable to work. Financial insecurity was much higher in these families: almost two in three families (64 per cent) where the main earner was self-employed and not working, and almost one in two families (49 per cent) where the main earner was furloughed were financially insecure. Further exploration of these findings revealed that financial insecurity was more likely in families of Pakistani heritage (43 per cent) than in White

British (29 per cent) families. Some of this inequality may be related to different types of employment, with more Pakistani heritage families (18 per cent) being self-employed and unable to work than White British families (4 per cent).

By the time of the Phase 2 survey, fewer of the main earners in families were furloughed (5 per cent), and none were self-employed but unable to work. This change in employment status may explain why 6 per cent fewer families reported being financially insecure at this time point. However, for some families things had become worse, with 4 per cent of mothers and 9 per cent of their partners having lost their job since the start of the pandemic. The loss of income during the pandemic had considerable implications for families, with one in five (20 per cent in Phase 1 and 17 per cent in Phase 2) being unable to always afford the food they needed, and just under one in ten reporting severe food insecurity by having to regularly skip meals (9 per cent and 7 per cent respectively). One in three families (37 per cent) were worried about the employment security of the main earner in Phase 1, and one in four (24 per cent) remained worried in Phase 2.

The Phase 1 free-text responses made clear that pre-pandemic, many families were managing on a financial tightrope. The abrupt change to their circumstances at the start of lockdown and the effect of the delay in furlough payments, particularly for self-employed people was very apparent:

'Loss of husband's job completely, now having to apply for Universal Credit which will not be based on figures that are actually relevant and we already have debts. I am behind on a lot of bills, fear that in a month they will spiral out of control.' (Adult, Phase 1)

'Worried about the financial impact of COVID-19. I am currently furloughed from work but I worry that the virus will have an impact on the business. My husband is self-employed and is not eligible to any funds.' (Adult, Phase 1)

At Phase 2, free-text responses indicated that families continued to struggle financially, with some suffering from severe long-term impacts of lost income: "I don't have enough money to look after my family" (Adult, Phase 2). "Sometimes it's eat or heat" (Adult, Phase 2).Recent job losses and the sustained job instability caused by certain job roles and industries that participants worked in were also common causes of financial worries: "Money – I've been given at risk redundancy notice" (Adult, Phase 2). "Our business is closed again because of the latest restrictions, I worry that we'll miss our much needed trade" (Adult, Phase 2).Financial insecurity was also a worry for some of the children who recognised that their families were severely financially vulnerable at this time: "No water or electricity" (Child, Phase 1). "Not enough money to get food" (Child, Phase 1). "Going homeless" (Child, Phase 2).

Mental ill health: "it's a battle not to slip each day"

The surveys also uncovered increases in the mental ill health of both parents and children (Dickerson et al, 2020; BIHR C-SAG, 2021; Dickerson et al, 2022). The number of women reporting clinically important depression/anxiety increased from 11 per cent to 19 per cent, and 10 per cent to 16 per cent respectively from before the pandemic to the first COVID-19 lockdown.[2] In Phase 2, 17 per cent continued to report clinically important symptoms of depression, and 13 per cent clinically important symptoms of anxiety.

We conducted further analyses to explore associations between key variables and a clinically important increase in anxiety and depression. We completed univariate logistical regression analyses using pre-pandemic and Phase 1 data. The findings from this analysis showed that the odds of a clinically important increase in depression were: more than eight times greater in mothers who felt lonely; more than six times greater in mothers who were financially insecure; and for depression (but not anxiety), more than three times greater for mothers who did no physical activity.

In White British mothers, the odds of an increase in clinically important depression were 12 per cent higher than in Pakistani heritage mothers. When we separated out the regression analyses by ethnicity, we found some interesting differences. Mothers of Pakistani heritage had greater odds of depression and anxiety if they were lonely or had an average/poor relationship with their partner than White British mothers. Pakistani heritage mothers had a much reduced odds in depression or anxiety if they lived in a large household compared to White British mothers. In contrast, mothers of White British ethnicity had greater odds of depression or anxiety if they were financially insecure and/or physically inactive compared to Pakistani heritage mothers reporting the same exposures.

In the free-text responses, mental ill health was frequently mentioned by respondents. Some parents expressed concerns over their own mental health having been affected by the pandemic: "I feel particularly anxious to even step out of the house even for food shopping or taking a walk/exercise" (Adult, Phase 1). "Keeping my own mental health up, it's a battle not to slip each day" (Adult, Phase 2). For those who had existing mental health issues before lockdown, the lockdown measures had often taken away their usual sources of support and methods of coping. Others reported being unable to access mental health services due to COVID-19 and lockdown measures:

'Mental health, I have had previous issues in the past and am struggling and don't feel like I can approach my GP at the minute as it isn't an emergency.' (Adult, Phase 1)

'I have anxiety and am not able to do the things I used to do as a coping mechanism. My son is autistic and challenging and I am unable to have quality "me" time.' (Adult, Phase 2)

Some responses uncovered complex experiences and intense pressures that had caused or exacerbated mental ill health:

'I have four children, one a disabled child and one a toddler. Being isolated from friends and family, and having no future plans because of the restrictions and being a stay-at-home mum and a carer for my son is extremely difficult mentally. I feel like since March I have lost my identity and my confidence. My anxiety has increased exponentially.' (Adult, Phase 2)

Many parents expressed concerns about their children's mental ill health, and children also reported concerns about their own mental health: "Mental health of children (especially youngest). Desperately missing social interaction with friends, school and all his sporting activities. He is getting increasingly angry" (Adult, Phase 1). "Daughter had mental health crisis which has impacted upon her ability to eat" (Adult, Phase 2). "Worry of developing a mental illness" (Child, Phase 1). "Getting depression" (Child, Phase 2).

Qualitative findings on children's mental health: "her whole little life has changed dramatically"

In response to the survey findings in Phase 1, and in consultation with our community steering group, a qualitative research study was undertaken to understand more about children's experiences of mental health during the pandemic. Parents and children were purposively sampled based on ethnicity and responses to the mental health questions in the Phase 1 child survey. Qualitative interviews were completed with 21 children and their parents (Lockyer et al, 2020). Four key themes emerged that were linked to the children's mental distress.

Many children had high levels of anxiety caused by COVID-19 and lockdown measures and many parents believed that the constant news and social media reporting on COVID-19 was making their children's anxiety worse. Parents also reported feeling unable to give reassurance because of their own confusion and worries, but many encouraged their children to avoid COVID-19-related stories:

'He's kind of, you know, nervous because he keeps hearing this many or how many people died, these people, you know, how many people are positive for this virus and this and this. So first, you know, for few weeks he was keep looking at those news, everybody every day, you know, telling me, telling me. Then I told him, "No, stop looking at this news, yeah, because it's too much for you." Yeah, because he was taking in that, you know, then he was worried, he was saying, "I'm not going outside," first'. (Family 14, Parent).

'She wouldn't even take the dog out, it seemed to really affect her … she's reading about the coronavirus every day and seeing things, so it did scare her at the beginning and she didn't, I don't think she left the house for about eight weeks'. (Family 11, Parent)

Children and their parents reported a lethargy caused by a lack of routine and/or regular sleep patterns, and children complained of days being boring, repetitive, lacking purpose, and of feeling stuck indoors:

'Everything from like going to school and going straight out after school, to being at home, it has, it stopped for her, her whole little life has changed dramatically. So the mood being down from being sociable to being at home all the time.' (Family 4, Parent)

'Because I used to wake up with, like, a plan for the day and what I was going to do. And now, there isn't really a big point in getting up so early, might as well have another hour in bed.' (Family 9, Child)

A major cause of children's boredom and lack of routine was because they were not able to go to school. In addition, home schooling was often reported as causing tension and arguments at home, with many children becoming disengaged, and both parents and children recognising that their concentration levels had decreased:

'I'd say we did have a lot of tears, a lot of kind of storming off saying he couldn't do his work and that kind of thing. And obviously then he'd got a lot, very, he'd have a lot of, well, I call them strops, tantrums, kind of thing, he'd just, yeah, he'd just storm off and kind of answer back and stuff. However, since kind of they did finish school and again, as a few things have started, since his football started again the change has been quite dramatic actually. He's just so much happier. And he does, he has settled down, he's stopped wetting the bed again. He's gone back to school today actually, first day back.' (Family 15, Parent)

Finally, children and parents both reported that being cut off from friends and family caused distress and unhappiness, and that virtual contact was strange compared to face-to-face interactions:

'I just missed hugging [my friends], even when I got to school I couldn't hug them. I was only able to keep in touch with my best friend because I don't think Mummy had any other, like any other of my friends emails or anybody, so.' (Family 16, Child)

'I mean, it's different [than seeing them face-to-face] because you're not really having a laugh and a joke about things you've just seen or what's just happened. It's kind of, trying to make up a random conversation about something. You're not, like, having a laugh with them. It feels more formal. It don't feel sort of laughy and jokey.' (Family 9, Child)

The concerns around school closures and periods of self-isolation for children have often focused on lost education, but it is clear from our findings here, and later on, that the impact for children on their mental health and physical activity is also of real concern.

Physical activity: "I'm scared to go out"

The findings from our survey highlighted that a large proportion of both adults and children were falling short of government recommendations for physical activity during the pandemic.[3] In our surveys, we found that more than one in ten adults (12 per cent Phase 1; 14 per cent Phase 2) were doing no exercise at all, and one in four (26 per cent Phase 1; 34 per cent Phase 2) were exercising only one to two times a week. A lack of any physical activity was far greater in Pakistani heritage parents (17 per cent) than in White British parents (7 per cent) (Dickerson et al, 2020).

We compared the physical activity data in the children's Phase 1 survey with pre-pandemic baseline physical activity data (Bingham et al, 2021). This analysis found a significant reduction in the number of children who were meeting the Government guidelines for physical activity during the first lockdown: two in three children (69 per cent) met the guidelines pre-pandemic, but fewer than one in three (29 per cent) did in Phase 1. There was a clear association between ethnicity and reduced physical activity, with significantly fewer Pakistani heritage children (23 per cent) meeting guidelines than White British children (34 per cent).

We used multivariable regression analysis to explore the factors associated with a child being sufficiently active. One key finding was that leaving the home for 30–60 minutes doubled the odds of a child being sufficiently active, and leaving the home for more than 60 minutes increased these odds to more than seven (Bingham et al, 2021). When frequency of leaving the home was controlled, the physical activity differences between ethnic groups no longer existed, highlighting a key need for Pakistani heritage children to be encouraged to leave the home regularly and for longer durations to be sufficiently physically active.

In the free-text responses, relatively few participants mentioned that they were worried about lack of exercise, which suggests that this was not a particular concern or priority for families during this time. However, in Phase 1, several parents mentioned that COVID-19 health anxiety had caused them to be fearful of going outside, which could explain the lack of activity for some families: "Even though we are allowed one walk outside I'm scared to go out for my kids especially my two months old baby so I decide not to go outside. We're only go for groceries once a week" (Adult, Phase 1). In the qualitative study on children's mental health (Lockyer et al, 2020), the lack of routine, inability to go out, or take part in extracurricular activities was highlighted as a cause of lethargy which affected activity levels in children:

'Now I'm that lazy, I do less. I'm less eager to be more active, like go outside. I'm like, "Oh, I have to go outside now," I'm like, I don't want to, I just want to, you know, lie down on my bed and just watch my phone all day ... And I used to be much more active before lockdown and now I can't do it.' (Family 18, Child)

The persistent patterns of low physical activity during the pandemic places adults and children at greater risk of developing, or exacerbating, non-communicable diseases and co-morbidities such as obesity, diabetes, and respiratory illnesses (Marmot et al, 2020; Born in Bradford, 2021). South Asian children are already at a higher risk of being overweight/obese, making regular physical activity even more important for these children (Sivasubramanian et al, 2021).

Methods reflection: free-text responses

The free-text questions completed by BiB participants gave families the opportunity to share their concerns in their own words and to elucidate the quantitative findings. We did not, however, anticipate the powerful effect that these free-text responses would have on our research team, key stakeholders, and the survey findings. Qualitative survey data of this type is often dismissed due to the brevity of some responses and the inability of the researcher to ask participants to expand or explain their meaning further (Braun et al, 2020). However, while individual responses in our survey may lack depth when viewed in isolation, when taken as a whole, they tell us a complex story of Bradford families' pandemic experiences. These responses have not only helped to illuminate the quantitative findings, but they have added detail and richness to our understanding that we would not have been able to reach through any other method.

These responses have influenced and informed several complementary research studies, including qualitative interview studies on experiences during pregnancy (BIHR C-SAG, 2021, Brawner et al, 2021), adolescent mental wellbeing (Lockyer et al, 2020), health beliefs (Lockyer et al, 2021), and vaccine hesitancy (Dickerson et al, 2021). These same questions have also been asked in other studies (for example Tower Hamlets study by Cameron et al, Chapter 6; Gibson et al, 2021). Most significantly, however, these findings have enabled us to rapidly inform local decision makers about the concerns and circumstances of families, using their own words. This enabled a more resonant and powerful communication of our research to those who could, and did, work to improve the situation of Bradford families.

Policy and practice implications of our findings

The results from our COVID-19 longitudinal BiB study reflect findings that are emerging around the country: that the response to the pandemic has had unintended negative consequences, with the greatest impact being on those families who were already vulnerable. It has exacerbated inequalities in financial security, mental ill health and physical activity and these impacts have continued throughout the pandemic. To recover effectively from the pandemic, additional support will be needed to support the most vulnerable families (Marmot et al, 2020), and the UK Government's pledge of 'levelling up' (to reduce the inequalities experienced by many) will require even more resources now than it did pre-pandemic.

While the furlough scheme and support to self-employed workers was introduced by the UK Government to provide financial support, our findings suggest that the loss of even a small proportion of income for those on low wages is enough to tip families into perilous financial difficulty, and potentially further exacerbate health inequalities. Economic support for communities in areas of high deprivation, and specific financial advice and support to families who have been hardest hit during the pandemic are needed as we enter the next phase of managing the recovery from the pandemic.

The self-reported worsening of mental ill health by parents and children during the pandemic is also of concern. More needs to be done to reach and support those with long-term mental ill health caused by the pandemic. Policy and decision makers should also make provision for the continuing need to support and protect vulnerable families from financial, food and housing insecurity, and loneliness, all of which were associated with poor mental health in adults in this study.

While there are plans in place to alleviate lost academic learning caused by school closures and self-isolation, it is far less widely acknowledged that many children are also struggling with their mental health, and many have also endured a significant amount of time with very low levels of physical activity. Education policymakers and schools need to be made aware that the impact of children not attending school is wider than just on their education; it also has a significant impact on their health and wellbeing which must be considered in the recovery plans as well as in future lockdowns and/or periods of isolation.

Being able to leave the home environment was found to be significantly associated with children being sufficiently physically active during the first COVID-19 lockdown. The Government guidance during the first and all subsequent lockdowns has been to minimise the time spent outside of the home, and in the first lockdown this was restricted to up to one hour a day. Our findings illustrate the importance of allowing extended time outside of the home for children to be physically active, with relevant public health messaging directed at parents to emphasise both the importance and safety of this.

Impact of our research and future research

By co-producing our research with communities, key policy and decision makers, we have produced findings that are both meaningful and readily translatable into local practice. Emerging findings have been rapidly disseminated to community and stakeholder groups using briefing notes, meetings, and informal communication channels (for example WhatsApp groups). This provided an opportunity to contextualise findings within our communities and to spark further conversations about emerging priorities, and also help to develop recovery plans within the city to address these (BIHR C-SAG, 2021).

We have also worked with our community steering group to co-produce accessible, bite-size summaries of key findings to share with our families and communities. Our community advisors were keen that we use these findings to empower local communities, so findings were combined with positive actions that could be taken to address the issues we had discovered. We will continue to follow our families during the recovery from the pandemic and look at the full trajectories of the COVID-19 Government responses on vulnerable families using our Phase 3 survey. Key areas for future research include understanding the persistence of (and resilience from) mental ill-health and physical inactivity triggered by the pandemic and how to best address these with culturally appropriate interventions.

The rich insights from our BiB COVID-19 research with seldom-listened-to communities has only been possible because of the enthusiasm and commitment of the children and parents in BiB. We are grateful to all of the families who have given their time to support this research in such a tough and onerous time, giving us the chance to highlight the issues that matter most to them. The applied focus of our research and the ability to transfer our findings into actions so quickly has only been possible due to the time that numerous key policy and decision makers across the Bradford District have given to shaping this research, and acting upon our findings to make real changes to policy and recovery strategies in our city. This in turn has only been possible from the time that our wonderful research team have spent building trusting and reciprocal relationships and a shared understanding of research priorities over many years. We hope that others are encouraged to work in such a collaborative way to develop applied and impactful research that can change a city.

Acknowledgements

We would like to acknowledge the input of the wider Bradford Institute for Health Research COVID-19 Scientific Advisory Group and the Community Steering group in this research programme.

Notes

[1] For financial insecurity we used the question: 'How well would you say you are managing financially right now?' Answer options are: living comfortably, doing all right, just about getting by, finding it quite difficult, finding it very difficult. The final three options were grouped and categorised as indicating current financial insecurity.

[2] For depression we used total scores on the PHQ8 and standard categorisations (0 to 4 no depression, 5 to 9 mild depression, 10 to 14 moderate depression, 15 to 19 moderately severe depression and 20 to 24 severe depression). Similarly, for anxiety we employed total scores on the GAD7 and standard categorisations (0 to 4 no anxiety, 5 to 9 mild anxiety, 10 to 14 moderate anxiety and 15 to 21 severe anxiety). Moderate, moderately severe, and severe categories were collapsed to indicate clinically important symptoms of depression and anxiety. For regression analyses, we used an increase of five or more points as a clinically important increase in symptoms.

[3] Government guidelines recommend that adults accumulate 150 minutes of moderate-to-vigorous physical activity (MVPA) across a week, with a suggested guide of 30 minutes' activity five days a week. For children, guidelines recommend achieving an average of 60 minutes of MVPA daily.

References

Bingham, D.D., Daly-Smith, A., Hall, J., Seims, A., Dogra, S.A., Fairclough, S.J. et al (2021) COVID-19 lockdown: ethnic differences in children's self-reported physical activity and the importance of leaving the home environment. A longitudinal and cross-sectional study from the Born in Bradford Birth Cohort Study. *International Journal Of Behavioral Nutrition And Physical Activity*. In press.

Born in Bradford (2021) Available at: https://borninbradford.nhs.uk/

Bradford Institute for Health Research COVID-19 Scientific Advisory Group (2021). Available at: www.bradfordresearch.nhs.uk/c-sag/

Braun, V., Clarke, V., Boulton, E., Davey, L., and McEvoy, C. (2020) The online survey as a qualitative research tool. *International Journal Of Social Research Methodology*, 1–14.

Brawner, J., Garcia Rodriguez, D., Jackson, C., Dickerson, J., Dharni, N., Smith, H., and Sheard, L. (2021) 'What if I'm on my own?' Interim report: experiences of pregnancy and birth during the COVID-19 pandemic. [Online]. Available at: https://www.bradfordresearch.nhs.uk/wp-content/uploads/2021/05/BiB-Qualitative-study_Pregnancy-in-COVID_brief-report_FINAL.pdf

Dickerson, J., Kelly, B., Lockyer, B., Bridges, S., Cartwright, C., Willan, K., et al (2020) Experiences of lockdown during the COVID-19 pandemic: descriptive findings from a survey of families in the Born in Bradford study. *Wellcome Open Research*, 5, 228.

Dickerson, J., Kelly, B., Lockyer, B., Bridges, S., Cartwright, C., Willan, K., et al (2022) 'When will this end? Will it end?' The impact of the March–June 2020 UK COVID-19 lockdown response on mental health: a longitudinal survey of mothers in the Born in Bradford study. BMJ Open 2022;12:e047748. doi:10.1136/bmjopen-2020-047748

Dickerson, J., Lockyer, B., Moss, R.H., Endacott, C., Kelly, B., Bridges, S., et al (2021) COVID-19 vaccine hesitancy in an ethnically diverse community: descriptive findings from the Born in Bradford study. *Wellcome Open Research*, 6, 23.

Gibson, L.Y., Lockyer, B., Dickerson, J., Endacott, C., Bridges, S., McEachan, R.R.C., et al (2021) Comparison of experiences in two birth cohorts comprising young families with children under four years during the initial COVID-19 lockdown in Australia and the UK: a qualitative study. *International Journal of Environmental Research and Public Health*, 18(17), 9119. https://doi.org/10.3390/ijerph18179119

Lockyer, B., Islam, S., Rahman, A., Dickerson, J., Pickett, K.E., Sheldon, T., et al (2021) Understanding COVID-19 misinformation and vaccine hesitancy in context: findings from a qualitative study involving citizens in Bradford, UK. *Health Expectations*, 24(4), 115867. DOI: 10.1111/Hex.13240.

Lockyer, B., Sheard, L., Smith, H., Dickerson, J., Kelly, B., McEachan, R.R.C., et al (2020) 'Her whole little life has changed dramatically': Findings of a qualitative study into children's mental wellbeing in Bradford during COVID-19. [Online]. Available at: https://www.bradfordresearch.nhs.uk/wp-content/uploads/2020/11/CSAGChildrens-Mental-Wellbeing-Report-11th-November-2020.pdf

Marmot, M., Allen, J., Boyce, T., Goldblatt, P., and Morrison, J. (2020) Build back fairer: the COVID-19 Marmot Review. London: Institute of Health Equity.

McEachan, R.R., Dickerson, J., Bridges, S., Bryant, M., Cartwright, C., Islam, S., et al (2020) The Born in Bradford COVID-19 research study: protocol for an adaptive mixed methods research study to gather actionable intelligence on the impact of COVID-19 on health inequalities among families living in Bradford. *Wellcome Open Research*, 5, 191.

Office for National Statistics (2011) 2011 Census: population and household estimates for England and Wales, March 2011. [Online]. Available at: www.ons.gov.uk/peoplepopulationandcommunity/populationandmigration/populationestimates/bulletins/2011censuspopulationandhouseholdestimatesforenglandandwales/2012-07-16

Office for National Statistics (2020) Coronavirus and depression in adults, Great Britain: June 2020. [Online]. Available at: www.ons.gov.uk/peoplepopulationandcommunity/wellbeing/articles/coronavirusanddepressioninadultsgreatbritain/June2020

Pierce, M., Hope, H., Ford, T., Hatch, S., Hotopf, M., John, A., et al (2020) Mental health before and during the COVID-19 pandemic: a longitudinal probability sample survey of the UK population. *The Lancet Psychiatry*, 7, 883–92.

Sivasubramanian, R., Malhotra, S., Fitch, A.K., and Singhal, V. (2021) Obesity and metabolic care of children of South Asian ethnicity in Western society. *Children*, 8, 447.

6

A tale of two cities in London's East End: impacts of COVID-19 on low- and high-income families with young children and pregnant women

Claire Cameron, Hanan Hauari, Michelle Heys, Katie Hollingworth, Margaret O'Brien, Sarah O'Toole, and Lydia Whitaker

Introduction

That rich and poor live side by side in London is not new; it is a legacy that Charles Dickens, whose first job, age 12, in 1824, was in a shoe blacking factory, would recognise today. Of 32 London boroughs, those in the east of the city feature most prominently in the 'most deprived' category and Tower Hamlets and Newham in particular are among the six most deprived boroughs overall (London Datastore, 2019). More than half of children resident in these two boroughs are living in poverty. These areas are also witnessing major population increases, and are home to very ethnically diverse populations. This chapter will describe findings from two parallel surveys of the impacts of COVID-19 on families with young children, or those expecting a child, that took place in the latter half of 2020 in Newham and Tower Hamlets. Survey data was collected as part of a larger study that investigated the intersections of place, income, ethnicity, and family status (Cameron et al, 2021), and was situated within the umbrella of a major programme evaluating initiatives supporting health and wellbeing outcomes called ActEarly (Wright et al, 2019). The chapter uses household income as its major variable and in particular examines how low- and high-income families were managing during the pandemic.

Characteristics of Tower Hamlets and Newham

Life expectancy in Tower Hamlets and Newham is about four years less than in Westminster, the London borough where residents live the longest (Trust for London, 2021b). Employment in these two boroughs for males in

2020 was close to the average for London (72.6 per cent in Tower Hamlets and 79.5 per cent in Newham vs 78.7 per cent in London) and lower for females (66 per cent and 66.1 per cent vs 71.3 per cent across London) (Nomis, 2020. Full-time salaries are above the London average (£759.40 pw for males and £670.80 pw for females) in Tower Hamlets (at £862.40 (males) and £701.50 (females), presumably due to the close proximity to the City and Canary Wharf business districts, while substantially lower in Newham (£634.50 and £609.20 respectively).

The proportion of children living in poverty, after housing costs, is 55 per cent in Tower Hamlets and 50 per cent in Newham, compared to 17 per cent in the much more affluent Richmond upon Thames. Housing costs effectively double the proportion of children living in poverty (Trust for London, 2020). Prior to the pandemic, the proportion of children in low income households in Tower Hamlets and Newham was around three times higher than in the least deprived boroughs in London (Trust for London, 2021a).

One of the hallmarks of both boroughs is rich ethnic diversity. In Tower Hamlets, over two thirds of the borough is not White British, while in Newham this is the case for around 85 per cent of residents and in London for 61 per cent (Table 6.1).

Families in Tower Hamlets and Newham studies

The disruption to family life once national lockdowns were announced was immediate, affecting access to early childhood education and care services, schools, health care, as well as leisure facilities and livelihoods. The aim of our studies was to assess the economic, social, and health impacts of the pandemic on families both expecting babies, and those with children under five, in two places where the impacts might be expected to be severe, and where, critically, recovery policies would be needed. The study design largely followed that of the Born in Bradford team's study of family life taking place concurrently (Chapter 5 in this collection), but a key difference was that our survey samples had to be constructed from scratch due to an absence of pre-existing sampling frames. We worked with the local authority public health, early years, and child health teams, and borough marketing, to invite mothers, mothers-to-be, fathers, and fathers-to-be, to take part in the survey via Qualtrics, an online survey tool, with availability in many languages and accessible in multiple formats. We also worked with specialist voluntary organisations in order to boost participation from frequently under-represented groups, such as Somali women, and those living in temporary accommodation. In Tower Hamlets, all those on Housing Benefit were invited to take part via a mailed-out postcard. All participants were offered a £10 shopping voucher as a thank you for their contribution.[1]

Table 6.1: Ethnic diversity in Tower Hamlets and Newham, compared to London

Ethnicity	Tower Hamlets[1] %	Newham[2] %	London %
Arab	1	1.3	1.6
Bangladeshi	32	12.4	2.9
Black African	4	11.1	7.3
Black Caribbean	2	4.1	3.8
Chinese	3	1.6	1.7
Indian	3	14.8	7.1
Other Asian	2	6.6	5.6
Other Black	1	2.6	2.3
Other Ethnic Group	1	2.8	2.4
Other Mixed	1	1.7	1.8
Other White	12	13.7	15.8
Pakistani	1	9.8	3.1
White and Asian	1	1.1	1.4
White and Black African	1	11	0.9
White and Black Caribbean	1	1.1	1.5
White British	31	13.2	38.6
White Irish	2	0.8	0.2

[1] Tower Hamlets (2013).

[2] Newham London (nd).

Here, we report selected findings from data collected between July and December 2020. Survey content was drawn from three main sources: (i) Born in Bradford's COVID-19 family survey; (ii) Work-care items from a survey run by the International Network on Leave Policies and Research; and (iii) *Understanding Society*, a large longitudinal household panel study. Most questions were standardised and offered Likert-type scales for responses, but three questions were open-ended, and asked about recent worries, challenges, and aspects of the pandemic that were enjoyable. We also include an anonymised case study, data for which is drawn from the second strand of the study design. This was in-depth interviews with household members, where possible with both mother and father. In total, 45 interviews were completed (Tower Hamlets: 32 interviews, 20 mothers and 12 fathers from 22 families; Newham: 13 interviews, all mothers). In both areas, interview respondents were purposively selected to ensure representation of low- (below £20,799 pa), middle- (£20,800–£51,999 pa) and high- (£52,000 and above pa) income households, household structures (for example, single-parent, couple-parent, or multi-adult households) and ethnic backgrounds.

The case study selected is a low-income, two-parent household of Black British origin.

Survey participants

Of 992 eligible responses in Tower Hamlets and 2,054 in Newham, the majority were female (Tower Hamlets 74 per cent; Newham 61 per cent) and had at least one child under five (Tower Hamlets 84 per cent; Newham 88 per cent). A small proportion were expecting their first child (6 per cent and 7 per cent respectively) or were expecting a child and had at least one already (6 per cent and 5 per cent).[2]

The sample over-represents White British respondents and under-represents Bangladeshi residents in Newham, and also under-represents people from a non-British White background in both boroughs (see Tables 6.1 and 6.2).

Initial investigation of the Tower Hamlets dataset suggested that income was a more important factor than ethnicity when looking at key outcomes such as mental health status (Cameron et al, 2021). For this reason, we will be focusing here on household income as a variable structuring respondents' experience of the pandemic in 2020, while not discounting the impacts of ethnicity.

Overview of main findings

Nearly 40 per cent of Tower Hamlets' survey respondents were from low-income households, while in Newham, 51 per cent[3] were from mid-income households. Median household incomes were £30,760 and £23,143 respectively (Table 6.3). Given the lower median salaries in Newham, the survey may under-represent the proportion with low income in that borough.

Respondents, particularly those from a low income, reported a worsening financial situation during the second half of 2020. Prior to the first lockdown, which began on 23 March 2020, a majority of respondents were employed or on leave from employment but receiving in-work benefits (Tower Hamlets

Table 6.2: Ethnic diversity in the Tower Hamlets and Newham survey data

	Tower Hamlets %	Newham %
White British/Irish	34.8	59.0
Bangladeshi	35.7	6.8
Other Asian (inc Indian, Pakistani, mixed)	8.2	11.2
Other White	8.5	5.7
Black (inc Somali, Black African, Caribbean, Mixed)	6.5	6.3
Other (inc Chinese, Vietnamese, other)	3.7	3.4
Prefer not to say/missing	1.4	1.5

Table 6.3: Household income of respondents by income band, compared to median

	Tower Hamlets	Newham
Low HH inc[1] (up to £20,799)	39%	16.7%
Mid HH inc (£20,800–51,999)	31.5%	51.3%
High HH inc (52,000 +)	21.9%	26.9%
Missing/not stated	143	178
Total n (excluding missing)	849	1,876
Median household income, 2019[2]	£30,760	£23,143

[1] Household income bands were selected to match the distribution of the sample and taking into account local median household income.
[2] Tower Hamlets Borough Statistics, 2019.

67 per cent; Newham 82 per cent). The remainder (Tower Hamlets 33 per cent; Newham 19 per cent) were unemployed or not working despite a self-employed status. That is, employment activity was precarious for a significant minority of the sample at the start of the pandemic.

At the point of data collection, employment rates were lower and unemployment higher in low-income households (Tables 6.4 and 6.5). These rates represented a disproportionate drop in employment compared to pre-March 2020 for low-income households. Tables 6.4 and 6.5 show that in Tower Hamlets 16 per cent fewer low-income households compared to 11 per cent high-income households were employed. In Newham, there was a drop of 10 per cent for low-income households but a rise in employment among high-income households of 3 per cent. However, low- and mid-income households were more likely than high-income families to be protected through the Coronavirus Job Retention Scheme (furlough).

Many respondents claimed social security benefits. Universal Credit was being claimed by 43 per cent of low-income respondents in Newham and 33 per cent in Tower Hamlets (Tables 6.6 and 6.7). However, the most commonly claimed benefit among low-income families in Tower Hamlets was the in-work child tax credit (52 per cent), vs 33 per cent of low-income respondents in Newham. Quite strikingly, only 39 per cent of high-income families were not claiming any benefits in Newham, compared to 81 per cent in Tower Hamlets. This may speak to a need to ensure families are claiming all they are entitled to in Tower Hamlets, or it may be that their incomes are higher than in Newham.

Food and housing insecurity

Alongside accessing the social security system, low-income respondents had considerable food and housing insecurity. Just over a third (36 per cent) of

Table 6.4: Tower Hamlets, respondent employment status, by household income

	Low income			Mid income			High income			Prefer not to say			DK/NA			All participants		
	N	%	Δ*	N	%	Δ	N	%	Δ	N	%	Δ	N	%	Δ	N	%	Δ
Employed	97	29.1	-15.6	127	47.4	-17.2	75	40.3	-11.8	12	19.4	-12.9	9	6.3	-6.3	320	32.3	-13.8
Furlough	22	6.6		24	9.0		7	3.8		2	3.2		2	1.4		57	5.7	
Parental leave	17	5.1	-0.3	34	12.7	+5.2	60	32.3	+10.2	8	12.9	+3.2	5	3.5	-0.7	124	12.5	+3.3
Self-employed (working)	21	6.3	-3.0	17	6.3	-2.2	15	8.1	0.0	3	4.8	+1.6	6	4.2	+0.7	62	6.3	-1.4
Self-employed (not working)	7	2.1	+1.5	2	0.7	0.0	1	0.5	-1.6	2	3.2	+1.6	2	1.4	-0.7	14	1.4	+0.2
Unemployed	84	25.2	+5.1	51	19.0	+4.5	23	12.4	-2.2	21	33.9	+1.6	31	21.7	+3.5	210	21.2	+3.1
Unemployed and receiving benefits	81	24.3	+5.7	10	3.7	+0.4	5	2.7	+1.6	11	17.7	+1.6	43	30.1	+4.2	150	15.1	+3.0
Don't know	0	0.0	0.0	0	0.0	0.0	0	0.0	0.0	0	0.0	0.0	0	0.0	0.0	0	0.0	0.0
N/A	4	1.2	0.0	3	1.1	+0.4	0	0.0	0.0	3	4.8	0.0	45	31.5	-2.1	55	5.5	-0.2

*Δ= Change of percentage of employment status compared to prior to March 2020

COVID-19 Collaborations

Table 6.5: Newham, respondent employment status, by household income

	Low income			Mid income			High income			Prefer not to say			All participants		
	N	%	Δ*	N	%	Δ	N	%	Δ	N	%	Δ	N	%	Δ
Employed	87	28.0	-9.9	602	62.6	-8.7	375	74.3	+2.6	23	25.8	-12.4	1087	58.3	-6.0
Furlough	22	7.1	-	92	9.6	-	7	1.4	-	5	5.6		126	6.8	-
Parental leave	37	11.9	+2.8	98	10.2	+5.7	43	8.5	+0.3	13	14.6	+4.5	191	10.2	+3.5
Self-employed (working)	12	3.9	-4.8	54	5.6	-7.4	46	9.1	+1.9	8	9.0	+9.0	120	6.4	-4.2
Self-employed (not working)	7	2.3	+0.4	21	2.2	-1.9	10	2.0	-7.0	3	3.4	-10.1	41	2.2	-2.6
Unemployed	68	21.9	+2.8	51	5.3	+0.1	15	3.0	-0.2	29	32.6	+4.5	163	8.7	+0.6
Unemployed and receiving benefits	78	25.1	+1.8	43	4.5	+2.5	9	1.8	+1.0	8	9.0	-1.1	138	7.4	+1.8
Don't know	0	0.0	0.0	0	0.0	0.0	0	0.0	0.0	0	0.0	0.0	0	0.0	0.0

*Δ= Change of percentage of employment status compared to prior to March 2020

Table 6.6: Tower Hamlets, benefits claimed, by household income

Benefits	Low income		Mid income		High income		Prefer not to say		DK/NA		All participants	
	N	%	N	%	N	%	N	%	N	%	N	%
Universal Credit	110	33.0	53	19.8	3	1.6	18	29.0	35	24.5	219	22.1
Work Tax Credit	110	33.0	27	10.1	1	0.5	7	11.3	9	6.3	154	15.5
Child Tax Credit	172	51.7	53	19.8	10	5.4	12	19.4	38	26.6	285	28.7
Jobseekers Allowance	27	8.1	32	11.9	2	1.1	3	4.8	2	1.4	66	6.7
Employment and Support Allowance	32	9.6	26	9.7	2	1.1	3	4.8	4	2.8	67	6.8
None of these	28	8.4	125	46.6	151	81.2	13	21.0	9	6.3	326	32.9
No recourse to public funds	10	3.0	12	4.5	17	9.1	3	4.8	0	0.0	42	4.2
Prefer not to say	8	2.4	7	2.6	0	0.0	17	27.4	8	5.6	40	4.0

Table 6.7: Newham, benefits claimed, by household income

Benefits	Low income		Mid income		High income		Prefer not to say		All participants	
	N	%	N	%	N	%	N	%	N	%
Universal Credit	134	42.7	260	27.0	79	15.6	10	10.6	483	25.7
Work Tax Credit	72	22.9	362	37.6	85	16.8	3	3.2	522	27.8
Child Tax Credit	104	33.1	346	35.9	95	18.8	9	9.6	554	29.5
Jobseekers Allowance	20	6.4	258	26.8	105	20.8	2	2.1	385	20.5
Employment and Support Allowance	25	8.0	228	23.7	127	25.1	3	3.2	383	20.4
None of these	32	10.2	144	15.0	196	38.8	44	46.8	416	22.2
No recourse to public funds	19	6.1	9	0.9	16	3.2	13	13.8	57	3.0
Prefer not to say	5	1.6	4	0.4	3	0.6	18	19.1	30	1.6

Table 6.8: Tower Hamlets, food bank use in most recent four weeks, by household income

	Low income		Mid income		High income		Prefer not to say		All participants	
	N	%	N	%	N	%	N	%	N	%
Never	203	64.2	208	78.5	166	90.2	46	78.0	676	75.3
Less than four times	80	25.3	53	20.0	18	9.8	10	16.9	178	19.8
Four times or more	33	10.4	4	1.5	-	-	3	5.1	44	4.9
Total	316	100	265	100	184	100	59	100	898	100

Table 6.9: Newham, food bank use in most recent four weeks, by household income

	Low income		Mid income		High income		Prefer not to say		All participants	
	N	%	N	%	N	%	N	%	N	%
Never	175	57.9	613	64.1	427	84.6	67	71.3	1,362	69.0
Less than four times	95	31.5	290	30.3	74	14.7	10	10.6	494	24.1
Four times or more	32	10.6	54	5.6	4	0.8	8	8.5	117	5.7
Do not know	12	3.8	6	0.6	-	-	9	9.6	27	1.4
Total	314	100	963	100	505	100	94	100	2000	100

respondents in Tower Hamlets and approaching half (42 per cent) in Newham had used a food bank in the preceding four weeks (Tables 6.8 and 6.9). Far fewer high-income households had used a food bank. In addition, two thirds of respondents in low-income households found that they could not always afford balanced meals (Tower Hamlets 67 per cent; Newham 63 per cent), or the food they bought did not last and there was no money for more (Tower Hamlets 68 per cent; Newham 68 per cent). Just under half skipped meals (Tower Hamlets 44 per cent; Newham 49 per cent). The links between low income and food insecurity were underscored by survey respondents, such as this mother who wrote about her worries: 'Not having enough money to even buy food for myself or my child and having to ask friends for money' (Black/Black British: Caribbean, £5,200–£10,399).

Low income was associated with rented accommodation and poor-quality housing. While the majority of high-income respondents owned or had a mortgage on their homes (Tower Hamlets 91 per cent; Newham 64 per cent), most low-income respondents lived in rented accommodation (Tower

Hamlets 76 per cent; Newham 58 per cent) (Tables 6.10 and 6.11). Those living in low-income households were also much more likely to experience damp and mould than their high-income peers (Tower Hamlets 41 per cent vs 15 per cent, Newham 49 per cent vs 12 per cent per cent).

Housing quality was associated with health problems and living through the pandemic-associated restrictions had exacerbated difficulties for some, as this father in Newham explained:

"My daughter is young and has heart problems since birth. My accommodation is unfit for her. The local authority is unwilling to help. I fear her steady progress will be disrupted. Continuity of her progress is essential to her living a normal childhood and beyond. I fear the virus has caused the entire support network to be disrupted, which has affected many people including me." (Bangladeshi, £10,400–£15,999)

Networks of support

In the face of often very difficult financial and housing circumstances, familial and particularly couple relationships became very important during COVID-19. Nearly 40 per cent of Tower Hamlets' respondents said that spending time as a family was an enjoyable aspect of life during the pandemic; a finding echoed in Chapters 5, 8, and 9 in this collection. The strength of a couple relationship, alongside income, were the two most important family assets in protecting respondents from the risk of mental health difficulties (Cameron et al, 2021. Most survey respondents said they had a good or excellent relationship with their partner (Tables 6.12 and 6.13). In Tower Hamlets, there was an income gradient to this, with an 18 percentage point difference between high-income households (84 per cent reporting good or excellent couple relationships) and low-income households (66 per cent). However, there was little difference by income in the Newham survey.

Support from outside the household from wider family, friends, and neighbours was more often mentioned in Newham (67 per cent) than in Tower Hamlets (51 per cent). In Newham, there was a clear difference by income; far fewer low-income households (12 per cent) than high income (25 per cent) or middle income (60 per cent) reported that they received help. Where they did have help, it was mostly from siblings. From all sources, those on a middle income reported more support. Help was given in relation to shopping, practical help with house and garden, meals, online access, lifts in cars, help with domestic chores, meeting basic personal needs, financial affairs, and looking after children.

On the other hand, being in lockdown could be a lonely experience, particularly for single parents – as echoed by Clery et al in Chapter 8. A mother in Newham summed up the sense of isolation and absence of

Table 6.10: Tower Hamlets, housing circumstances, by household income

	Low income		Mid income		High income		Prefer not to say		DK/NA		All participants	
	N	%	N	%	N	%	N	%	N	%	N	%
Own it outright	15	4.5	118	44.0	56	30.1	2	3.2	5	4.1	196	20.3
Mortgage/loan	17	5.2	30	11.2	63	33.9	5	8.1	6	5.0	121	12.5
Shared ownership	24	7.3	12	4.5	12	6.5	3	4.8	2	1.7	53	5.5
Renting	249	75.5	97	36.2	53	28.5	49	79.0	94	77.7	542	56.0
Living rent free	6	1.8	6	2.2	2	1.1	1	1.6	3	2.5	18	1.9
Temporary accommodation	19	5.8	5	1.9	-	-	2	3.2	10	8.3	36	3.7
Squatting	-	-	-	-	-	-	-	-	1	0.8	1	0.1
Total	330	100	268	100	186	100	62	100	121	100	967	100

Table 6.11: Newham, housing circumstances, by household income

	Low income		Mid income		High income		Prefer not to say		All participants	
	N	%	N	%	N	%	N	%	N	%
Own it outright	24	7.7	378	39.3	272	54.0	12	13.2	686	36.7
Mortgage/loan	31	9.9	312	32.4	186	36.9	21	23.1	550	29.4
Shared ownership	23	7.4	108	11.2	16	3.2	-	-	147	7.9
Renting	181	58.0	146	15.2	22	4.4	44	48.4	393	21.0
Living rent free	15	4.8	15	1.6	8	1.6	9	9.9	47	2.5
Temporary accommodation	36	11.5	3	0.3	-	-	5	5.5	44	2.4
Squatting	2	0.6	-	-	-	-	-	-	2	0.1
Total	312	100	962	100	504	100	91	100	1,869	100

Table 6.12: Tower Hamlets, relationship quality, by household income

	Low income		Mid income		High income		Prefer not to say		All participants	
Quality of relationship	N	%	N	%	N	%	N	%	N	%
Excellent/good	152	65.8	193	79.1	149	84.2	38	71.7	532	75.5
Average	41	17.7	35	14.3	21	11.9	4	7.5	101	14.3
Poor/very poor	35	15.2	10	4.1	7	4.0	2	3.8	54	7.7
Prefer not to say	3	1.3	6	2.5	-	-	9	17.0	18	2.6
Total	231	100	244	100	177	100	53	100	705	100

Table 6.13: Newham, relationship quality, by household income

	Low income		Mid income		High income		Prefer not to say		All participants	
Quality of relationship	N	%	N	%	N	%	N	%	N	%
Excellent/good	168	71.2	699	72.4	347	71.3	61	79.2	1,275	72.2
Average	36	15.3	228	23.6	124	25.5	4	5.2	392	22.2
Poor/very poor	25	10.6	34	3.5	15	3.1	2	2.6	76	4.3
Prefer not to say	7	3.0	4	0.4	1	0.2	10	13.0	22	1.2
Total	236	100	965	100	487	100	77	100	1,765	100

help she felt: "Being in self-isolation on my own with two little children and no help from anyone. Being so far away from family and friends and facing consequences of recent divorce" (White British, prefer not to say income). In Tower Hamlets, over half (53 per cent), said they had felt lonely during the past week. Of those who felt lonely most of the time, over half (53 per cent) were from low-income households, compared to a third from middle- and 11 per cent from high-income households.

Study findings show that across the two East London boroughs, there were similar experiences of the pandemic. The pre-existing inequalities of income, housing, and environment were amplified during lockdown with reductions in employment and job security. However, at the time of the survey, parents' reports of their parenting were showing considerable resilience with most children's learning being supported at home, with reports of strengthened bonds through spending more time together, as illustrated by this mother from Newham: "Early lockdown I was pregnant and with only one child (2.5yrs old) so I had more time on my hands to do more educational things with her. Had fun cooking with her and giving her more 1 to 1 time" (Indian, £26,000–£36,399). We now turn to a case study of the Campbells, a 'just about managing' family running a business prior to the pandemic whose losses were multiple and immediate.

Case study

In 2020, the Campbells and their four children, went from self-employment at the point when the COVID-19 pandemic struck, to a potentially ruinous level of debt. They are a case of a family falling through the government's financial support net with adverse consequences for health and wellbeing and thwarted dreams of moving house.

The Campbells live in a Housing Association two-bedroom house with their children aged between three and 15. Before the COVID-19 pandemic, both parents were running a small business, which they had built up over time. Business profits were low and the majority of their after-tax household income came from tax credits. The family were living in overcrowded conditions and had been saving for a deposit to buy a house under the 'right to buy' scheme.

The immediate concern was exposure to the virus as the mother and youngest daughter both had respiratory health issues and were at high risk if they contracted COVID-19. Moreover, the paternal grandmother was recovering from an operation to remove a brain tumour. Both parents stopped work and closed their business to protect the family's health.

By August 2020, the household income was £5,200–£10,399 pa. The government support scheme for the self-employed (SEISS), while announced at the end of March

2020, did not commence making payments until June 2020. The Campbells applied, but their application was unsuccessful as their profits for the preceding tax year were too low and did not meet the threshold criteria.

Further stress arose when, because of applying for SEISS, the family came under investigation over the tax they had been paying (even though they had been paying tax through the Construction Industry Scheme). In the meantime, rent arrears quickly accumulated as did significant credit card debt. When they contacted the credit card companies to ask for help they were told that no 'payment holiday' systems were in place and were advised to call back a month later. By the time they tried again, after delays due to COVID-19-related bereavements, the credit card debt had risen so much they were told they were not eligible for payment holidays.

The Campbells appealed to the financial ombudsman because there had been no COVID-19 financial support available for them and the mitigating factors around the delay in applying for a payment holiday. Their case is still ongoing.

The rapid deterioration in finances and absence of help was significant in the parents' level of worry and stress about both managing day to day and providing for their children in the future. Mr Campbell's anxiety about getting a mortgage and his credit rating dominated his account. He said: "You work for years just to build your credit and then to see it just taken away."

He found he could no longer manage the appeals process, felt suicidal, and sought therapy. Mrs Campbell took on the responsibility for the appeal. In her interview, she talked about how she had to stay strong for her children and her husband and how she has been holding the family together, doing most of the work caring for and home-schooling the children. The parents' perception of vulnerability to the virus meant they and their children "locked themselves inside", not only during lockdowns but also when restrictions were lifted. Time spent indoors with the children involved playing board games and baking, and both parents appreciated getting to know their kids better.

By early 2021, Mr Campbell had found employment but with the burden of accumulated debt, rent arrears, and a poor credit rating, their application to be moved to a larger home or to be put on the housing exchange list has been rejected. He reflected that: "because of the whole COVID situation we're stuck here and ... it's just ... bills upon bills to get sorted and debt to clear".

They have not been able to re-start their own business. Their family and friends can support them emotionally and keep in contact, but there is no financial or practical help available. This low-income self-employed working family was dramatically propelled from 'just managing' with a good credit rating and clear plans for the future into a situation of spiralling debt and a decimated credit rating that will impact their recovery and futures for many years to come.

Policy implications

Emerging evidence from across the UK suggests that adverse impacts of the pandemic are distributed unevenly (Marmot et al, 2021). Nationally, the impact of the pandemic has been felt disproportionately by families with children and especially those on a low income (Collard et al, 2021). Low-income families of Tower Hamlets and Newham were highly vulnerable to adverse impacts in the immediate and perhaps the longer term, and they are dependent on public policies to support their recovery.

Secure and well-paid employment is the best defence against poverty and dual-earner households are better protected against poverty than those with a single earner (European Commission, 2015). The generation of new jobs and arguably local jobs that reduce the need for time spent commuting and contribute to ecological sustainability is highly significant for recovery (Organisation for Economic Co-operation and Development [OECD], 2020). In Tower Hamlets, economic growth and associated increase in jobs has been rapid (Tower Hamlets, 2018). However, jobs are unevenly distributed and employment among mothers is comparatively low, said to be a personal choice among families particularly those from some minority ethnic backgrounds. Recovery from the pandemic will require a redoubling of efforts to match jobs and economic growth to residents' skill profiles and potential, as well as linking educational success in the boroughs to employment options and further work on any lifecourse and cultural barriers to enable mothers to earn an income and make use of early childhood education and care services to support parental employment (Dale et al, 2002).

In terms of family support, couple relationships were largely described as good or excellent, while wider familial and community networks were much less frequently reported. Where informal support was available it was most often reported by middle-income households, and from siblings, in Newham, which might speak to the strength of longer-established communities. Many respondents were lonely, especially among the low-income group. Many, as in our case study of the Campbells, developed poor mental health during the pandemic. Again, this mirrors the national data (Collard et al, 2021), with those living alone or with poorer health or living conditions more likely to report loneliness. There was considerable effort in Tower Hamlets to bring people together, so the low figures for informal support and engagement were a surprise. However, national data suggests that the increase in community spirit was most likely to be felt by those from wealthier backgrounds and in better health (Collard et al, 2021). The implication is that community-based mutual help has to be nurtured and even more embedded in daily life alongside attending to the fundamental issues of health and income. Our twin surveys of families with young children in Tower Hamlets and Newham largely confirm national data on the exacerbation of inequality during the pandemic. However, the concentration of income and housing disadvantage in these two highly urbanised and dense living environments, coupled with the lockdown measures of closure of services which closed off much social interaction and informal support created a multiplier of impacts. The longer-term impact on children, and on parental mental health, remains highly uncertain. Inspired and concerted political action and public policy will be required to 'level up' resources and opportunities within London boroughs, and beyond.

Acknowledgements

Francisco Figueroa Zamorano helped produce the tables and Diana Rosenthal supported recruitment and data curation in Newham. UKRI ESRC Award number ESRC Grant Ref: ES/V004891/1. We are grateful to all the families responding to our survey and Borough officers in both Tower Hamlets and Newham who supported the research.

Notes
[1] Ethical approval for the study was awarded by the UCL Institute of Education Research Ethics Committee (REC1366) and the NHS Health Research Authority (20/LO/1039).
[2] Some respondents did not report their gender or household structure.
[3] In-text reporting uses rounding of decimal points to ease reading.

References

Cameron, C., Hauari, H., Hollingworth, K., O'Brien, M. and Whitaker, L. (2021) The impact of COVID-19 on families, children aged 0–4 and pregnant women in Tower Hamlets: Wave One Survey Findings. Available at: Families in Tower Hamlets: impacts of COVID-19 | IOE – Faculty of Education and Society – UCL – University College London.

Cameron, C., O'Brien, M., Whitaker, L., Hollingworth, K. and Hauari, H. (2021) Income, ethnic diversity and family life in East London during the first wave of the pandemic: an assets approach. *Journal of Family Research*. Early View. Available at https://ubp.uni-bamberg.de/jfr/index.php/jfr/article/view/725

Collard, S., Collings, D., Kempson, E., and Evans, J. (2021) Bearing the brunt: the impact of the crisis on families with children. Standard Life Foundation. Available at: www.standardlifefoundation.org.uk/en/our-work/coronavirus-financial-tracker

Dale, A., Fieldhouse, E, Shaheen, N. and Virinder, K. (2002) The labour market prospects for Pakistani and Bangladeshi women. *Work, Employment and Society*, 16(1), 5–25.

European Commission (2015) Employment and social developments in Europe 2015. Available at: https://ec.europa.eu/social/main.jsp?catId=738&langId=en&pubId=7859&furtherPubs=yes

London Datastore (2019) Indices of deprivation 2019 initial analysis. Available at: https://data.london.gov.uk/blog/indices-of-deprivation-2019-initial-analysis/

Marmot, M., Allen, J., Boyce, T., Goldblatt, P. and Morrison, J. (2021) Building back fairer in Greater Manchester: health equity and dignified lives. London: Institute of Health Equity.

Newham London (nd) Population. Available at: https://www.newham.info/population/#/view-report/1ee4f94e929141d0bb9e4792ecdd8e89/___iaFirstFeature

Nomis (2020) Official labour market statistics. Available at: www.nomisweb.co.uk/reports/lmp/la/1946157257/printable.aspx

Organisation for Economic Co-operation and Development (OECD) (2020) Building back better: a sustainable, resilient recovery after COVID-19. Available at: www.oecd.org/coronavirus/policy-responses/building-back-better-a-sustainable-resilient-recovery-after-covid-19-52b869f5/

Tower Hamlets (2018) Tower Hamlets growth and economic development plan 2018–2023. Available at: www.towerhamlets.gov.uk/Documents/Consultation/Growth_and_Economic_Development_Plan_2018_2023/GrowthEconomicPlan_2.pdf

Tower Hamlets borough statistics (2019) Household income 2019. Available at: www.towerhamlets.gov.uk/Documents/Borough_statistics/Income_poverty_and_welfare/income_2019_l.pdf

Trust for London (2020) London's Poverty Profile. Available at: https://trustforlondon.fra1.cdn.digitaloceanspaces.com/media/documents/Londons_Poverty_Profile_2020.pdf

Trust for London (2021a) London's poverty profile 2021. Available at: www.trustforlondon.org.uk/londons-poverty-profile-2021-covid-19-and-poverty-in-london/

Trust for London (2021b) Life expectancy at birth by London borough (2017-19), available at: https://www.trustforlondon.org.uk/data/life-expectancy-borough/

Wright, J., Hayward, A.C., West, J., Pickett, K., McEachan, R., Mon-Williams, M., et al (2019) ActEarly: a City Collaboratory approach to early promotion of good health and wellbeing [version 1; peer review: 2 approved]. *Wellcome Open Research*, 4,156. Available at: https://doi.org/10.12688/wellcomeopenres.15443.1

7

Size matters: experiences of larger families on a low income during COVID-19

Mary Reader and Kate Andersen

Introduction

Children in larger families entered the pandemic at disproportionate risk of poverty. Children in households with three or more children (our marker for larger families) were twice as likely as those in smaller families to be living in poverty in 2019/20, and most of the increase in child poverty since 2012/13 has been driven by increases in poverty among larger families (Stewart et al, 2021).

Larger families have always faced a disproportionate risk of poverty (Bradshaw et al, 2006). This is due to a double bind of higher household needs and lower average work intensity: more children mean more mouths to feed, more childcare to pay, and if childcare is unaffordable, fewer hours left in the day to conduct paid work. Historically, the tax-benefit system has played a large role in mitigating poverty risk among larger families, but cuts to social security since 2012/13 have left larger families more exposed to poverty, despite increases in employment and education (Cooper and Hills, 2021; Stewart et al, 2021). On the eve of the pandemic, larger families on a low income were, therefore, in a particularly precarious financial position.

Yet despite the importance of family size to recent child poverty trends, and the acknowledgement that poverty shaped experiences of the pandemic, little is known about the distributional impact of the pandemic by family size. This is surprising given that the disproportionate burden of COVID-19 for larger families has been evident across the income distribution. The demands of childcare, home schooling, and the risk of children's school bubbles bursting are inevitably enlarged for households with a greater number of children.

This chapter addresses this gap in our knowledge by using quantitative and qualitative data to explore the experiences of low-income larger families during the pandemic. In particular, the chapter investigates the extent to which larger families' experiences of the pandemic have differed from those of other family groups.

Our methodological approach

We draw on quantitative and qualitative evidence generated as part of the Benefit Changes and Larger Families research project. This project is investigating the two-child limit and the benefit cap, both key 'welfare reforms' that have significantly affected larger families.

For the quantitative analysis presented here, we draw on individual-level data throughout the pandemic from Understanding Society (the UK Household Longitudinal Survey), a high-quality panel survey based on probability sampling (University of Essex, Institute for Social and Economic Research, 2021a, 2021b). We use regular monthly and quarterly data from Waves 1–8 of the COVID-19 survey over the period April 2020 to March 2021 and match respondents longitudinally to pre-pandemic data from Wave 10 of the main survey (based on fieldwork from 2017 to 2019).[1] Longitudinal weights are applied to correct for non-response and are customised versions of those described in Benzeval et al (2021).[2] We use this survey data to track and compare outcomes for four distinct groups, by family size and receipt of means-tested social security benefits. This enables us to separate out the contribution of family size and income to the experiences of families with children during the pandemic. We use means-tested social security benefits as a proxy for low income because this is the mechanism through which the two-child limit and benefit cap are implemented.[3] Segmenting our quantitative sample by social security status thereby enables us to integrate insights from our qualitative and quantitative research.

We also draw on early interviews conducted as part of ongoing qualitative longitudinal research for the Benefit Changes and Larger Families project. This research explores how families are impacted by the two-child limit and the benefit cap, and how they respond to these policy changes, by interviewing 44 parents or carers three times over the course of 18 months. The research takes place in Bradford, London, and York. As this project focuses on larger families, our sample is composed of parents or carers with three or more children who are subject to either the benefit cap or the two-child limit, or both. To obtain in-depth data relevant to the participants' experiences of these welfare reforms, we conduct semi-structured individual interviews. The interviews uphold good ethical practice and particular attention is paid to informed consent, confidentiality, and anonymity, prevention of harm (for example, though handling participants' accounts sensitively), and reciprocity. This chapter reports on findings from the first 12 interviews. All of these interviews were conducted by telephone due to COVID-19 regulations.

Impact on employment

As the UK first locked down in March 2020, working hours plummeted and, although the furlough scheme staved off a surge in unemployment, there was a significant reduction in household earnings at the bottom of the income distribution, particularly among younger workers, those from minority ethnic groups, and those in precarious work (Benzeval et al, 2020; Crossley et al, 2021). Larger families on a low income were no exception. In fact, Figure 7.1 shows that among families with children, larger families on benefits saw the sharpest falls in working hours. Average working hours for respondents in larger families on benefits halved between January and May 2020, while they fell by roughly a third for smaller families on benefits.

These large falls in working hours for larger families on benefits appear to be driven by two factors: the labour market position of low-income families; and larger families' household needs. First, low-income families were more exposed to reductions in working hours, redundancies, and furlough as a result of their labour market position prior to the pandemic. Of those in work at the beginning of the pandemic, families on benefits were significantly more likely to be working part-time: 51 per cent of respondents in families on benefits were in part-time work, compared to 38

Figure 7.1: Mean weekly working hours during the pandemic by family type

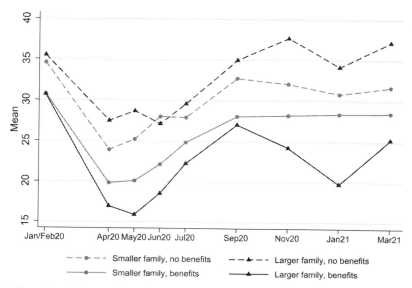

Note: Sample is adult respondents who were in paid work (employment or self-employment) at the COVID-19 survey baseline in January–February 2020. N=2862, 2701, 2243, 2040, 1996, 1777, 1584, 1490 and 1732 in each wave.

per cent of respondents in families who were not on benefits. Families on benefits were also 12 percentage points more likely to be working in routine occupations. These jobs were likely to be more affected by reductions in demand and less likely to be able to continue on a work-from-home basis (Joyce and Xu, 2020). As Figure 7.2 shows, families on benefits, and larger families in particular, were significantly less likely to be able to work from home during the pandemic: just 33 per cent of respondents from larger families on benefits were able to work from home.

However, as Figure 7.2 shows, despite their reduced ability to work from home, families on benefits were not statistically more likely to be classed as key workers. This appears to be explained in part by the high concentration of low-income families in industries such as manufacturing, construction, wholesale and retail, accommodation, food, and other service industries. For many workers in these industries, it was not possible to work from home, yet these respondents were excluded from the government's definition of key worker status.[4] The survey data shows that workers in these industries were more likely than the wider working population to be in precarious work at the beginning of the pandemic, with no minimum hours guaranteed by their employer. At best, where there was some continuity of demand, workers in these industries were able to continue going to work (albeit facing the additional health risks that entailed, with none of the social rights and status of the 'key worker' label). At worst, these workers were more likely to experience redundancy, reductions in working hours, or furlough (Crossley et al, 2021; see also Chapters 3 and 8).

A second driver of reduced working hours that became particularly salient for larger families was caring and home-schooling responsibilities. As Figure 7.3 shows, parents in larger families spent more time helping their children with home schooling within both low-income and higher-income groups. However, parents in low-income larger families spent the most time of all: 3.9 hours every day on average compared to 2.9 hours among higher-income larger families.[5] This is likely to be both a consequence of reduced working hours and a further contributor towards it. Additionally, fewer home learning resources among low-income larger families – including working space, laptops, and books – may have made parental involvement and supervision of home schooling more intensive. While 39 per cent of smaller families on benefits had a designated computer for each child when home schooling, just 25 per cent of larger families on benefits did. Parents in larger families on benefits may therefore have had to be more actively involved in home schooling.

This greater burden of home schooling and childcare is likely to have contributed towards the higher rates of furlough among larger families on benefits in Figure 7.4 – a dynamic which holds both relative to smaller families on benefits and relative to larger families not on benefits. In April

Figure 7.2: Proportion of adult respondents who identify as key workers and are able to work from home some or all of the time by family type, April 2020

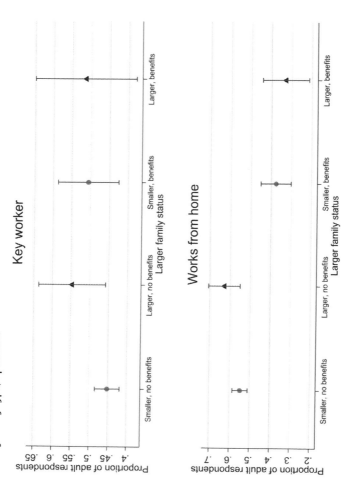

Note: Sample is adult respondents who were in paid work (employment or self-employment) at the COVID-19 survey baseline in January–February 2020. N = 2709 and 2708 respectively. Ninety-five per cent confidence intervals are shown. These indicate a range of values which we can be 95 per cent confident includes the true value. If confidence intervals between two groups do not overlap, there is a statistically significant difference between the two groups.

Figure 7.3: Average hours reported by parents and family members helping children with home schooling by family type, April 2020

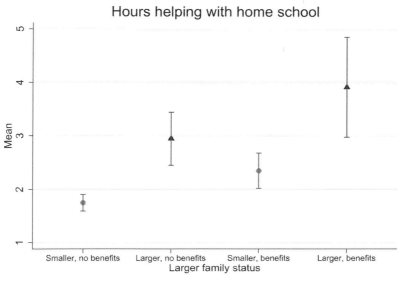

Note: Sample is adult respondents with school-aged children who are not attending school in April 2020, N=3484. Ninety-five per cent confidence intervals are shown. These indicate a range of values which we can be 95 per cent confident includes the true value. If confidence intervals between two groups do not overlap, there is a statistically significant difference between the two groups.

2020, the government confirmed that caring responsibilities were a legitimate reason for furloughing staff (Palmer, 2020). Employers may therefore have been more likely to furlough workers with larger numbers of children. In particular, the timing of the government's clarification is likely to explain the sharper rise in furlough among larger families after April 2020.

Furlough may have afforded some benefits to larger families, enabling more time for bonding with babies and children, and protecting job security and earnings in the short term (see Chapter 9; also, Power et al, 2020; Tarrant et al, 2020). However, being on long-term furlough or reduced working hours has potential scarring effects and puts workers at increased risk of redundancy (Cominetti et al, 2021). By September 2020, when schools had reopened, working hours had recovered to pre-pandemic levels for most families, but larger families on benefits saw the largest shortfall, of 3.6 hours on average. This suggests that there were indeed scarring effects on this group's working patterns from furlough and reduced working hours, even in the short term.

Furlough and reduced working hours also pose a particular challenge for larger families who are at risk of the benefit cap, as they can be pushed onto

Figure 7.4: Proportion of adult respondents who have ever been furloughed by family type, April–July 2020

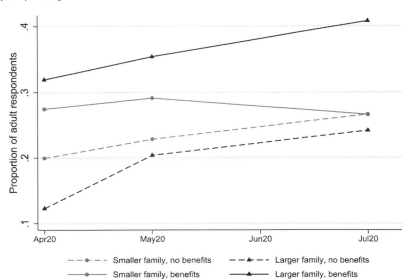

Note: Sample is adult respondents who were in paid work (employment or self-employment) at the COVID-19 survey baseline in January–February 2020. N=2174, 1803, 1617 for each wave. Since it should not be possible for there to be a fall in the proportion of people who have ever been furloughed, the slight fall from May to July 2020 among smaller families on benefits is likely due to changes in the sample of respondents.

the cap by even a small reduction in hours or reduced furlough pay. This was the case for one of the project's participants, Ifemelu,[6] a factory worker in the food industry who was working full-time before the pandemic hit. During the first lockdown, she did not obtain any hours of paid work from her employer and has only been given part-time hours since then. As a result, she had to claim social security benefits for the first time. Ifemelu has been subject to the benefit cap since claiming Universal Credit (UC), as although she now has part-time work, her earnings are just under the threshold for exemption. She is also subject to the two-child limit. She explained that her benefit payments were inadequate and resulted in debt and inability to pay bills: "What they're even giving me is not even enough and you're still removing one benefit cap ... [I have] debt which keeps piling up, but I don't have a choice ... I'm not able to pay all the bills I'm supposed to pay" (Ifemelu, single mother, three children, subject to the two-child limit and benefit cap). As a result of the levels of benefit payments and policies such as the two-child limit and benefit cap, Ifemelu faced a considerable shortfall in income when her work hours were reduced. For many larger families, such loss of income was exacerbated by increased household costs.

Impact on meeting and accessing basic needs

Households in professional sectors who were able to work from home largely saw their household earnings and job security unchanged throughout the crisis. Some managed to accrue significant savings as they cut back on non-essential purchases. However, for low-income households, a higher proportion of their incomes is spent on essentials, and their household costs increased during the pandemic (Brewer and Patrick, 2021). Increased costs were commonly associated with higher food bills, the costs of home schooling and of trying to keep children entertained during lockdown. These increased costs are likely to have a greater impact on larger families due to their larger household consumption needs. As a result, larger families found it particularly difficult to meet basic essential needs during the pandemic. According to the Understanding Society data, in April 2020 11 per cent of larger families on benefits had used a food bank in the last month compared with 6 per cent of smaller families on benefits.[7]

Our qualitative research evidences the difficulties larger families faced during the pandemic in meeting basic needs. Several participants reported that they struggled to afford food and had to resort to using food banks. As well as having difficulty affording basic living costs, some of the participants also found it hard to access necessities including clothes and furniture, as well as food. One participant's comments illuminate the difficulties of trying to go food shopping with multiple children during the pandemic: "And I couldn't get to Asda cos of the queue, like if you saw the queue and you try to take four kids to a COVID two-metre queue and like it's mental, especially, and three of us have asthma so my anxiety levels are going [up]" (Amanda, single mother, four children, subject to the benefit cap and the two-child limit). The qualitative data suggests that larger families experienced particular difficulties in affording food and negotiating the new procedures for shopping brought about by the pandemic. As Amanda's comment also indicates, this impacted on her mental health, which we turn to next.

Impact on mental health

Mental health worsened considerably at the beginning of the pandemic, and there are reasons to think that this would impact disproportionately on larger families given the distributive effects detailed earlier (Banks and Xu, 2020). In addition, there is causal evidence that school closures had greater impacts on the mental health of mothers who had more than one child (Blanden et al, 2021). Later in the year, larger families were particularly negatively affected by social distancing regulations that were put in place in September 2020 through the 'rule of six', which in its initial form meant that many larger families were less able to meet up with others outside of their household

(BBC, 2020). It was not until April 2021, when restrictions were lifted after the winter lockdown, that in England the rule was amended to include '6 people or 2 households', whichever was larger (iNews, 2020). In practice, this meant that both parents and children in larger families were less able to meet others outside their household during lockdown, especially if they had young children who could not be left at home.

Several participants spoke of the isolation they experienced during the lockdowns. They explained that it was very difficult not being able to visit anyone or have anyone come and visit them. This put a lot of strain on the parents and negatively impacted their children. One of the participants explained: "The lockdown was hard, especially for the kids and being stuck at home ... not being able to do normal kids' stuff, and the baby she didn't really experience the outside life cos she's just been stuck at home with you" (Kalima, single mother, five children, subject to the benefit cap and the two-child limit). Somewhat to our surprise, however, the quantitative survey data does not suggest that the change in mental health due to the pandemic was larger among low-income larger families relative to other families. Figure 7.5 charts the General Health Questionnaire (GHQ-12) measure of mental health, distress, and wellbeing in the COVID-19 survey data from the pre-pandemic main survey (2017–19) to March 2021, with higher scores signifying a worsening of mental health over the period prior to survey. Larger families on benefits entered the pandemic with the worst mental health. In the immediate stages of the crisis, mental health worsened for all groups but particularly sharply among higher-income groups. Meanwhile, larger families on benefits saw the least relative change in mental health at the beginning of the pandemic.

Looking at the change in GHQ subscales between the pre-pandemic period and April 2020, all families saw a decline in their ability to enjoy day-to-day activities and an increase in feeling under strain. Higher-income families and smaller families on benefits saw increases in being unable to concentrate, feeling depressed, losing sleep due to worry, problems overcoming difficulties, losing confidence, feeling worthless, and reductions in happiness. Low-income larger families saw less relative change in these aspects of wellbeing.

However, it is crucial to note that low-income larger families entered the pandemic with the worst wellbeing across these indicators, and these measures are relative by construction because responses refer to respondents' 'usual' experiences as a baseline.[8] The low base of larger families in terms of wellbeing in the pre-pandemic period therefore meant that there was less room for decline across these measures. What these results collectively suggest is that larger families on benefits were experiencing poor mental wellbeing and high psychological distress prior to the pandemic, and that the initial onset of COVID-19 did not change this significantly.

Figure 7.5: GHQ-12 mental health scores from a pre-pandemic baseline to March 2021 by family type (higher scores indicate worse mental health)

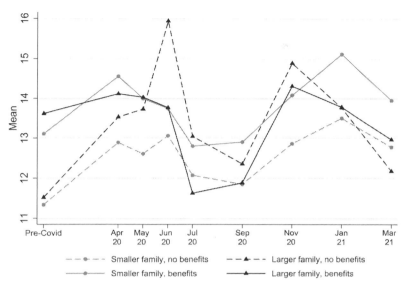

Note: GHQ-12 scores are based on a Likert scale, with a higher score denoting worse mental health. N=7274, 3034, 2631, 2384, 2343, 2026, 1825, 1738 and 2036 for each wave.

Additionally, high-income families were more likely to work from home during the pandemic, and low-income smaller families were more likely to be single-parent households. Single parents and those working from home saw particularly large declines to wellbeing at the beginning of the pandemic. This may have contributed further to the trends in Figure 7.5.

Case study: "I've just been kinda struggling to get back on my feet at the moment due to this COVID"

Daneen's experiences of COVID-19 illuminate some of the challenges that larger families in receipt of social security have faced during the pandemic, particularly when subject to the two-child limit. Daneen has three children and is a single parent. She receives UC and has been subject to the two-child limit since her youngest child was born just under two years ago. The financial impacts of COVID-19 have been keenly felt by Daneen and her family. When asked what impact COVID-19 and the lockdowns had on her family, she replied, "Well, to be honest with you, it's been absolutely terrible. Since the COVID-19, I've gotten into so much debt; I've got a credit card that I've had to use … that card is pretty much maxed out." As the interview progressed, it became clear that the application of the two-child limit had left Daneen particularly vulnerable to the negative financial impacts of COVID-19. Daneen explained that during the COVID-19 lockdowns, she did not have enough money to pay basic living costs as she was only receiving the child element of UC for only two of her three children: "It [the two-child limit] has affected me because since having my little one that's why I've gotten into like a lot of credit card debt because I couldn't fund bills with the three kids at home when the COVID hit us." Daneen mentioned her struggle to afford food for the family during the lockdowns:

'I do receive like things like school vouchers but £15 a week; I mean, I shop from Lidl and Aldi which is like you can't go below Aldi and Lidl, there is no other store that's going to be cheaper than them two stores, and I shop the bare minimum ... when the COVID hit it was like before from breakfast to just, you know, teatime meal it went from three set meals a day ... But then this is what I'm saying that what are we supposed to do as parents? Do we starve our kids, you know, where do we go from here?'

Daneen incurred additional costs as she had to provide more food for her children (see Brewer and Patrick, 2021), including a lunchtime meal, which was difficult to do despite sourcing low-priced food. Although she was receiving free school meals vouchers, she found that this was insufficient to cover the extra spending on food that the pandemic necessitated.

As well as financial hardship, Daneen also experienced isolation during the COVID-19 pandemic. Her children only saw their father on an ad hoc basis and her parents were not able to help with the children due to health problems. Consequently, she had almost sole responsibility for the care of her children and, as a result of the pandemic, ended up staying at home a lot with the children and did not interact very much with other people. She explained: "I don't usually speak to people a lot ... I haven't spoken to someone in a long time."

Daneen cited not being able to get out much as a negative impact of the pandemic. However, in line with the quantitative mental health findings outlined earlier, she also explained that in some ways, the pandemic relieved some pressure from her interactions with her children given her financial circumstances: "I can't imagine if the COVID wasn't here what we'd be doing ... COVID is an excuse for everything, like, oh, we can't do this because everything's closed." Daneen's comment indicates larger families who are subject to the two-child limit will continue to struggle financially once the pandemic and associated restrictions ease. Some additional household expenditure incurred by the pandemic may no longer be needed, but many larger families in receipt of benefits will still face difficulties affording basic necessities. This is partly due to the two-child limit and the benefit cap, introduced before the pandemic, which break the link between entitlement and need, and disproportionately affect larger families who were already at greater risk of poverty. The government's refusal to suspend these policies during the pandemic, thereby undermining its own efforts to support low-income families, signals a tenacious commitment to retain these policies to the detriment of larger families in receipt of benefits.

Conclusions and implications

The research presented in this chapter demonstrates that family size played a crucial and largely unrecognised role in shaping families' experiences of the COVID-19 pandemic. Larger families on a low income were particularly vulnerable to the economic shock of the pandemic. In part due to their labour market position and in part due to greater caring responsibilities, they experienced the sharpest falls in working hours and were consistently more likely to be on furlough. This puts them at risk of labour market scarring as the economy recovers. It also means that the future of the furlough scheme is a particularly salient issue for larger families. Unless job support is extended until the economy fully recovers, we can expect a wave of redundancies that will hit larger families especially hard. Investment will be required to ensure that those who have been on low working hours throughout the pandemic or on long-term furlough receive employment support to prevent permanent scarring in labour market prospects.

One of the most striking and counter-intuitive conclusions of this chapter, however, is that the relative change in mental health due to the pandemic appears to have been more muted among larger families on a low income. The survey data and qualitative interviews conducted so far give some indications of what might be driving this, including the lower baseline of mental health that larger families on benefits entered the pandemic. These findings are a sobering demonstration that larger families on benefits had the odds stacked against them going into the pandemic, hence why they simultaneously saw greater economic impacts and less relative change in mental health than other groups. Our qualitative interviews have shown that the benefit cap and two-child limit have a significant impact on families' ability to meet basic needs in 'good times', let alone the bad (Hills, 2017). Further qualitative longitudinal research as part of the project will help us explore whether mental health 'bounces back' among larger families on benefits, or whether their mental health sees little change while the rest of the economy and society recovers.

The government has refused to suspend or modify two policies which disproportionately affect larger families: the two-child limit, and the household benefit cap. These policies were driven by a 'machinery' of 'anti-welfare commonsense' (Jensen and Tyler, 2015) that was forged in the aftermath of the financial crisis of 2008. For many, the assumptions behind these policies were thrown into stark relief by the pandemic. The two-child limit in particular upheld an assumption that families could and should make decisions about how many children to have by forecasting the financial risks of unemployment, sickness, or disability, and absorbing those risks as a family. The widely unanticipated and sudden nature of the COVID-19 crisis proved a counterexample to this logic. Additionally, the two mechanisms proposed by the government for households to escape the benefit cap – seeking more paid work and moving to cheaper accommodation – were impossible during the pandemic.

Finally, COVID-19 exposed a wider group of families to these punitive social security policies: smaller families have been become increasingly likely to be affected by the benefit cap over the course of the pandemic (Hirsch, 2020; Department for Work and Pensions [DWP], 2021). These factors may have led to a realignment in public attitudes towards social security, the benefit cap, and the two-child limit, though the extent and permanence of this realignment is unclear as of yet. Recent polling indicated that 61 per cent of the British public supported the suspension of the two-child limit during COVID-19 (British Pregnancy Advisory Service [BPAS], 2021). Is this an early sign of a new, pro-welfare 'commonsense' to emerge from the crisis? Perhaps. Regardless, if a new social security settlement is to reverse the hardship inflicted on larger families – not least by the benefit cap and two-child limit – it will need to make an overdue acknowledgement that family size matters.

Notes

[1] There were approximately 34,000 adult respondents in Wave 10 of the main Understanding Society survey and 12,000 in each COVID-19 survey wave. We restricted our main sample to respondents with children aged under 16 in their household at the time of survey. This resulted in a total unweighted sample of 10,082 adult respondents in Wave 10 of the main survey, 5,319 in Wave 1 of the COVID-19, 3,932 in Wave 2, 3,583 in Wave 3, 3,505 in Wave 4, 3,118 in Wave 5, 2,773 in Wave 6, 2,672 in Wave 7, and 2,999 in Wave 8.

[2] We are grateful to Dr Jamie Moore for his assistance in customising these weights for the purposes of this chapter.

[3] In the survey analysis, we define a household as being on benefits if they were in receipt of Universal Credit or Child Tax Credit at any point up to and including the wave in question within the Understanding Society COVID-19 survey, including the baseline in January–February 2020. For data points with Wave 10 of the Main Survey, benefit receipt is derived exclusively from this wave. We define a household as being a larger family if they report having three or more children aged under 16 in the given wave or if they reported this in Wave 10 of the Main Survey. We rely on the latter to minimise under-reporting of larger families within the COVID-19 survey, since it does not contain an exact measure of the number of children in the household but instead reports the number of children in different age categories with a binned frequency approach. For example, if an individual reports having '2+' children aged 0–4 and no children aged 5–15, we would code them as a smaller family with two children based on the COVID-19 survey alone, even though it is technically possible that they have three children aged 0–5 and

are in fact a larger family. By drawing on the exact number of children reported in Wave 10 of the Main Survey, we reduce this underestimation of the number of larger families.

4   Children of critical workers and vulnerable children who can access schools or educational settings. Available at: www.gov.uk/government/publications/coronavirus-covid-19-maintaining-educational-provision/guidance-for-schools-colleges-and-local-authorities-on-maintaining-educational-provision

5   A further contributory factor may also be that younger children require more supervision at home, and larger families on benefits are more likely to have young children due to the link between caring responsibilities, work intensity, and benefits receipt (the average of school-age children among larger families on benefits is 9.9 years compared to 10.4 years for larger families not on benefits).

6   All participant names given in this chapter are pseudonyms.

7   These differences are not statistically significant, however, due to the small number of people using food banks.

8   Survey response options for each GHQ subscale are typically of the form: 'Better than usual'; 'Same as usual'; 'Less than usual'; 'Much less than usual'. They are therefore inherently relative and tied to a baseline level of wellbeing.

References

Banks, J. and Xu, X. (2020) The mental health effects of the first two months of lockdown and social distancing during the COVID-19 pandemic in the UK. London: Institute for Fiscal Studies.

BBC (2020) Coronavirus: 'rule of six' hits larger families. 11 September. Available at: https://www.bbc.co.uk/news/uk-england-54101524

Benzeval, M., Burton, J., Crossley, T.F., Fisher, P., Jäckle, A., Low, H. and Read, B. (2020) The idiosyncratic impact of an aggregate shock: the distributional consequences of COVID-19. *Understanding Society Working Paper 2020–09*. Colchester: University of Essex.

Benzeval, M., Burton, J., Crossley, T.F., Fisher, P., Gardiner, P., Gardiner, C., Jäckle, A. and Moore, J. (2021) High frequency online data collection in an annual household panel study: some evidence on bias prevention and bias adjustment. *Understanding Society Working Paper Series 2021–03*. Colchester: University of Essex.

Blanden, J., Crawford, C., Fumagalli, L., and Rabe, B. (2021). School closures and parents' mental health. ISER briefing note. Colchester: University of Essex.

Bradshaw, J., Finch, N., Mayhew, E., Ritakallio, V-M. and Skinner, C. (2006) *Child Poverty in Large Families*. Bristol: Joseph Rowntree Foundation, Policy Press.

Brewer, M. and Patrick, R. (2021) Pandemic pressures: why families on low-income are spending more during Covid-19. London: Resolution Foundation.

British Pregnancy Advisory Service (BPAS) (2021) New polling shows majority of the public now oppose the government's two-child limit policy. Available at: www.bpas.org/about-our-charity/press-office/press-releases/new-polling-shows-majority-of-the-public-now-oppose-the-government-s-two-child-limit-policy/

Cominetti, N., Henehan, K., Slaughter, H. and Thwaites, G. (2021) Long Covid in the labour market: the impact on the labour market of COVID-19 a year into the crisis, and how to secure a strong recovery. London: Resolution Foundation.

Cooper, K. and Hills, J. (2021) The Conservative Governments' Record on Social Security from May 2015 to pre-COVID 2020: Policies, Spending and Outcomes. SPDO research paper. London: Centre for Analysis of Social Exclusion.

Crossley, T.F., Fisher, P. and Low, H. (2021) The heterogeneous and regressive consequences of COVID-19: evidence from high quality panel data. *Journal of Public Economics*, 193.

Department for Work and Pensions (DWP) (2021) Benefit cap statistics. Available at: www.gov.uk/government/collections/benefit-cap-statistics

Hills, J. (2017) *Good Times, Bad Times* (2nd edition). Bristol: Policy Press.

Hirsch, D. (2020) How the benefit cap has gone from a selective punishment for having high family needs to a generalised curb on benefit incomes. Welfare Reform and Larger Families Blog. Available at: https://largerfamilies.study/blog/how-the-benefit-cap-has-gone-from-a-selective-punishment-for-having-high-family-needs-to-a

iNews (2020) Rule of 6 explained: what new two households rule means for meeting outdoors, after lockdown restrictions ease. *Independent News*. 11 April. Available at: https://inews.co.uk/news/uk/rule-of-6-explained-what-mean-two-households-outdoors-england-lockdown-restrictions-roadmap-934387

Jensen, T. and Tyler, I. (2015) 'Benefits broods': the cultural and political crafting of anti-welfare commonsense. *Critical Social Policy*, 35(4), 470–91.

Joyce, R. and Xu, X. (2020) Sector shutdowns during the coronavirus crisis: which workers are most exposed? Institute for Fiscal Studies.

Palmer, S. (2020). Employees can be furloughed to carry out caring responsibilities, government confirms. People Management. Available at: https://www.peoplemanagement.co.uk/news/articles/employees-can-be-furloughed-to-carry-out-caring-responsibilities#gref

Power, M., Patrick, R., Garthwaite, K. and Page, G. (2020) COVID realities: everyday life for families on a low income during the pandemic. Covid Realities briefing paper.

Stewart, K., Reeves, A. and Patrick, R. (2021) A time of need: exploring the changing poverty risk facing larger families in the UK. CASEpaper 224. London: Centre for Analysis of Social Exclusion.

Tarrant, A., Way, L. and Ladlow, L. (2020) Negotiating 'earning' and 'caring' through the COVID-19 crisis: change and continuities in the parenting and employment trajectories of young fathers. University of Lincoln: Following Young Fathers Further Project. https://followingyoungfathersfurther.org/asset/working-papers/

University of Essex, Institute for Social and Economic Research (2021a) Understanding society: Waves 1–10, 2009–2019 and Harmonised BHPS: Waves 1–18, 1991–2009. [data collection]. (13th edition). UK Data Service. SN: 6614. Available at: http://doi.org/10.5255/UKDA-SN-6614-14

University of Essex, Institute for Social and Economic Research (2021b) Understanding society: COVID-19 Study, 2020–2021. [data collection]. (9th edition). UK Data Service. SN: 8644. Available at: http://doi.org/10.5255/UKDA-SN-8644-9

8

Caring without Sharing: how single parents worked and cared during the pandemic

Elizabeth Clery and Laura Dewar

Introduction

Our Caring without Sharing research project, funded by the Standard Life Foundation (now known as abrdn Financial Fairness Trust) and undertaken by Gingerbread and the Institute for Employment Studies (IES), was designed to fill a gap in the evidence base regarding the differential impacts of the COVID-19 pandemic on single-parent families. While, during the first national lockdown (March–June 2020), there was a considerable focus by policymakers and researchers on the experiences of certain groups including women, those in work, those on low incomes, and parents, for example, there was little specific consideration of the lived experiences of single parents, who frequently encapsulate a number of these identities. 'Caring without Sharing' sought to fill this gap, by exploring the working and caring situations of single parents in early 2020 and by following their working and caring journeys over the first year of the pandemic. It focused on the sub-group of single parents who it was envisaged would face the greatest challenges during the COVID-19 lockdowns, namely those who were not classified as 'critical workers' by the government. These single parents were unable to access emergency education and childcare, and so were required to work and care for their children both simultaneously and in isolation, given that childcare provided by those outside of the household was prohibited in the first lockdown.

A mixed methods design was adopted. Secondary quantitative data was analysed to understand the prevalence of different experiences and challenges among single parents, and how this compared with other family types, while new qualitative data was collected to enable us to understand the ways in which these experiences interacted to inform the lived experiences of single parents through the COVID-19 pandemic. We recruited a qualitative sample of 40 single parents in the summer of 2020, with quotas employed to ensure diversity on various work- and family-related characteristics, which it was envisaged would influence their experiences of working and caring during the pandemic. Work-related characteristics included: hours worked, employment status, and experience of being furloughed, while family-related characteristics included number of children and the age of the youngest child. In line with the national picture where around nine in ten single parents are women, the vast majority (36 out of 40) of the single parents we interviewed were female. While other chapters focus on the gendered impacts of the pandemic (see Chapters 7 and 9), this was less feasible from our data, given we only interviewed a handful of single fathers.

Each of these 40 single parents participated in a semi-structured qualitative interview in July or August 2020, as the UK emerged from the first national lockdown. Six months later, 33 of the original parents, who were contactable and willing to talk to us again, were re-interviewed. The two sets of interviews had a primarily retrospective focus, examining changes to, and challenges in, single parents' working and caring lives over the previous six months in each instance, along with their expectations and concerns for the future. The opportunity to collect and analyse longitudinal qualitative data from single parents was invaluable, as it enabled us to track not just their actual working and caring journeys but to understand how these reflected and were informed by their expectations and fears (see Chapters 1, 3, and 9 for other examples of qualitative longitudinal research). Alongside this qualitative strand of work, IES undertook analysis of the government's Labour Force Survey (LFS), to understand the extent to which single parents experienced various work-related developments, such as being furloughed, working from home, and becoming unemployed, compared with other family types (see Gingerbread, 2020, 2021). However, it is the qualitative longitudinal data collected from single parents on which this chapter concentrates, when exploring and illustrating their journeys through the COVID-19 pandemic.

Overview of findings

The single parents interviewed for this project provided a wealth of data about their experiences of working and caring during 2020 and 2021. Data from Caring without Sharing will serve as a historic record of single parents' experiences during the COVID-19 pandemic, as well as informing policymaking going forward and contributing to its evaluation. In this chapter, we focus on three key themes to emerge from the data. While the first has been selected as it broadly encapsulates the difficulties facing single parents during the pandemic, the second and third were chosen as they are highly relevant to single parents' future working and caring journeys, with employers, government, and policymakers having the potential to significantly improve the caring experiences and job outcomes for single parents in these particular areas.

Caring without sharing: an impossible balancing act

In relation to many aspects of their lives, single parents characterised the experience of caring without sharing during the COVID-19 pandemic as "an impossible balancing act". While many single parents described their working and caring situations prior to March 2020 in terms of balancing a range of routines and considerations, it was widely felt that the imposition of additional responsibilities on them (in terms of home-schooling) and the loss of wider support in the first lockdown, converted the "challenging" balancing act into the "impossible". Single parents frequently found themselves having to balance a range of roles and responsibilities, with insufficient time or support or with conflicting demands on their time or resources – without being able to share the load with a partner. This experience was particularly pronounced during the first and third lockdowns, when many single parents were required to work from home and undertake home-schooling with their children simultaneously. Single parents described how they were unable to fit in all that was required of them within the available hours of the day, forcing them to make compromises – some of which they were deeply uncomfortable with. Reflecting on the first lockdown and her primary-aged child, Jasmine, who worked part-time in administration, recalled: "I'd do two hours' work and just think, do you know what, I'm not doing it, and take her out for a walk or something because it did get really hard with having to try and balance the both of them (work and care)." Similarly, Emily, who was self-employed as a personal shopper, described how: "it was fine the first few weeks, but when you're in the middle of doing, say, Maths, and a client rings me, then Maths went by the by. And then I'd feel guilty." Experiencing their working and caring roles as an "impossible balancing act" was pronounced during those periods in the autumn of 2020 where some single parents' children were required to self-isolate, due to positive COVID-19 cases in their children's school class bubbles. Single parents described how what was required from them by government guidance, schools, and their employers was frequently impossible to achieve in combination and sometimes contradictory. As Penny, who worked outside the home and whose young primary-aged child was sent home to isolate from school, explained:

'We have to follow the protocol of isolating. I can go to work apparently, but my son can't go to school, but he can't actually leave the house. So I am a single parent (and) you're saying it's okay for me to go to work but what do I do with my son if he's obviously been in contact with somebody, so I can't leave him with anyone? It just doesn't make any sense.'

To deal with these conflicting requirements, the single parents we interviewed took a variety of approaches including taking annual or unpaid leave or, in a small number of instances, taking their children with them to work and ensuring they did not interact with others.

Such experiences, and the feelings of worry and guilt they engendered, contributed to widespread concerns among single parents about their and their children's mental health. The impacts on mental health reflects a wider body of research, as well as our own analysis of LFS data, which shows that single parent families remain particularly at risk of negative outcomes in this area (Child Poverty Action Group, 2020; Fawcett Society, 2020). Our analysis found that, even at the outset of the pandemic, single parents were substantially more likely to report depression or bad nerves, compared with parents in couples, and these differences were sustained, as reports of negative mental health outcomes rose for all throughout the first year of the pandemic (see also Chapter 5).

More positively, however, our research did unearth evidence of mediating factors, which could improve the experiences of single parents working and caring in isolation and lessen the burden of responsibility placed upon them. Many single parents found that the introduction of support bubbles for single adult households in June 2020 eased their situations, as did the availability of pre-school childcare (and the greater availability of school places) in the third lockdown although, as single parents noted themselves, this was often offered at the discretion of schools, rather than reflecting national policy. Similarly, the greater level of provision and communication from schools, including the availability of live teaching, in the third lockdown reduced the responsibility placed on single parents to 'teach' their children – although it is worth noting that challenges remained for those with primary-aged children in particular, where considerable supervision was still required.

One of the most significant mediating factors discussed by single parents which helped them to balance their work and caring responsibilities was the flexibility of their employers. This had a particularly positive impact when single parents were allowed to fit their working hours around their caring responsibilities. In the summer of 2020, one single parent we interviewed, Carla, who worked as a bookkeeper, said:

'Because I worked five hours a day … they said that rather than me doing them between ten and three, which was the core school hours (where) I was getting distracted by children asking me questions and me trying to help them with their schoolwork as well. So work said that when the school day had finished, I could do my working day then. So my workday would then start at 3:30 until nine, ten o'clock in the evening.'

Analysis of time-use data identified similar trends in the working hours of parents in general who worked from home, with these being fitted around their childcare obligations, making work more likely to occur in the morning and at night (Office for National Statistics, 2020). While the single parents we interviewed were grateful to their employers for their flexibility in allowing them to fit their work hours around their caring responsibilities, it was commonly described how this could lead to very long days, with early starts and late finishes and little time for any relaxation. Feelings of stress, exhaustion, and burnout were very common. Moreover, such flexibility was by no means universally experienced by single parents in the first lockdown. Esther, for instance, who worked for an energy company, recounted how:

'They did at one point tell me that it would be more flexible and I could log off and log back on later on if it suited me better, but when I tried doing that they complained to me and told me that I should be working to my hours.'

Encouragingly, however, data from our second set of interviews with single parents shows that employer flexibility was much more universal in the third lockdown (January–March 2021). While most employers were allowing single parents to fit their working hours around their caring responsibilities, some went even further, offering additional support with home-schooling in terms of resources, such as digital technology and time off for parents. However, in the minority of cases where employers were not supportive or flexible, this considerably exacerbated the challenges facing single parents and their feeling of stress – as a result of the necessity of making uncomfortable compromises, discussed previously.

In the next two sections, we examine two specific aspects of single parents' working and caring journeys over the first year of the COVID-19 pandemic, both of which have significant long-term policy relevance – the shift to home-working and experiences of job insecurity.

A shift to home-working

The majority of single parents interviewed for this project moved to working from home in March 2020 and continued to do so into the early part of 2021, although LFS data shows that the proportionate increase in home-working was less pronounced among this group of single parents compared with other family types (Gingerbread, 2020) – likely to result from the fact that home-working has been shown to be more common among those in professional occupations, where single parents are less likely to be represented. Single parents' experiences of and attitudes to home-working were highly polarised, but also evolved considerably throughout this period. When we interviewed single parents in the summer of 2020, they identified a variety of benefits and drawbacks to home-working. Chief among the benefits identified were the fact that it enables flexibility, reduces travel time and costs, and so allows single parents to potentially work a greater number of hours. However, home-working was viewed negatively by other single parents, who attributed it with the experience of increased social isolation. Isolation was seen to produce a range of negative impacts including making team-working more challenging and reducing visibility, which single parents thought might limit opportunities for career progression in the future. While some single parents recognised both the benefits and drawbacks of home-working, when it came to their own lives, perceptions regarding its impact and desirability were highly polarised. In the summer of 2020, Jasmine, who worked in administration, described the benefits to her situation of working from home, explaining:

'for one, saving petrol. I used to spend £40 a week driving to [LOCATION] for four days ... So obviously money wise I've saved. I can do hours that are quite suited to me, so if I've got something silly like a delivery coming between 10 and 11 I know not to work between then, or be on a call. So I can kind of cater it to me.'

On the other hand, Bethan, who worked as an analyst for a bank, described the limitations home-working placed on social interaction within her organisation and its negative impacts from a work perspective, emphasising: "Everything is harder remotely, everything. Everything has to be written up, every conversation, nothing happens easily. If I were at work, I'd pop to someone's desk if I needed to chat about something work-related, and now you can't do that, you have to schedule it in." When we re-interviewed single parents in early 2021, attitudes to home-working had evolved markedly. For many, home-working had come to be viewed as the 'new normal', and there was clear evidence of a greater appreciation of its advantages and, among those who had originally disliked it, a resigned acceptance of its continuation. While Esther told us that: "Now I've got used to it, I think I actually prefer working from home than actually going into the office. I've just found it, as I've got into a routine, it's easier," Rowena emphasised that: "I miss people. [But] it is the norm now. It's been almost a year." Moreover, those single parents who viewed home-working negatively because of its impact on isolation, increasingly recognised the role of the national lockdowns in this regard and the fact that a return to office-based working would not resolve this problem entirely. This was the case for Kelly, who told us that:

'If I asked to go in the office, it won't be the same as what I had before, so I won't be any happier, I don't think, because I want to be with people, I want to sit with people ... so I don't think I'd be any happier going back in the office with all this social distancing.'

Experiences of job insecurity

Similarly, single parents' experiences of job insecurity were far from homogenous, and evolved throughout the pandemic. When we interviewed single parents in the summer of 2020, many were concerned about the security of their jobs, a feeling which was sometimes triggered by actual (or anticipated) reductions in hours and pay. Concerns about job insecurity also reflected more general feelings of uncertainty at the start of the pandemic, as emphasised by Lindsay, who worked as a receptionist in the plastics industry, who told us that:

'it's all a bit uncertain for a lot of companies at the moment. The industry we're in, it's taken a big dip financially with the whole COVID-19, so it is a bit worrying. I don't know if we're going to survive this, but at the moment we're just taking every day as it comes.'

By the start of 2021, however, single parents' views had diverged. While some single parents felt that the organisations they worked for had survived, adapted, and prospered during the pandemic, others felt increasingly insecure; this was particularly the case for those who had been on long-term furlough, who felt distanced from their employers and therefore more vulnerable. As Karen explained: "I think then it's just been that the firm has managed without me, to be honest, which is then making me very concerned for the security of my job going forward." Indeed, such concerns dissuaded some single parents from pursuing furlough during the third national lockdown, even when their employers had furloughed them in the first lockdown. As Bethan recounted of her employer: "We've never really spoken about it. I think the worry is that if you're furloughed you'll be first out. So everybody just wants a job." In fact, even working from home could create for single parents a perception of a lack of visibility, which heightened concerns about the security of their jobs. As Shona explained:

'I just worry about job security which I think everybody does ... it's something that's started to worry me more. I think being at home, because I'm so used to being out busy travelling, talking to people, I'm worrying that I'm not doing enough ... no one has said anything, I think it's just something that's playing on my mind.'

The translation of job insecurity into actual job losses was comparatively rare among the single parents we interviewed. Of our 40 research participants, six lost their jobs at some point between the summer of 2020 and early spring of 2021, with three having already found new jobs or entered self-employment by the end of our second round of interviewing in February 2021. Those single parents who had secured new positions tended to have done so through existing contacts and networks, rather than through contact with Jobcentre Plus. At the time of writing, LFS data similarly shows little change in the level of single-parent unemployment (Clery et al, 2021). However, the proportion of the single-parent workforce that was unemployed was already higher before the pandemic at 12 per cent, compared with 5 per cent for coupled parents, with single parents being more likely to be working in routine occupations such as retail, hospitality, and restaurants (46 per cent, compared with 26 per cent of coupled parents) – industries which are likely to see further job losses. It was widely recognised, a the time of writing, that the economic impact of the pandemic on single-parent unemployment might not be fully realised until the furlough scheme ends in September 2021. There is also mounting evidence that single parents are likely to be disproportionately impacted in this regard (for instance, as they are much more likely to work part-time, compared with other family types – a characteristic likely to be associated with more negative outcomes as the furlough scheme ends (Timewise, 2021).

Case study

We can see how the themes described thus far can interact and inform the lived experiences of single parents, by considering the case of Marilyn – a single parent who we interviewed in the summer of 2020 and again in early 2021. Marilyn's case demonstrates the particularly precarious nature of balancing work and care for single parents during the pandemic.

In March 2020, Marilyn was working in administration in a shop for 20 hours a week across four days, to fit around the schooling of her secondary-aged daughter. She used family for childcare in the school holidays during her working hours; her child did not have any contact with their father. Balancing her working and caring roles became an immediate challenge for Marilyn when it was announced that schools would shut on 20 March 2020. As her role needed to be performed on-site, she took the decision to take unpaid leave for a week, before finding out she was to be placed on furlough (due to the shop shutting) at the start of April. Recalling her manager's reaction, Marilyn described how: "I kind of felt backed into a corner because I was basically telling her I am not prepared to go to work; I'm not bringing my daughter in and I'm not leaving her with anybody else so it makes me unable to work. She wasn't very happy about it." After being on furlough for three months, Marilyn was informed in early July that she was being made redundant. Over the subsequent six months, she had regular interaction with a work coach from Jobcentre Plus. However, he often suggested jobs to her that did not fit with her caring commitments, which only allowed her to work part-time during school hours. As Marilyn described:

'he went through a point where he was ringing with jobs and then they would turn out not to be suitable ... he rang me with a few that were weekends and even though my mother is in my social bubble with me, she couldn't really babysit because she is furloughed but when she goes back to work she is contracted every other weekend, so that wasn't suitable.'

In early 2021, Marilyn also described how some companies who were initially interested in employing her to undertake call-centre work, lost interest when it became clear she could not attend the required full-time training courses before beginning part-time working-from-home roles.

When we spoke to Marilyn in the summer of 2020, she told us that she had already applied for over 50 jobs and was struggling to find work, an experience she had never encountered before. When we interviewed her again in early 2021, she explained that she had just started a role as a personal assistant, which she had found through a friend. While this job was not ideal, as it involved a lower number of hours, lower earnings, and cleaning, Marilyn concluded that it would "do for now" as it fitted in with her current caring commitments. Marilyn expressed an interest in retraining in the beauty industry at both points we spoke to her, but did not view this as a realistic option at the current point in time.

When we spoke in early 2021, a family member was helping to home-school Marilyn's daughter, while she was out working. Marilyn acknowledged, however, that, had she been working during the autumn of 2020, it would have been extremely challenging to manage the several periods of self-isolation required of her daughter's bubble, and that in all likelihood she would have needed to give up her job.

Policy implications

Since the end of the Caring without Sharing research project, the UK has come out of the third national lockdown and for single parents on out-of-work benefits there are renewed expectations for them to seek work through the work conditionality regime and reflected in their claimant commitment. The pandemic has significantly increased the number of single parents on Universal Credit (UC) to 1,271,057 in February 2021; they now make up a quarter of all UC claimants. In addition, UC rules mean that single parents must look for work when their youngest child is aged three. As we discovered during this research project, single-parent unemployment levels are already at 12 per cent and because of the nature of the jobs in which they worked were more likely to have been furloughed than other family types. When the furlough scheme ends, it is anticipated that some jobs will not exist in the same way and as such, single parents face further unemployment as the scheme ends. Policies to support single parents into work and to progress into better-paid employment are needed as the UK moves forward from the pandemic. However, there remain three significant challenges for single parents: limited access to flexible working, particularly quality part-time work; the availability and costs of childcare; and single parents' concentration in industries that have been hard hit by the pandemic, which may necessitate them to move into new areas of work.

The greater prevalence of home-working which emerged during the pandemic should not be viewed as the only solution to flexible working. Many single parents work in jobs that cannot be done from home. The Timewise Flexible Jobs Index showed that, at the start of 2020, just two in ten jobs were advertised with options to work flexibly (Timewise, 2020). A few months later, following the impact of the pandemic on work including a big shift towards home-working, 'the dial barely moved in the jobs market', other than a notable drop in advertised part-time roles. The Timewise Index concludes that there is a fractured job market with part-time work more likely among the lowest-paid jobs. Conversely, home-working and other flexible working options are disproportionately offered at higher salary levels. In other words, those single parents, on low incomes and in part-time roles, who are most likely to lose their jobs in the coming months are the least likely to benefit from the shift to home-working available to many during the pandemic – and so require other solutions to enable flexible working. For single parents, a broader change to how work is structured, including greater access to good-quality part-time work, is therefore needed.

At the end of our research project, we were disappointed that the government's Employment Bill was delayed; a Bill that offered the legislative push for jobs to be advertised as flexible by default. While we wait for the Bill to progress, the government could legislate through amending the Flexible Working Regulations 2014 to make it a day-one right for employees to make a flexible working request. We also want the government to work with employers and employer bodies to emphasise the business case for greater flexibility in job roles and consider financially incentivising employers to divide full-time roles into job shares. To support this, we urge the Chartered Institute of Personnel and Development and the Flexible Working Task Force to work together to develop job-sharing as part of the flexible working menu in adapting to new ways of working after the pandemic.

The availability and cost of childcare will remain a significant barrier for single parents entering or moving into employment after the pandemic.

The pandemic has had a significant impact on the already volatile childcare market. Coram Family and Childcare Trust (2021) suggest that over a third (35 per cent) of local authorities had reported that the number of childcare providers permanently closing in their area had gone up in the last year and those that remained had increased their prices to remain sustainable. The government's own figures (Ofsted, 2021) showed that, in the first three months of 2021, over 2,000 childcare providers had closed their doors.

The cost of childcare also remains an ongoing concern for parents, and this is a particular issue for single parents who rely on one income to pay for childcare. While childcare costs can be supported within UC for those on a low income, those single parents who participated in our research who had moved over to the benefit during the pandemic expressed concern about meeting childcare costs and having to claim them back later. Single parents worried about being able to meet these costs when they moved into work or took on more hours of work and that the payment in arrears could push them into debt. The Department for Work and Pensions (DWP) needs to change the payment structure under UC so that childcare costs are made upfront rather than paying in arrears. In addition, the government needs to offer greater support for childcare including a national childcare deposit fund to help parents meet any other upfront costs of childcare when they enter work (such as deposits required by nurseries). The level of childcare costs that can be claimed under UC is also capped at a level set back in 2005 which means that, for many single parents, the promised 85 per cent of childcare support is not delivered. These caps need to be urgently reviewed by the Department for Education (DfE).

The concentration of single parents in the industries that have been hit hardest by the pandemic means that they are vulnerable to anticipated job cuts, including when the furlough scheme ends. Back-to-work support needs to address both the requirements of single parents to work and care on their own and the big hit to sectors which may not exist to the same extent after the pandemic. Single parents who were interviewed for the project and who lost their jobs during the first year of the pandemic were often unclear about where they should start in their job search or retraining. Since the start of the pandemic, the government has introduced a series of employment support schemes for claimants including the Restart scheme for those who have been unemployed for at least a year (GOV.UK, 2021). The government has almost doubled the number of work coaches (to 26,500) since the start of the pandemic including specialist support for disabled claimants and young people. Both these measures of support are welcome but there needs to be much more emphasis on tailored support within the government schemes and from work coaches for single parents. A change in mindset is also needed with longer-term job outcomes at the forefront of the design of back-to-work services for single parents. Many single parents will need support to retrain and reskill, and it is vital that this is backed up with affordable access to childcare.

Conclusion

The Caring without Sharing research project provides vital insights into how the inequalities that single parents routinely face in their interactions with paid employment, and how these relate to the care demands they face, were intensified during the pandemic. There is the very real risk that these inequalities will worsen yet further unless policy action is directed at helping single parents to both work and care. While all types of families struggled to work and care during the pandemic our research shines a light on the additional barriers and challenges that single parents faced.

The pandemic has also shown that things can be done better; work can be structured in a more flexible way, and the Government can act quickly to develop new schemes of back-to-work support. But for single parents, the good practice of some employers and generalist back-to-work programmes will not be enough. A holistic view of the needs of single parents in their caring and working roles is needed by Government, in particular legislative change to ensure that more jobs are advertised as flexible by default and specialist back to work support. As the country moves on from the pandemic we want to ensure that single parents are not left behind, that they have the opportunities to move into sustainable jobs, work that makes the most of their skills with potential to progress while giving them time to also care for their children. Our next project, also funded by the Standard Life Foundation (now renamed as adrdn Financial Fairness Trust), will allow us to examine the experiences of unemployed single parents of finding new work and the roles and impact of new government employment schemes to support this.

References

Child Poverty Action Group and The Church of England (2020) Poverty in the pandemic: the impact of coronavirus on low-income families and children. Available at: https://cpag.org.uk/policy-and-campaigns/report/poverty-pandemic-impact-coronavirus-low-income-families-and-children

Coram Family and Childcare Trust (2021) Childcare survey. Available at: www.familyandchildcaretrust.org/sites/default/files/Resource%20Library/Childcare%20Survey%202021_Coram%20Family%20and%20Childcare.pdf

Fawcett Society (2020) Parenting and Covid-19: research evidence. Available at: www.fawcettsociety.org.uk/Handlers/Download.ashx?IDMF=f1d5b1c3-d5e0-4497-8078-1bad6ca4eb5a

Gingerbread (2020) Caring without sharing: single parents' journeys through the Covid-19 crisis: interim report. Available at: www.gingerbread.org.uk/wp-content/uploads/2020/11/Gingerbread-Caringwithoutsharing-v3.pdf

Gingerbread (2021) Caring without sharing: single parents' journeys through the COVID-19 pandemic: final report. Available at: www.gingerbread.org.uk/wp-content/uploads/2021/05/Gingerbread-Caring-Without-Sharing-Final-Report.pdf

Gingerbread (2022) The single parent employment challenge: job loss and job seeking after the pandemic. Interim report. Available at: https://www.gingerbread.org.uk/wp-content/uploads/2022/03/The-Single-Parent-Employment-Challenge-interim-report-final-design.pdf

GOV.UK (2021) How the Restart scheme will work. Available at: www.gov.uk/government/publications/restart-scheme/how-the-restart-scheme-will-work

Office for National Statistics (2020) Parenting in lockdown: Coronavirus and the effects on work-life balance. Available at: www.ons.gov.uk/peoplepopulationandcommunity/healthandsocialcare/conditionsanddiseases/articles/parentinginlockdowncoronavirusandtheeffectsonworklifebalance/2020-07-22

Ofsted (2021) Joiners and leavers in the childcare sector. Available at: www.gov.uk/government/publications/joiners-and-leavers-in-the-childcare-sector

Timewise (2020) The Timewise Flexible Jobs Index 2020. Available at: https://timewise.co.uk/wp-content/uploads/2020/12/Timewise-Flexible-Job-Index-2020.pdf

Timewise (2021) The impact of COVID-19 on part-time employees. Available at: https://timewise.co.uk/wp-content/uploads/2021/06/Impact-of-Covid-19-on-part-time-employees.pdf

9

The impacts of the COVID-19 pandemic on young fathers and the services that support them

Anna Tarrant, Laura Way, and Linzi Ladlow

Introduction

In this chapter, we draw on insights from the first wave of semi-structured interviews for a qualitative longitudinal study called Following Young Fathers Further[1] (hereafter FYFF). The substantive foci of the interviews were adapted to explore the diverse impacts of the COVID-19 pandemic on young fathers and the services that engage them. Evidence suggests that even prior to the pandemic, these young men were already more likely to be experiencing family poverty and/or social disadvantage (Hadley, 2017; Neale et al, 2015) and to be living in low-income families and contexts. They also negotiate stigma because of their young age and gender (Beggs Weber, 2012; Neale et al, 2015a) and therefore face a unique set of challenges in their transitions to parenthood and throughout their parenting journeys.

The unanticipated character of the pandemic meant that it was not our intention at the outset of the study to explore how young fathers and support professionals would fare at a time of global crisis. The study set out to explore and challenge the persistent problematisation of young parents, who continue to be constructed as a 'problem' (Duncan, 2007) in the UK welfare policy context and to be held largely responsible for their own marginalisation. These young men may face any combination of disadvantages including poverty; limited support in education, training, or employment; unstable homes; volatile family backgrounds and periods in care; mental health issues; and experiences of offending and domestic violence (as both victims and perpetrators). The qualitative longitudinal design of the study supported exploration of these complexities and their dynamics, as well as the effects of the major economic, social, and policy shifts wrought by the pandemic as it emerged. These were captured through retrospective and prospective accounts generated with young fathers and professionals working for national organisations that support young fathers in their parenting journeys.

In this chapter, we illustrate how existing inequalities experienced by young fathers were exacerbated in the new policy climate produced by the pandemic. These findings are placed alongside those generated via interviews with professionals who were forced to quickly adapt their support offers to mitigate its effects on low-income families.

Following Young Fathers Further

FYFF is a four-year participatory, qualitative longitudinal and comparative study of the lives and support needs of young fathers. Throughout the study, the team has been researching *with* young fathers and professionals, albeit remotely, to understand the lived experiences and parenting journeys of young fathers and their contexts of social support through the pandemic. By social support we refer to informal (that is, family, friends, and communities) and formal (that is, provided by institutions, agencies, and support services) mechanisms of support that comprise what Hall (2019) conceptualises as the everyday social infrastructures and tapestries of care that enable families to 'get by' when on a low income. The project has also continued to drive social change for young fathers through the co-creation of models of father-inclusive practice. As well as working across comparative national contexts and localities in the study, we are also collaborating with academic partners in Sweden to explore experiences of young fatherhood in different welfare contexts. We do not specifically develop a comparative analysis of the international impacts of the COVID-19 pandemic on young fathers in this chapter because the research is still ongoing, but we are already identifying interesting differences in how young fathers in both contexts have fared. The social security system in Sweden, for example, has meant that the economic impacts of the pandemic appear to have produced less precarity for young fathers there than in the UK. Uniquely, our study also builds on a baseline study called Following Young Fathers (Neale et al, 2015a), which tracked the lives and support needs of a cohort of 31 young fathers between 2012 and 2015. Via these existing connections, we have followed up with a sub-sample of participants, allowing us to explore the changes and challenges wrought by the pandemic on the working and caring trajectories of an otherwise stigmatised and marginalised group of fathers in low-income contexts.

A cohort of 17 fathers, aged between 15 and 30 years old, were interviewed within months of the imposition of the first national lockdown in the UK in March 2020. While all fathers were under the age of 25 when they entered parenthood, some of the participants were over the age of 25 at the time of the interviews. This is reflective of our sampling strategy whereby some of the young fathers we interviewed were recruited from the baseline study. A diverse range of work and family circumstances were described.

There was a patchwork of employment circumstances, including variation in number of hours worked and the extent of employment precarity, a mix of home-based working and those classified as key workers, experiences of furlough (and in one case redundancy), and unemployment. The youngest of the dads were still in education, living with parents, and had limited resources. There was also diversity in relation to the number of children, experiences of being a father (some became fathers during lockdown while others had been fathers for nearly a decade), and in terms of relationship and residence status.

We also interviewed 17 professionals working for the voluntary sector and other generic and specialist family and youth support services. These were professionals and service managers addressing the broad range of complex needs that may be experienced by those in low-income families or deprived contexts, including some of the young fathers who participated in the FYFF study. These multi-agency services included youth, housing, mental health, and parenting support services.

In the remainder of this chapter, we explore the impacts of the pandemic and lockdown as a policy intervention on young fathers and support organisations in greater depth, before bringing the findings together as part of a short, illustrative case study about how interactions between the two were both affected and navigated to ensure vital social connections were maintained. We conclude with recommendations for practice and policy that centre on how more father-inclusive approaches might be instigated and embedded in the emergent post-COVID-19 era.

The trajectories of young fathers

The social disadvantages that many young fathers experience mean that adhering to contemporary cultural expectations of involved and engaged fatherhood (Dermott and Miller, 2015) can be difficult to fulfil. Even prior to the pandemic, many young fathers were navigating a complex variety of relational, socio-economic, and environmental challenges, some of which constrained their aspirations towards involvement (Neale et al, 2015b). Yet regardless of their young age, gender, and resources, young fathers still express their intentions to 'be there' for their children and engage in a variety of strategies to achieve this (Neale et al, 2015b).

Transitions into fatherhood during the lockdown were highly varied. Some of the new fathers who participated reported being subject to significant visiting restrictions when their partners were in hospital and one witnessed the birth of his child via a video call (Tarrant et al, 2020a). Once home, however, lockdown provided an unanticipated opportunity to bond with babies and engage in their care. Reflective of the national picture for fathers (Burgess and Goldman, 2021), several of the young men said they valued the time that lockdown afforded them to be at home with their children. Bradley became a first-time father during the lockdown and explained:

> 'It's been surprisingly good actually because we've had all this time to isolate in the house by ourselves. We've got to know her, like, we've had so much time with her, it's actually turned out, I'm not gonna say good cause obviously everything that's happened with [the pandemic], but us being isolated in the house, it's been good.' (Bradley, aged 15, in education, 1 child)

Several of the fathers with school-age children also engaged in remote learning, which was especially enjoyable to those with the time and material resources to invest in it. There were differing levels of engagement and uptake among the sample, however, and access to reliable technology was problematic for those who were unemployed or on a limited budget (see also Chapters 12 and 14). For those who were furloughed, had the threat of redundancy hanging over them, or who had lost work and were looking for alternative employment, remote learning was an additional pressure. Compounded by the loss of social contact and support beyond households, these pressures impacted on the mental health of the fathers but also meant that mothers predominantly shouldered the additional burdens of children being at home (see Chapter 8).

Non-resident fathers were perhaps the most disadvantaged by the lockdown with regards to fulfilling their fathering responsibilities. Of the 13 participants that were non-resident, two were in relationships with the mother of their children while the remainder were separated. 7 explained that their contact time with children had been restricted, either because of requirements to isolate, quarantine (one father contracted the virus), or because relatives were shielding. While gatekeeping by maternal family members was also identified prior to the pandemic (Lau Clayton, 2015) it became especially apparent during lockdown. The young men explained that the mothers and grandmothers of their children expressed concerns about the risks of spreading the virus and therefore limited contact (Tarrant et al, 2020b). Later in the chapter we consider the significant role that support services played in supporting young men in their relationships with their children's mothers to distil the continued value of father involvement for children despite the risks associated with spreading the virus. However, for young men without existing support networks or access to professional support, the pandemic was a period of heightened risk around losing contact with children altogether, with the potential for much longer-term consequences for their relationships and fathering identities.

Increasing employment precarity and family finances

Even prior to the pandemic, many of the young fathers we were researching with had tenuous connections to the labour market and expressed varied education, employment, and training pathways that also intersected with their expectations around involved fatherhood (see, for example, Neale and Davies, 2015; Davies, 2016). The impacts of the upheaval wrought by the pandemic most notably fell disproportionately on those who were already living in contexts of socio-economic disadvantage (see Chapters 1 and 11 in this collection). Notably, the older dads in the sample, who we re-accessed from the Following Young Fathers baseline study and some of whom were being interviewed for the sixth time, had relatively secure employment trajectories and were able to work from home. The younger men, who were only just embarking on their parenting journeys, were more likely to be among those experiencing the complex mix of job loss, furlough with the threat of redundancy, complexities organising zero-hours contracts, and risk associated with front line work that had the potential to expose them, and therefore their families, to the virus.

At the time of interview, six of the fathers were in secure employment and two of these were working from home. Of the entire sample, four were furloughed and one lost his job when the business he was working for went into administration. The young fathers who were furloughed described a range of strategies for making up for lost income. One young dad took on extra shifts at his second job and another took 'cash in hand' jobs. Others were glad of the reduced involvement and requirements of job centres and advisors although this made it more challenging to identify secure work (see Chapter 11 in this collection). These young men therefore continued to navigate a labour market that has long been characterised by low-paid and precarious work that marginalises young men (McDowell, 2003; MacDonald and Giazitzoglu, 2019).

The precarity of work was especially apparent for those with zero-hours work contracts for whom balancing work and caregiving was an 'impossible balancing act' (see Cain 2016; Chapter 8, this collection). For Raymond and his partner, the need to balance childcare responsibilities around two zero-hours contracts, was a significant source of distress, making them vulnerable to a loss of employment:

'I was supposed to start work at 5pm today. I can no longer do that so I've had to give my partner my shift ... whatever she gets taxed she's gonna have to pay me my shift in cash kinda thing ... either way there's no winning ... then when I work, she's gonna have to be home. I'm gonna have to cancel one of my shifts in the week and she's gonna have to cancel two of her's and give them away. So ... there's nothing really we can do. And this whole furlough business stops on the 31st October 2020 which doesn't help ... it's just when we have to give up our shift at the end of the week only because like this whole COVID thing. We're not getting paid for it at all. We give that up, our hours get reduced. And then we're below contracted hours and then we're in trouble kind of thing ... as much as we try we have to take each day at a time. We just can't do it.' (Raymond, aged 26, on furlough, working a second job on a zero-hours contract, two children)

The young men employed in precarious positions also struggled to achieve the right balance between doing enough hours to maintain employment and sustain household finances while also managing the increasing food, energy and other costs associated with having children at home. As we explore later in the chapter, some young fathers were not entitled to furlough and became increasingly vulnerable to losing work altogether.

Informal support and community participation

The previous section demonstrates how restricted contact with children contributed to the social isolation of some young fathers and mitigated against their intentions to 'be there' for their children. Yet, the pandemic also produced new and more extensive practices of family and community participation. Whereas maternal grandparents were described by non-resident fathers as engaging in gatekeeping around access to children, the parents and grandparents of those still in a relationship provided vital financial and material support. Early in the lockdown when essential items like food and toilet paper were being stockpiled, for example, father of four Craig, aged 28, had to rely on his partner's parents to source key items for their baby:

'[partner] and me were getting worried that we couldn't get baby milk in or nappies or stuff like that ... the only thing that we've been really short of is baby formula for [youngest child] but that's because the supermarket near us hasn't had any in for a bit now ... we did run out at one point but she rang her dad up and said, "Look, can you go to [the supermarket] near you, get some baby formula and send it down?" and he did.' (Craig, aged 28, unemployed, 4 children)

While some young parents are often assumed to be dependent on their parents, financially, emotionally, and practically, the pandemic provided opportunities for increased family participation and engagement in the support of others. Many of the young fathers we spoke with had parents and/or grandparents who were shielding and required support to gain access to essentials like food and medicines. Several described doing the weekly shopping for family members, a practice that for some was already established but for others became more essential: "I've gone to the shop for my mum a few times" (Jonny, aged 21, unemployed, 1 child). "I do all the shopping runs for everyone. ... I pretty much do all the shopping runs and I get like paint for the house and stuff and just general stuff like that" (Cole, aged 19, in education, 1 child). One of the participants also distributed food to local community members when the restaurant he worked at closed. Local social solidarity and community spirit were evidently heightened during the early days of the lockdown among those living in contexts of deprivation, although these have long been observed as compelling features of family and community lives in deprived localities (for example, MacDonald et al, 2005).

Schools were also key sources of support and resource for low-income fathers and their families, especially in the absence or reduction of formalised or specialised support services. Some of the families received food parcels from their children's schools, for example, and in another case, a teacher gained notoriety among the community for going out on foot to deliver school meals and work to children at home. These were essential strategies as low-income families tried to 'get by' at a time of major flux and change (see also Chapters 1 and 11).

Service sustainability and relationship building at a distance

Beyond families, support from locally embedded services and institutions was essential for many of the young fathers we interviewed. Yet support organisations and professionals working with young fathers and low-income families also needed to adjust rapidly to the new context produced by the pandemic, shifting from face-to-face to remote working, and adapting and tailoring their support offers accordingly. Some of the young men in our study were already engaged with a wide variety of statutory and voluntary agencies prior to the pandemic, accessing them for different purposes and at different times in their parenting journeys (for example, Neale et al, 2015b). Indeed, the complex needs that many young fathers experience mean that they often come into the orbit of a variety of different services and agencies when they become a parent (Neale and Davies, 2015).

Relationship building and maintenance between professionals and young fathers has been identified as essential to service sustainability and for ensuring that services are accessible to young men (Davies,

2016). In the early days of the first lockdown, relationships were more challenging to establish and sustain. Services therefore sought to facilitate continued connection and engagement with young fathers in a context of enforced distancing and isolation. Many practitioners commented on the challenge of establishing relationships with new referrals to services and with young men with whom relationships of trust were not already established. Building relationships of trust was more challenged by newly imposed constraints on flexible, tailored interactions like simply being there with an open door (see also Chapter 11). A support worker for a mental health charity noted:

'normally people would just come in, 'cause we have like a drop-in there between one and four too, so people could come in and maybe do a universal, sorry, a job search for the Universal Credit, or they could just come in and get a meal and things like that, so those things have gone'.

Lockdown rules also meant that it was difficult to reach out to people in their local communities to maintain visibility and actively offer support, making services harder for families to access. Several professionals also reflected on the loss of more subtle or less visible aspects of support, such as observations of body language to read emotional cues. A specialist learning mentor for a local council commented: "They don't always articulate to you, as you know, the way that they're feeling and the emotions that they're going through and the stress that they're under but you can read it through the body language. And then that leads to better conversations cause then you can explore things." Paradoxically, professionals were perceived by some to be more accessible and reachable during the pandemic than they had been before. The shift to remote support therefore meant that contact with families increased, albeit outside of traditional work hours. A family service manager explained that remote working had "eased people to be able to send us messages at odd random times during the day, during the weekend and things that they normally probably wouldn't send". Services therefore found new ways of relationship building via their new digital offers, and the pandemic created new opportunities for implementing alternative working practices that were previously constrained by established working cultures; see Chapter 14 for a discussion of the challenges of remote working in a pandemic context.

We now explore insights generated by a community-based support group for young fathers and professionals who adapted to a digital offer to continue their mission to tackle the loneliness and isolation that many young men experience. The themes identified so far in the chapter were commented on by the professionals working this service and in combination, provide a multi-perspective account of how services adapted to maintain a continuous source of support for young men and their families.

Community support for young fathers: an illustrative case study

The North East Young Dads and Lads (hereafter NEYDL) are a dedicated and established organisation that provides specialist, community-based support to young fathers. Professionals engaged with the organisation are 'local champions' (hereafter referred to as support workers) for young fathers and support them with a broad range of complex issues, some of which we captured through the research, conducted both with them and the fathers they were supporting. Some of these issues were specific to, and exacerbated by the pandemic, while others were prevalent beforehand. Distinct pandemic-related concerns included: difficulties around reduced contact with children, higher levels of social isolation and loneliness, and greater employment precarity, and impacts on finances associated with having children at home, as we see in several chapters across the collection, such as Chapters 5 and 11. The findings reported as part of this case study include reflections from three support workers from NEYDL who took part in a focus group for Wave one of the FYFF study.

Supporting the accounts from the non-resident fathers, support workers reported that the pandemic had exacerbated tensions between parents residing in different households, linked to changes in contact arrangements for children. Here, one of the support workers at NEYDL explains his role in supporting one young father to navigate these issues during the pandemic:

> '[T]here's a particular case at the moment where, we went into lockdown so the young man's contact completely stopped. And then the mother a' the child's changed her phone number so he couldn't make any phone calls, he couldn't arrange contact. So he asked if I could support so I, I was calling Mum to try and facilitate the contact happening because the relationship had ended and they couldn't, you know, it was very hard for the mum and dad to be able to talk to each other without it breaking down. Between myself and the maternal mum [child's grandmother on the mother's side], we managed to organise to re-establish contact when it was safe to do it that way. So yeah, that was quite a lot a' work to be done there.'

Where young dads had daily contact with their children, there were also drawbacks, linked to the additional costs and emotional pressures of managing multiple children at home. These were not uniformly experienced and the support workers described a range of circumstances reflective of the complex needs young fathers either experience themselves or navigate on behalf of family members:

'It's the challenge of having one or two children at home all the time. We've got some young dads where their children have got learning difficulties and other needs and the challenge of just that lack of support. And also about the fact that we're often working with young men in low-income families and suddenly the lights are all on, all the consoles are on and they're having to feed their children all the time. So there's that whole economic impact as well as the social impact and the challenge of educating their kids at home. So yeah there's a lot of other aspects there that the young men are telling us are really, are really challenging them.'

Higher costs of living also ran in parallel with experiences of job insecurity and associated challenges securing a stable source of income. Here, one of the support workers reveals experiences of job insecurity similar to that described by Raymond earlier, confirming that those on precarious contracts or employed by agencies were especially vulnerable to job loss and social isolation:

'a lot a' the young men that we've worked with in the past and previously, and there's a few that I've been working with during lockdown where they weren't furloughed because they were on temporary contracts, they were working for agencies. So they were doing a little bit a' work during lockdown and then changes to lockdown and then they just lost their jobs. So then they were in that limbo of waiting to go back on to Universal Credit and having to make that. So that was ... none a' the young men were, that I was working with got, were, eligible to be furloughed. They were all just let go because they were on temporary contracts or like I say agency work.'

While these examples illustrate clear parallels between the lived experiences reported by the young fathers who participated in our study and accounts given by professionals working at support organisations, they are also revealing of a diverse range of gendered experiences among young men produced in the pandemic context. For some families, dads were able to be more involved because they spent more time at home. For non-resident fathers, access to children was more likely to be reduced. Significantly, these observations reflect the importance of continued service support for young fathers at a time of crisis where welfare support has limitations. The support provided, however, was not delivered in ways the organisation would have pre-COVID-19, as we explore next.

Creating a digital support offer

Support workers were also reflective about the impacts of the shift to remote ways of working on their offer to young fathers. NEYDL adapted their offer to ensure that the young men continued to receive the support they needed, albeit with interactions online, via telephone or text. In so doing, they also experienced alternative ways of working with young fathers. A key observation was that while the amount of time spent supporting the young men remained the same, the nature of the support had had to change by necessity. One support worker explained:

> 'I haven't had a decrease in the amount of contact time with the young men. It's just how I've contacted them and talking to them has changed. For me it's really hard. I'm a very tactile person. You know, if the lads are all right I give them a cuddle. And I'll shake their hand and walk alongside them. So for me that's been really hard not to go, "Hello, mate, how you doing?"'

The loss of physical contact and co-presence in these formal support relationships was further exacerbated by digital exclusion. Not all of the young men who required support from the service had access to technology, which isolated them both from local and informal support, and from support services during the pandemic: "there's this automatic assumption that all young people have access to digital media and smart phones and internet connection. They've got, you know, data on their phones and they haven't." It is evident that remote working is not a straightforward replacement for face-to-face, locally accessible support. The requirement of professionals to adapt and develop a new digital offer does mean, however, that in the post-pandemic support context, a combination of face-to-face and digital support can be combined to increase service sustainability and facilitate preventative work, enabling professionals to build and establish trusting relationships with a much wider constituency of young fathers. However, should services move towards a blended or online approach, young fathers may require support to access appropriate digital technology and to develop the digital skills needed to ensure services remain accessible to them.

Implications for policy and practice

The COVID-19 pandemic and lockdowns engendered major changes in the organisation of work and family life for young fathers and their families. Accounts of the pandemic, by both young fathers and professionals, has revealed the complex ways that the lockdowns have contributed to increased social, economic, and relational precarity, especially among young fathers who were already living in socially disadvantaged contexts. The lockdowns also altered the informal and formal support landscapes of these fathers, impacting specifically on the wide variety of specialist, generic, statutory, and voluntary services that engage with low-income and marginalised families.

Our findings offer timely evidence that speak to a variety of policy areas. Significantly, time to bond with babies and engage in childcare was highly valued, although for the younger fathers or fathers who were not in employment, financial precarity and uncertainty was problematic. These findings also lend weight to the need for affordable and accessible paternal and/or shared leave for all fathers, regardless of their employment status. Indeed, research demonstrates that the earlier fathers are involved in caregiving in their parenting journeys the better this is for fathers, mothers, and for children and their developmental outcomes (Cundy, 2016). Young fathers increasingly face a variety of obstacles and structural challenges that limit their opportunities to access the labour market and secure employment. Their precarity is further compounded by limited access to affordable and flexible childcare. Change in organisational cultures in workplaces would also be beneficial, driven through recognition that fathers also benefit from home working, shorter hours, and greater flexibility to enable care sharing. Legislation that ensures flexible working as a default for everyone would be welcome and would challenge gendered assumptions around work and childcare.

The findings about how services adapted their offers to support young fathers at a physical distance also evidence the crucial roles that specialist, community, and locality-based support groups play in addressing some of the complex social, economic, and relational issues that young fathers navigate across their parenting journeys. Not only do these groups provide peer support and help young fathers to remain engaged in their children's lives, they also support them to build confidence, and to flourish as part of a local community. Yet, the availability and accessibility of these groups for young fathers remains a postcode lottery (Tarrant and Neale, 2017). Fragmented and time-limited funding and inadequate policy support impacts on the sustainability of services, with real potential to marginalise disadvantaged young fathers further in the longer term. The pandemic has proven the adaptability of professionals in this sector and its vital role in filling gaps where the social security system fails, or where informal mechanisms of support are lacking. Sustainable funding to enable these kinds of new innovations among community-based groups for young fathers is sorely needed if young men are to reach their full potential, both as fathers and as citizens.

Note

[1] Funded by the UK Research & Innovation Future Leaders Fellowship scheme (2020–2024, grant number: MR/S031723/1). Website: https://followingyoungfathersfurther.org

References

Beggs Weber, J. (2012) Becoming teen fathers: stories of teen pregnancy, responsibility, and masculinity. *Men and Masculinities*, 16(6), 900–21.

Burgess, A. and Goldman, R. (2021) *Lockdown fathers: the untold story (full report). Contemporary fathers in the UK*. Full report available at: www. fatherhoodinstitute.org/wp-content/uploads/2021/05/Lockdown-Fathers-Full-Report.pdf

Cain, R. (2016) Responsibilising recovery: lone and low paid parents, Universal Credit and the gendered contradictions of UK welfare reform. *British Politics*, 11(4), 488–507.

Cundy, J. (2016) Supporting young dads' journeys through fatherhood. *Social Policy and Society*, 15(1), 141–53.

Davies, L. (2016) Are young fathers 'hard to reach'? Understanding the importance of relationship building and service sustainability. *Journal of Children's Services: Research Informing Policy and Practice*, 11(4), 317–29.

Dermott, E. and Miller, T. (2015) More than the sum of its parts? Contemporary fatherhood policy, practice and discourse. *Families, Relationships and Societies*, 4(2): 183-95.

Duncan, S. (2007) What's the problem with teenage parents? And what's the problem with policy?. *Critical Social Policy*, 27(3), 307–34.

Hadley, A. (2017) *Teenage Pregnancy and Young Parenthood: Effective Policy and Practice*. London: Routledge.

Hall, S-M (2019) *Everyday Life in Austerity: Family, Friends and Intimate Relations*. Basingstoke: Palgrave Macmillan.

Lau Clayton, C. (2015) Young fatherhood: sharing care with the mother of the child. Briefing Paper no. 2. Available at: https://followingfathers.leeds. ac.uk/wp-content/uploads/sites/79/2015/10/Brieifing-Paper-2-V8.pdf

MacDonald, R. and Giazitzoglu, A. (2019) Youth, enterprise and precarity: or, what is, and what is wrong with, the 'gig economy'?. *Journal of Sociology*, 55(4), 724–40.

MacDonald, R., Shildrick, T., Webster, C. and Simpson, D. (2005) Growing up in poor neighbourhoods: the significance of class and place in the extended transitions of 'socially excluded' young adults. *Sociology*, 39(5), 873–91.

McDowell, L. (2003) *Redundant Masculinities? Employment Change and White Working Class Youth*. Oxford: Blackwell.

Neale, B. and Davies, L. (2015) Becoming a young breadwinner? The education, employment and training trajectories of young fathers. *Social Policy and Society*, 15(1), 85–98.

Neale, B., Lau Clayton, C., Davies, L. and Ladlow, L. (2015a) Researching the lives of young fathers: the following young fathers study and dataset. Briefing Paper no. 8. Available at: https://followingfathers.leeds.ac.uk/wp-content/uploads/sites/79/2015/10/Researching-the-Lives-of-Young-Fathers-updated-Oct-22.pdf

Neale, B., Patrick, R. and Lau Clayton, C. (2015b) Becoming a young father: transitions into early parenthood. Briefing Paper no. 1. Available at: https://followingfathers.leeds.ac.uk/wp-content/uploads/sites/79/2015/10/Brieifing-Paper-1-web.pdf

Tarrant, A. and Neale, B. (2017) *Learning to support young dads, responding to young fathers in a different way.* Project report available at: https://followingfathers.leeds.ac.uk/wp-content/uploads/sites/79/2017/04/SYD-final-report.pdf

Tarrant, A., Way, L. and Ladlow, L. (2020a) Negotiating 'earning' and 'caring' through the COVID-19 crisis: change and continuities in the parenting and employment trajectories of young fathers. Briefing Paper One. Available at: https://followingyoungfathersfurther.org/asset/working-papers/

Tarrant, A., Ladlow, L. and Way, L. (2020b) From social isolation to local support: relational change and continuities for young fathers in the context of the COVID 19 crisis. Briefing Paper Two. Available at: https://followingyoungfathersfurther.org/asset/working-papers/

Tarrant, A., Way, L. and Ladlow, L. (2021) Supporting at a distance: the challenges and opportunities of supporting young fathers through the COVID-19 pandemic. Briefing Paper Three. Available at: https://followingyoungfathersfurther.org/asset/working-papers/

10

Social security during COVID-19: the experiences of military veterans

Lisa Scullion, Philip Martin, Celia Hynes, and David Young

Introduction

Research published prior to COVID-19 has illustrated some of the difficulties that veterans can experience within the benefits system (Scullion et al, 2018; 2019; Scullion and Curchin, 2021). For example, those with Service-attributed mental health conditions can face challenges interacting with various aspects of the system from Work Capability Assessments (WCAs) through to Work Focused Interviews (WFIs) (Scullion and Curchin, 2021). Accounts within pre-COVID-19 research also highlight the significant role of informal peer networks and third sector organisations in supporting veterans in relation to both benefits processes but also wider issues relating to health and wellbeing, particularly where there is an absence of close family connections and relationships (Scullion et al, 2018; 2019). Drawing on emerging findings from interviews with veterans undertaken during COVID-19, this chapter revisits some of these pre-COVID-19 issues around mental health, benefits processes, and support networks to explore the impact of the pandemic.

In this chapter we discuss two key issues. First, we reflect on some of the changes that occurred to the benefits system during COVID-19 (albeit temporary). More specifically we focus on (i) the suspension of, or changes to, benefit assessment processes; and (ii) the suspension of conditionality. We acknowledge that experiences of these particular (and sometimes challenging) aspects of the benefits system apply equally to non-veterans. However, by drawing on the accounts of a cohort of veterans who have complex needs, we provide important insights for policy and practice in relation to the need for careful consideration of *when*, *how* (or indeed *whether*), we return to 'business as usual' within the benefits system.

Second, we explore the importance of taking a wider perspective on the nature of *family* when considering how people experience, and are supported through, periods of crisis. Indeed, the Covid Realities project is documenting the experiences of *families* during this unprecedented time. Drawing on the accounts of our cohort of veterans provides an important contribution from those whose families are 'fractured' or where 'family', in the traditional sense, is *absent*. Here we highlight the importance of peer networks in delivering many of the support functions associated with families and provide an understanding of the impact when such networks are broken, even temporarily.

The Sanctions, Support and Service Leavers project: background, methods, and participants

Each year a proportion of people leave the UK Armed Forces and enter civilian life. For the vast majority, the transition to civilian life is relatively unproblematic. However, it is recognised that 'those who do encounter difficulties often experience multiple and complex problems' (Warren et al, 2015: 38). This can include concerns around mental health and/or physical impairment following active Service (Hynes and Thomas, 2016; Hynes et al, 2020), and experiences of homelessness (Johnsen et al, 2008), drug and alcohol use (The Centre for Social Justice, 2014), the criminal justice system (Fossey et al, 2017), and gambling (Roberts et al, 2017). In response to the recognition that those leaving the military need supporting appropriately, there has been an increasing focus in UK policy and practice on the needs of veterans. Notable policy changes include the publication of the *Armed Forces Covenant* (2011) and the ten-year *Strategy for our Veterans* (2018), but also through the creation of the first ever Office for Veterans' Affairs (OVA) (2019) and the new Armed Forces Bill (2021) which proposes enshrining the Armed Forces Covenant in law. Each of these measures aims to ensure that veterans are not disadvantaged when accessing public services and focus on 'helping the nation fulfil its lifelong duty to those who have served in the Armed Forces' (OVA, nd). However, how far this support has extended to those navigating the UK social security system was largely unknown. To address this gap, the Sanctions, Support and Service Leavers project [hereafter SSSL[1]] was developed to explore the experiences of veterans within the benefits system. SSSL is a qualitative longitudinal research (QLR) project, which began in early 2017 and originally ran for two years. Following significant policy and practice impact (Scullion et al, 2021), in early 2020 the research was extended to 2023 to ensure that the experiences of veterans were considered during the ongoing implementation of Universal Credit (UC).

Responding to COVID-19: changing our focus and methods

As a longitudinal project that was designed and commissioned pre-COVID-19, the pandemic required a shift in both *focus* (that is, consideration of the changing benefits processes, such as the acceleration to digital/telephone interactions, the suspension of benefits assessments, the temporary removal of conditionality) and *methods* (that is, switching to remote interviews).

The project started with a baseline sample of 68 veterans at Wave A (2017–18), with 52 veterans re-interviewed at Wave B (2018–19). Wave C commenced in December 2020, with 28 interviews completed (at the time of writing) with our original cohort. With the exception of a very small number of telephone interviews in Wave A and B, face-to-face interviewing was our main (and preferred) approach; however, the Wave C interviews with our original cohort have all been undertaken 'remotely' via telephone or other virtual platforms such as MS Teams or Zoom. Although the original participants have been accepting of the shift to remote methods, as we will discuss later in relation to benefits assessments, some expressed a strong preference for face-to-face interactions.

In parallel with our Wave C fieldwork, we have also recruited new participants as part of the continuation of the project. To date, 30 new participants (all claiming UC) have been added to the project, all of whom have been interviewed via remote methods. The findings presented in this chapter are therefore based on the analysis of 58 interviews undertaken during COVID-19. The original cohort were recruited from four main geographical areas in England (the North West, North East, London, Yorkshire), reflecting areas with large proportions of Armed Forces Service leavers or garrisons, but also pragmatically relating to maximising the available fieldwork travel resources. However, with the recruitment of the new UC cohort, the use of remote interviews has meant that we have been able to widen the study to veterans from across the UK. The new cohort includes a number of veterans from Scotland, for example.

Background to our participants

Although our project focuses on experiences of the benefits system, the data reflects the range of complex needs experienced by the participants in our sample. This is important for understanding the context within which our participants were claiming benefits, and their subsequent experiences during COVID-19. The sample was overwhelmingly male, with only two female veterans (who were part of our original cohort). Through our Wave A interviews, we captured a range of issues relating to transitions from military to civilian life, including health, housing, employment, and relationships. Across our original cohort of 68 participants, 59 identified as having a mental health impairment. The new UC cohort demonstrated remarkably similar patterns of mental ill health, with (at the time of writing) 22 out of 30 stating that they had a mental health issue. Across both cohorts, PTSD, anxiety, and depression were mentioned most frequently, and the majority attributed their mental health issues to their time in the Armed Forces. Research suggests that comorbidity is frequent among veterans seeking mental health support (Murphy et al, 2017) and it was evident that some participants in our study were experiencing multiple mental health issues (with some also experiencing physical health problems). In many accounts, the symptoms and effects of mental ill health were simultaneously described by participants as having longer-term debilitating impacts but also being episodic in their severity. A small number of participants had also been sectioned under the Mental Health Act (2007) or had spent time in a mental health institution since leaving the Armed Forces. Although many participants were clear about the role they believed their experiences within the Armed Forces had played in relation to their mental ill health, it is important to acknowledge the presence of longer-term trauma that was unrelated to the Armed Forces (Iversen et al, 2007; Van Voorhees at al., 2012; Scullion and Curchin, 2021). As such, there was sometimes a complex mix of pre-existing trauma, experiences during Service, and wider post-Service events that impacted on people's mental health.

Alcohol misuse also featured within the accounts of some of our participants, with a smaller number referring to drug use as well. The use of alcohol was sometimes described by veterans as being part of the 'culture' within the military (Jones and Fear, 2011). However, for others it was a response to difficulties relating to health, relationships, employment, and other aspects of the transition to civilian life (Scullion et al, 2018). There were also participants who described experiencing periods of housing insecurity, including some episodes of street homelessness.

For many of our participants, benefit claims had been instigated following a period of crisis, where mental ill health (and the related experiences described earlier) impacted on their ability to sustain employment. As such, within our original cohort over half were claiming Employment Support Allowance (ESA) (primarily within the Support Group), and within our new UC cohort a similar number had 'limited capability for work or work-related activity'. Additionally, several participants were also claiming (or in the process of claiming) Personal Independence Payment (PIP). The remainder of the sample were classed as 'jobseekers' and subject to varying degrees of conditionality.

It is also important here to mention the complex family and relationship circumstances of many of our participants. Almost half of the sample had experienced a relationship breakdown, which was often attributed to two key issues: (i) difficulties in adjusting to civilian life as a couple when Service life had required so much time apart; and (ii) the impact of the mental health issues described earlier. Most of the participants had children; however, a consequence of relationship breakdown was often estrangement, with a number of participants having limited or no contact with their children.

Welcome reprieve? Experiences of the COVID-19 benefits system

In our pre-COVID-19 interviews, benefits assessments processes and interactions relating to managing the conditions of their claim were articulated as provoking significant anxiety (Scullion et al, 2019) or even experienced as re-traumatising for some (Scullion and Curchin, 2021). Here we turn our attention to the interviews that took place during COVID-19, whereby participants reflected on these aspects of their experience.

Like many other benefit claimants, the veterans we interviewed described the suspension, cancellation, or delay of benefits assessment processes during COVID-19 and indicated that original categorisations and payments had been extended: "I have heard nothing from ESA to reassess me or anything else, and I got a letter recently on the PIP side, saying that, due to the virus, my award has been extended by another year" (ESA Support Group claimant, Wave C). Given some of the previous negative experiences of our participants, one might assume that the suspension of assessments would be a welcome intervention. However, although there was evidence of some 'relief' at the suspension of assessments, overall, the interviews suggested that more commonly there was anxiety around the uncertainty of *when* and *how* they would take place. Additionally, for those who were making new claims or those who were hoping that a re-assessment would increase their payment level, such delays were articulated as having financial repercussions. One participant, for example, explained that in February 2020, he had been invited to attend a re-assessment, which he was hoping would give him the opportunity to provide his full medical records and would subsequently lead to a higher payment. However, when interviewed in December 2020, he explained that "then this COVID came along, so I'm still waiting" (UC claimant, Wave C). Another participant, from the new cohort of UC participants, described feeling in 'limbo' having waited 16 weeks for his new PIP claim to be processed. Frustrated at a PIP assessment being delayed, he commented:

'As hard as I try there is just no way of getting it right now because they say, "Oh well, we can't do it, everything is locked down with COVID." Surely they can look at somebody's medical records and say, "Hold on, he is at least eligible for some [support]."' (UC claimant, Wave A, new cohort)

Within our sample, four participants had experienced a PIP assessment during the COVID-19 period and one of these had also had a WCA. Like many other benefits processes, these assessments had shifted to remote methods (Work and Pensions Committee, 2020). As such, participants described having a telephone assessment, where previously it had been face-to-face. Again, there were mixed views on this method. Some welcomed the removal of the requirement to attend a face-to-face assessment at an assessment centre (for example those who experienced anxiety when leaving the house). However, for others telephone assessments were problematic due to the inability to judge how the assessor was reacting to the conversation, to make a connection with the assessor, or not knowing if other people were present in the background:

'I like to try and get my point across to someone on a personal level, so you can see people, you can gauge people's reactions. It's a lot easier to do it by body language and stuff when you see people than it is over the phone because you don't know ... it could be a party call sort of thing where they've got their bosses listening in, or other people prompting them, or it might be a trainee on their first day. You've no idea, do you, it's just a voice? It's very hard to build up any sort of connection over the telephone.' (UC claimant, Wave C)

For those participants who were classed as 'jobseekers', the emphasis was more on managing the requirements that are set to continue receiving benefits. Our pre-COVID-19 interviews highlighted acknowledged concerns around the effectiveness of conditionality (Dwyer et al, 2018), particularly where mental ill health was a significant issue (Dwyer et al, 2020; Scullion and Curchin, 2021). With the onset of the pandemic, another significant change to the benefits system was the temporary suspension of conditionality (under the Social Security (Coronavirus) (Further Measures) Regulations 2020), and there were examples from across the sample of people experiencing "a lot more leeway" (UC claimant, Wave A, new cohort). This participant, for example, had struggled to access his online account and had missed an appointment with his work coach. He described his perception that ordinarily this would result in a sanction; however: "My benefit didn't stop, whereas it would do usually. If you don't keep an appointment, your benefit stops."

Several participants talked positively about the supportive nature of the interactions with DWP staff, who were described as 'light touch' in their approach. For example, one veteran referred to a phone call he received at the very beginning of the pandemic (March/April 2020): "and they literally said, 'You're not coming in. You're not doing anything. Payments are all automatic. Don't do anything'" (UC claimant, Wave C). One participant, who was having to shield due to multiple health conditions, also described a conversation with his work coach where he had told them that he was struggling to manage the monthly payment, particularly in relation to the expense of food shopping. Although this raises much broader – and important – questions about the adequacy of the benefits system (see also Chapters 2, 3, 4, and 11), it was evident that on a practical level his work coach had tried to help and had subsequently quickly changed his payments from monthly to twice monthly:

'I was speaking to this [lady] from the DWP who's my work coach basically. She said, "How are you getting on?" I said, "I'm struggling with this lockdown because I can only get food once a month, and it's expensive." … She said, "I'll tell you what I'll do. You're in between payments now. Your next payment will be less than what your first payment is, the one just gone." So I get my payment every fortnight on Universal Credit, and the way it's fallen, this is better for me in a way; 4th February coming up, I get my Universal Credit that day, and I get my PIP that day, so I've got just under £1,000 coming in less than two weeks.' (UC claimant, Wave C)

Overall, the interactions with work coaches were described positively and were perceived as reassuring given that people had limited options to engage in work-related activity, but also given the anxiety that was experienced by so many people during this unprecedented period. However, it was evident that participants did not expect this "light touch" approach to remain indefinitely and there were indications in the interviews carried out later in the pandemic that the nature of the interactions had already begun to change. This is presented in the case study of 'Patrick'.[2]

Case study: 'Patrick'

Patrick was in his 50s and was one of the new UC claimants within our sample. He had left school before completing his secondary education, and joined the Armed Forces, where he had served for six years before leaving as he wanted to spend more time with his family. However, Patrick's marriage had broken down after he left the Armed Forces and although his children lived quite near, he did not have any contact with them. After a period of homelessness, he was offered accommodation by his local authority. He had worked in a number of different jobs since leaving the Armed Forces, often short-term in duration, and described "a series of jobs from one job to another just trying to find my place in life".

It was around 15 years after leaving the Armed Forces that he began to experience issues with stress and alcohol. He experienced a range of long-term physical and mental health challenges, indicating that his mental wellbeing had declined considerably over the last year, to the point where he didn't want to open the door to anybody or answer the telephone: "I just refused to engage." After experiencing a more significant mental health crisis in mid-2021, he was now supported by a mental health social work team.

He had claimed ESA for a short period of time in 2019/2020, where he described 'failing' a WCA and being transferred to JSA. He had subsequently found a job, but it was only for a short, three-week period in early 2020. On leaving this job, he had lived off some savings for a while, before applying for UC at the onset of the pandemic. We interviewed Patrick in early July 2021, and he indicated that for over a year (from his initial claim at the beginning of the pandemic up until May 2021) he had been categorised as 'fit for work'. He describes how all his contact with the DWP had been online or over the phone, and made reference to the early positive nature of his interactions with his work coach:

'I had a lovely woman ring me up and she says, "I've got your claim. I hope you're aware that it's going to take me some time. There's a backlog. There's millions of people." She was very empathetic .... She said, "You can't come into the office because nobody can go in. We're all working from home." She said, "We're going to do it all remotely. Do you have a problem with that?" I said, "No." She goes, "Okay then, we'll keep in touch. Don't bother about stressing out and whatever, we'll keep in touch once a month."'

He continued to say that he was contacted once a month and that the conversations focused on checking that he was okay: "The person didn't give me any grief ... they would just ring me up and say, 'Are you alive? Are you well? Are you basically happy? Okay, then I'll call you back next ... I'll call you again next month.'" This situation had lasted until around May 2021. At that point, he described experiencing what he perceived as a notable shift in attitude and approach from the previous "very friendly telephone conversation", when a new work coach phoned from his local JCP "asking me to come in and they would like to interrogate me further on what I was doing with my time." He described how the new work coach had stated explicitly: "The softly, softly approach was ending, and it was going to be, you know, forensically look at whether you've been doing enough ... He just explained that things were opening up, the lockdown as far as the Jobcentre was concerned was over and that things were getting back to normal." When asked how he felt about the change in approach, he replied, "Depressed, depressed, depressed." Fearing what would happen to him, and particularly the potential that he might experience a benefit sanction, he had contacted a third sector organisation that had supported him to get a sick note and he was currently not expected to engage in work-related activity.

Patrick's case study illustrates the need to consider *when* and *how* conditionality is (re)introduced in the aftermath of the pandemic. Reflecting existing research on the counterproductive nature of conditionality (Wright and Dwyer, 2020), Patrick's account demonstrates how his 'jarring' introduction to conditionality had not led to engagement with work-related activity; rather, it had led to Patrick moving further away from engagement with paid employment.

The absence of 'family': the importance of peer support

The Covid Realities project is focusing on documenting and understanding the experiences of *families* during an unprecedented time and existing research highlights the central role of *families* and *relational support* when managing on a low income (Daly and Kelly, 2015). However, an important contribution of the SSSL study is exploring experiences where families are fractured or where 'family', in the traditional sense, is absent. The absence of family was a notable feature of many of the accounts of the veterans who were experiencing mental ill health, and in addition to relationship breakdown and separation from children (referred to earlier in our background to participants), some also described limited contact with parents, siblings, and other family members.

Consequently*, even before* the pandemic many participants spoke of feeling isolated. In some cases, this isolation deepened considerably during COVID-19, leading to worsening mental health. For those who had limited family support or contact, the support provided by peers through local veteran-specific networks (both formal and informal) was described (pre-COVID-19) as vital. These networks provided a space for veterans to talk through a range of issues and concerns including sharing or comparing experiences of the benefits system. However, the suspension of such forms of support due to COVID-19 restrictions had impacted significantly on a number of participants:

'I'm constantly up, constantly down. … Obviously, the COVID's affecting us massively because of not being able to get out and go to these Breakfast Clubs [Armed Forces and Veterans' Breakfast Clubs[3]]. I don't really have any mates, but the mates that I do have I can't go and see because obviously, we're in lockdown.' (UC claimant, Wave C)

'Up at a church in the borough … they've got mental health advisers there. There's a guy that's an ex-squaddie. You just go there and have a chat, and just sit down and have a cup and talk through stuff, but obviously that stopped. That's all been lost because of the Covid … a lot of lads [referring to veterans] haven't coped very well.' (UC claimant, Wave C)

The importance of being able to resume attending these support groups was evident, not just in terms of addressing the isolation people felt but also as places that provided support across a range of issues. This is illustrated through the case study of 'Mark'.

Case study: 'Mark'

Mark was 49 years old and living on his own in a flat provided through a local veterans' support organisation. He had served three years in the Armed Forces, having had to leave after an 'administrative misunderstanding'. Upon leaving, he had moved straight into work; however, he had gone from the relative stability of his Armed Forces role to moving in and out of various lower-skilled roles, much of which had been agency work. Around ten years ago, he began to experience depression and anxiety but also became a full-time carer for his father, the stress of which saw his drinking increase to problematic levels. Mark was interviewed in March 2021 and described the difficulty he experienced in early 2020 after the death of a close family member, followed shortly after by the onset of COVID-19. As such, he described having no close family connections or support during that time:

> 'So, I don't really have anybody now, as regards family ... I mean, I've got sisters and that, but I don't interfere with them and then, vice versa, they don't interfere with me. She's [referring to the family member who passed away] the only one, still living, who was there for me, you know what I mean? So, it's like I've lost everybody now. ... Then COVID, I was stuck in all day.'

Mark had been through many years of treatment and support for his addiction and had actively engaged with a local veterans' group. In the absence of family, his main support was therefore from other veterans who were part of the local network and addiction support groups. It was also evident that beyond the support provided around his health and wellbeing, these groups had previously supported him with issues relating to his benefit claim. For example, he had been claiming ESA for over four years, and described how, with the help of other veterans, he had won an appeal against a WCA that had recommended transferring him to JSA and been granted two further years in the ESA Support Group. The veterans support group had also helped him to successfully challenge a refusal to award PIP in 2020. At the time of interview, he indicated that he was due another PIP assessment and had received the relevant paperwork to complete and knew that he would be required to attend a WCA at some point too (although he was uncertain when that would be).

It was evident that these assessments were at the forefront of his mind: "It's playing on me mind now thinking about it," and that the peer networks he had established would be vital forms of support through these processes. The ability to meet with these support networks has been suspended during COVID-19; however, with the relaxation of restrictions it was evident that he was grateful to be able to re-engage with these networks: "They've been rocks for me, they really have and, obviously, I'm back in with [veterans' group], now … So, I'm happy about that." Mark hoped that the reintroduction of these groups would come at the right time to provide support with his upcoming assessments.

For individuals like Mark, veterans' peer networks had delivered many of the support functions often associated with close families.

Policy implications

Drawing on interviews with veterans navigating the benefits system during COVID-19, this chapter has provided unique insights in relation to two key issues. First, it provides an understanding of experiences of the *suspension and subsequent (re)introduction* of specific aspects of the benefits system; namely benefits assessments and conditionality. With regards to benefits assessments, it was evident that suspension of these processes offered relief for some. However, overall, there was significant uncertainty and anxiety about *when* and *how* they would resume, which needs addressing through clearer communication. With regards to how the *assessment*s would be carried out when they did resume, although telephone methods had been welcomed by some, they were not appropriate for all participants, with face-to-face interactions still important for many. We therefore recommend giving *choice* to people in relation to how their assessments are undertaken. This would apply equally to other benefits interactions (for example WFIs), where providing *choice* to claimants about how those interactions take place would improve their experiences (Scullion and Curchin, 2021).

With regards to conditionality, participants valued the positive interactions with work coaches that had centred around wellbeing during the pandemic. However, our interviews suggest that, in some areas, there has been a return to more punitive compliance-based interactions. Similar to benefits assessments, the *when* and *how* of the (re)introduction of conditionality needs careful consideration and needs communicating appropriately with claimants. As evidenced in our findings, sudden shifts can destabilise those with ongoing mental health issues. However, more broadly we question (as we and many others have done previously) the effectiveness of conditionality (Dwyer et al, 2018; Scullion et al, 2019; Wright and Dwyer, 2020) given the evidence that it can be counterproductive in supporting movements towards or into paid employment.

Second, our interviews have raised questions about conceptualisations of 'family', highlighting the importance of peer networks and service support for those whose families are fractured or where there is an absence of family support. We therefore signal a need for a wider recognition of non-familial support when trying to understand how people experience, and are supported through, periods of crisis. Indeed, COVID-19 has helped us to understand which connections were most important and instrumental to participants, and what can happen when such connections are broken, even temporarily. Although we draw upon the case of veterans, we acknowledge that many of the issues highlighted in this chapter apply to *all* of those who have experienced challenges in navigating the benefits system and likewise apply to anyone who may have experienced losing vital support networks during a period of crisis.

Notes

[1] The project was funded by the Forces in Mind Trust (FiMT); www.fim-trust.org/
[2] Participants have been given pseudonyms to protect anonymity.
[3] www.afvbc.net/

References

The Centre for Social Justice (2014) *Doing our duty? Improving transitions for military leavers.* London: The Centre for Social Justice.

Daly, M. and Kelly, G. (2015) *Families and Poverty: Everyday Life on a Low Income.* Bristol: Policy Press.

Dwyer, P., Batty, E., Blenkinsopp, J., Fitzpatrick, S., Fletcher, D., Flint, J., et al (2018) *Final findings report: Welfare Conditionality Project 2013–2018.* York: Welfare Conditionality Project.

Dwyer, P., Scullion, L., Jones, K., McNeill, J. and Stewart, A.B. (2020) Work, welfare, and wellbeing: the impacts of welfare conditionality on people with mental health impairments in the UK. *Social Policy and Administration,* 54(2), 311–26.

Fossey, M., Cooper, L., Godier, L. and Cooper, A. (2017) *A pilot study to support veterans in the criminal justice system: final report.* Cambridge: Anglia Ruskin University. [Online]. Available at: www.fim-trust.org/wp-content/uploads/2017/04/Project-Nova-Report.pdf

Hynes, C. and Thomas, M. (2016) What does the literature say about the needs of veterans in the areas of health?. *Nurse Education Today,* 47, 81–8.

Hynes, C., Scullion, L., Lawler, C., Boland, P. and Steel, R. (2020) *Lives in transition: returning to civilian life with a physical injury or condition.* Preston: College for Military Veterans and Emergency Services.

Iversen, A.C., Fear, N.T., Simonoff, E., Hull, L., Horn, O., Greenberg, N., Hotopf, M., Rona, R. and Wessely, S. (2007) Influence of childhood adversity on health among male UK military personnel. *British Journal of Psychiatry,* 191, 506–11.

Johnsen, S., Jones, A. and Rugg, J. (2008) *The experience of homeless ex-service personnel in London.* York: Centre for Housing Policy.

Jones, E. and Fear, N.T. (2011) Alcohol use and misuse within the military: a review. *International Review of Psychiatry*, 23, 166–72.

Murphy, D., Ashwick, R., Palmer, E. and Busuttil, W. (2017) Describing the profile of a population of UK veterans seeking support for mental health difficulties. *Journal of Mental Health*. DOI: 10.1080/09638237.2017.1385739.

Office for Veterans' Affairs (OVA) (nd) About us. [Online]. Available at: www.gov.uk/government/organisations/office-for-veterans-affairs/about

Roberts, E., Dighton, G., Fossey, M., Hogan, L., Kitchiner, N., Rogers, R.D. and Dymond, S. (2017) *Gambling problems in UK Armed Forces veterans: preliminary findings*. [Online]. Available at: www.fim-trust.org/wp-content/uploads/2017/06/Gambling-Report-FINAL.compressed.pdf

Scullion, L. and Curchin, K. (2021) Examining veterans' interactions with the UK social security system through a trauma-informed lens. *Journal of Social Policy*, 1–18. DOI: 10.1017/S0047279420000719.

Scullion, L., Dwyer, P., Jones, K., Martin, P. and Hynes, C. (2018) *Sanctions, support and service leavers: social security benefits, welfare conditionality and transitions from military to civilian life: first wave findings*. Salford/York: University of Salford/University of York.

Scullion, L., Dwyer, P., Jones, K., Martin, P. and Hynes, C. (2019) *Sanctions, support and service leavers: social security and transitions from military to civilian life: final report*. Salford: University of Salford.

Scullion, L., Jones, K., Dwyer, P., Hynes, C. and Martin, P. (2021) Military veterans and welfare reform: bridging two policy worlds through qualitative longitudinal research. *Social Policy and Society*, 1–14. DOI: 10.1017/S1474746421000166.

Van Voorhees, E.E., Dedert, E.A., Calhoun, P.S., Branco, M., Runnels, J. and Beckham, J.C. (2012) Childhood trauma exposure in Iraq and Afghanistan war era veterans: implications for post traumatic stress disorder symptoms and adult functional social support. *Child Abuse and Neglect*, 36, 423–32.

Warren, J., Garthwaite, K. and Bambra, C. (2015) Help for heroes? Evaluating a case management programme for ex-service personnel in the United Kingdom. *Perspectives in Public Health*, 135(1), 37–42.

Work and Pensions Committee (2020) *DWP's response to the coronavirus outbreak: Government response to the committee's first report*. [Online]. Available at: https://publications.parliament.uk/pa/cm5801/cmselect/cmworpen/732/73202.htm

Wright, S. and Dwyer, P. (2020) In-work Universal Credit: claimant experiences of conditionality mismatches and counterproductive benefit sanctions. *Journal of Social Policy*. Available at: https://doi.org/10.1017/S0047279420000562

PART III

Innovating in sharing experiences during COVID-19

"Together we are making a difference": participatory research with families living on a low income during the pandemic

Geoff Page and Katie Pybus

Introduction

Almost as soon as the COVID-19 pandemic began to grip the UK, indications of its unequal impacts started to appear. Early evidence highlighted elevated morbidity and mortality from the virus in ethnically minoritised groups, elevated risks and exposure for keyworkers, and patterns of increased financial insecurity as a result of people's employment status, age, housing, income, and occupation (Institute for Fiscal Studies [IFS], 2020a; Judge and Rahman, 2020; Norman, 2020; Office for National Statistics [ONS], 2020; Public Health England [PHE], 2020). Once home schooling began, the impact on children – and their futures – quickly became apparent, as access to educational tools and resources fell along established social lines (Child Poverty Action Group [CPAG], 2020; Education Endowment Foundation, 2020). It was clear that 'the new normal' wrought by the COVID-19 pandemic had exacerbated and exposed pre-existing inequalities (IFS, 2020b; Marmot et al, 2020) and was starting to affect people in greater numbers than before. As economic shocks and uncertainty took hold, millions more people turned to the social security system for support – in just under a year (March 2020 to January 2021), for example, the number of Universal Credit (UC) claimants doubled (Department for Work and Pensions [DWP], 2021).

These troubling new social conditions emerged as Government discourse presented a more egalitarian view: that COVID-19 was a great leveller; that, like austerity, 'we are all in this together' (Nolan, 2021). It was this gap between rhetoric and reality that spurred the creation of the Covid Realities research programme. Establishing a partnership between the Universities of York and Birmingham, and working closely with the Child Poverty Action Group (CPAG), Covid Realities sought to develop a living archive of the experiences of families living on a low income during the pandemic.

A driving goal has been to understand what needs to change, and why, and to ensure that families living on a low income have a say in shaping the policies that affect them.

The mainstay of Covid Realities is a website, http://covidrealities.org. Here, parents can sign into a secure personal dashboard to write diary entries or answer themed 'Big Questions of the Week' – a weekly question posed by a member of the research team, a participant, or a guest from an external organisation. Monthly online discussion groups and arts-based activities such as zine-making provide more interactive opportunities for engagement. In the 12 months from June 2020, 172 parents from across the UK signed up, with 120 logging at least one diary entry, and 47 posting ten or more. Some participants only posted one-word or one-sentence entries, while our most prolific diarist accounted for just over a quarter of the 2,526 entries to July 2021, and a second accounted for just under a quarter of the 294,499 submitted words. Of those who entered demographic details, 93 per cent were female and 91 per cent White British[1] with an average age of 38.7 years old (range: 19–58). Over a third were in work, with a quarter unable to work due to disability. Slightly over half received UC, and 46 per cent of households in the sample had children who were eligible for free school meals.

Entries were coded through NVivo software using both inductive and deductive themes. Multiple iterations of pilot coding, team discussion, and refinement led to an agreed final framework. The sections that follow provide illustrative findings from four dominant and interconnected themes: the struggle to get by; the inadequacy of social security; the additional pressures of lockdown; and the impact of social security and poverty on parents' mental health. These themes are explored further in case studies of two participants. We conclude with participant-informed recommendations for policy change.

Key themes

Getting by

Within their diaries, families described extensive budgeting practices such as shopping carefully for reduced or lower-priced items; avoiding luxuries; planning and replanning monthly spends; buying gift cards each month where possible to save for Christmas, and calculating everything to the last penny. Still, families consistently struggled to get by, with every cost eating into social security payments that were inadequate to begin with. Coming into the pandemic, payment levels for key benefits such as UC and Employment Support Allowance were at least 9 per cent lower than they should have been if uprated according to the Consumer Price Index since 2010 (Brien et al, 2021) and the additional costs of lockdown pushed budgets to breaking point, as Erik describes:

'The money I receive has not increased in several years ... so [an increasing broadband bill] will mean even less food in the cupboard and a really tough time during the winter as I ... will not be able to afford the cost of heating our home even for a short period of time each day.' (Erik J, June 2020)

Meanwhile, as a result of restrictions, families were unable to employ some of their usual strategies to make tight budgets go further, such as visiting family and friends for meals or using charity shops to buy clothing and toys (Brewer and Patrick, 2021). With household finances already at – or beyond – their limit, there was no room for unavoidable additional expenses such as school uniforms and unpredictable costs such as car MOTs, as Alannah and Howie told us: "Anxious and financially broke, paying £310 pound for school uniform when I only receive £556 a month" (Alannah, September 2020). "[My car] is so neglected from [having] no spare cash ... that it overheated in the emissions test and damaged the water pump – they wouldn't let me drive it home" (Howie, February 2021). Families described accessing every available means of support – borrowing from family, using food banks, scouring local resources for additional support. Still, nutritious food and warm clothing were hard to sustain, and parents like Alex regularly went hungry: "Lying in bed. Tummy rumbling. Started to wait and see if daughter leaves food on plate and finish it off to save money. We finished her plate tonight" (November 2020). The struggles faced by Covid Realities families contrasted with the experiences of higher-income neighbours and acquaintances as stay-at-home rules and the rise of online engagement heightened and made social comparisons more visceral. For Gracie, her neighbours' new hot tub emphasised how little she had:

'I can't even afford a paddling pool and it's due to be 38 degrees tomorrow. My neighbours just bought a hot tub. I honestly want the thing to break in its first week. Sounds awful but I am sick to death of seeing and hearing everyone else having a marvellous time.' (August 2020)

While for Nicole's daughter, home learning drove home their poverty: "Dance teacher showing all the individual dancers videos of them dancing at home. My daughter is upset and embarrassed about our flat. The others have lovely big homes and beautiful show home furniture" (February 2021). Television and social media made comparisons still more painful, with *Scotland's Home of the Year* and "photos of sledging and snowboarding kids" driving home for Nicole that "[h]aving a decent income really makes a difference".

Evidence from Covid Realities parents and carers highlighted not only the detrimental material impact of trying to get by on a low income, but also the psychosocial effects. Poverty is stigmatising, and shame and embarrassment about social status is detrimental to wellbeing and self-esteem (Ridge, 2009; Corrigan et al, 2011; Bell, 2012). New ways of living and interacting during the pandemic may have intensified experiences of stigma and inequality.

Social security

For many Covid Realities participants, the pressures of getting by were rooted in the structure and processes of the social security system. Those who had moved on to UC both before and during the pandemic – over half of our participants – faced profound difficulties in managing the five-week 'initial assessment period', during which they received no income. Charlie, for example, spoke of how he was driven to use a food bank for the first time: "We used a food bank because of splitting from my wife ... and going from Child Tax Credits over to Universal Credit. And the six-week delay had a massive, massive impact and knock on with no money for six weeks coming in" (May 2021). This experience is not uncommon. Evidence suggests that in the 12 months after UC is rolled out in an area, there is on average a 30 per cent increase in referrals to Trussell Trust food banks (The Trussell Trust, 2019) and this statistic does not include independent food aid providers, so could represent an underestimation of the number of people in need of emergency food aid while awaiting their first UC payment.

Advance payments are available to provide financial support until first payments arrive, however these must be paid back over the following months, meaning that subsequent payments will be lower. Lexie spoke about how in order to avoid this debt, she and her family had to survive on just their Child Benefit payments each week:

'We went nearly 9 weeks trying to survive as a family of six on £60 per week, I tried desperately not to get into debt ... Luckily [the village school] were happy to start my children on free school meals, it was a little bit of relief knowing they would get at least one decent meal a day.' (January 2021)

While some finance companies provided payment holidays, and homeowners were able to take advantage of mortgage holidays to weather the financial difficulties caused by COVID-19, following a pause in the first few months of the pandemic the Government has continued to deduct debt repayments (for advances and other debts such as housing arrears) throughout the past year, leading to further hardship (see also Chapters 1 and 3). Evidence suggests in August 2020 that 41 per cent (1.85 million) of households on UC were subject to some form of debt deduction, and this rose to two thirds (63 per cent) of those who had started claiming in the first few months of the pandemic (Patrick and Lee, 2021).

Sometimes, parents transferred to UC because of erroneous advice to do so at the beginning of the pandemic (later revised). Ted reported he was told that he would retain his Child and Working Tax Credits (WTC) – and so switched to UC, only to be face unmanageable debt: "I was worried at the amount they deducted this month (£192 which leaves £864) … They said … at the time of accepting it I said I could afford [repayments], I pointed out that at the time of taking that advance … no one had told me the legacy [benefits] would stop" (October 2020). Meanwhile, policies such as the benefit cap continued throughout the pandemic, adding further pressure to households who already had little flexibility in monthly budgets. Aurora explains how the benefit cap impacted upon her and her family: "We are capped on UC. I'm a widowed parent of two primary-aged children. Our rent alone is over 95 per cent of our total benefits" (October 2020). The £20 uplift applied to WTC and UC in April 2020 provided a welcome boost to households, though frequently served only to cover pre-existing deficits in monthly budgets. A series of temporary extensions to the uplift generated uncertainty among those households who received this and at the time of writing, the uplift will stop altogether in October 2021. Many Covid Realities participants did not benefit from the extra £20 per week at all because they were in receipt of legacy benefits. Applying the uplift to some benefits but not others has created a two-tiered system of deservingness that leaves behind legacy benefit claimants, the majority of whom may have health conditions and disabilities, or who are carers (Cameron, 2021).

Locked down, locked in: compounded pressure

The stresses and strains caused by the struggle of getting by and the social security system were exacerbated by stay-at-home restrictions. Both school and structured work ended for many, bringing new financial pressures and new dynamics at home, as Lexie explains: "The new lockdown means more meals to find to keep them full, more stress of trying to become one teacher between four kids all in different age groups, just more worry" (Lexie, January 2021). Although the first summer of the pandemic brought opportunities to spend time outdoors and to reconnect as a family, the stigma and restrictions of poverty were again thrown into sharp relief when pubs and restaurants reopened in August. Schemes such as 'Eat Out to Help Out' were inaccessible to families without disposable income and did little to help with feelings of shame and exclusion. As summer turned into winter, and nights became colder and longer with few resources for entertainment and little prospect of escape or relief, a grinding sense of monotony set in. Deb reflected: "Every day is the same. Nowhere to go. Nothing is exciting any more like things used to be. Feel trapped inside" (November 2020). While Callie described feeling like a "zombie" through the seemingly endless "groundhog day of isolation and house imprisonment" (April 2021). In this context, possibilities for escape gained heightened significance but commonly experiences simply served to emphasise the inescapability of lockdown and of poverty. Connie planned a brief break, only for a burst bubble to render this impossible:

'We were meant to be away for three nights in my parents' new caravan. Unfortunately my eldest was sent home to self-isolate for 14 days from school so we are unable to go ... I am feeling incredibly fed up ... So many people still seem to be going out and enjoying fun experiences but I don't feel able to do that.' (October 2020)

The grinding budgets, inadequate social security payments, and the compressed tension of lockdown had consequences. By the end of March 2021, one in three Covid Realities diary entries made reference to some aspect(s) of mental health – predominantly anxiety and low mood.

Mental health

The uneven distribution of mental illness in society is well-documented, with those in the most deprived fifth of households two to three times more likely to suffer mental ill health than those in the top fifth (Marmot et al, 2010; Mental Health Foundation, 2021) – inequalities that have been exacerbated by lockdown (NatCen 2021; Royal College of Psychiatrists, 2021). In Covid Realities, we saw the immediate anxieties at the beginning of the pandemic give way to chronic stresses and worries over time. Regularly, poor mental health was tied to living conditions. For Callie, it was the constant struggle of balancing inadequate income with her children's needs: "I'm so anxious and depressed, I've never felt this bad. I was put on antidepressants last week by my GP over all the stress and worries I have over feeding and clothing my children and keeping the heating and lights on. I'm in despair, it's desperate" (December 2020). Indeed, throughout parents' accounts was a sense of the vulnerability of life at the margins. Families with few resources were exposed to constant stress, with lockdown removing coping and support mechanisms. Participants longed for the potential to laugh, relax, and talk through problems in healing face-to-face chats. Many also missed the rewards and comforts of physical touch, as described by May: "Apart from my seven-year-old I haven't had a hug or hugged anyone since March. Just thinking about that makes me feel low" (November 2020). For a subset of women, past experiences of domestic abuse exacerbated the pains of lockdown and compounded existing trauma.

As Meg describes, forced confinement echoed her abuser's strategies: "My son's dad would lock me in the house to prevent me from leaving when I felt under threat from him. Now [going out] is prohibited and I'm finding that aspect hard – it has definitely affected my mental health negatively, despite already taking long-term antidepressants" (June 2020). The social security system frequently added to the stresses and strains of getting by on a low-income through inadequate payments and uncertainty about the future (Pybus et al, 2021). Decision-making around the continuation of the £20 uplift, for example, left families feeling precarious – Winter O, told us: "The proposed change [removing £20 uplift] is the difference between paying our bills and not being able to pay some of them. And if one-off expenses crop up (like new shoes for kids etc) then you can't cover it. Any changes to benefits are very stressful" (January 2021). Perhaps unsurprisingly, lone parents often felt particularly alone with their struggles (see also Chapter 8 in this collection). Participants told us that taking part in Covid Realities, in a small way, helped to reduce some of these feelings of isolation. As well as the research and policy engagement functions of the project, parents and carers reflected that taking part in online discussion groups and arts-based workshops had provided a space to connect and to meet others going through similar experiences, so improving wellbeing:

'It feels like a community. Hearing other people's life experiences and thoughts and opinions is helpful. Knowing other people are going through similar to you makes you feel like you are not alone. Knowing we're trying to make a difference between us to everyone's lives is also empowering! Together we are making a difference.' (Isla F, March 2021)

Alex and Victoria

Echoing several chapters throughout this collection, Covid Realities speaks to the feminisation of poverty (for example Chant, 2007; 2008; see also discussion in Lister, 2020). It may be in part an artefact of online diary methods, but 13 in every 14 participants were female; two thirds were parenting alone.[2] Sole parenting *and* domestic abuse played significant roles in many of our participants' pathways into poverty, and Alex and Victoria's sharp choice between financial security and terrifying (male) violence stood as a powerful indicator of gendered dynamics. Strikingly, drawing on Luxembourg Income Study (LIS) data, Hakitova et al (2019) estimate that 60 per cent of all lone parent families in the UK could be lifted out of poverty by adequate child maintenance payments (Hakitova et al, 2019: 16).

To highlight this, we now show how the themes developed so far played out in gendered ways within the lives of two women who took part in Covid Realities. Alex is a single mother in Scotland, with a daughter recently diagnosed with autism. Victoria is a lone parent in the North of England with two children with additional needs. Each engaged with Covid Realities for their own reasons. Victoria wanted to be a part of history, and to speak to future generations:

'To the future people who read this study, who read about the plights of us low-income families, know that I thank you for taking time to look back on our nation's past. And heed this: learn from our mistakes. Value your undervalued. Prioritise potential over tax ability. How many minds are wasted in the drains of societies?' (July 2020)

Victoria attended a wide range of participatory events available to Covid Realities participants, and was keen to drive social change. Alex engaged with Covid Realities for different reasons – finding a space to offload, free of judgement: "[In my diary] I can say exactly how I feel without others dismissing/calling me depressing/negative/bitter" (March 2021). Alex's engagement was one-way. She shared how she was feeling almost every day, but – almost uniquely – provided no functional email address and participated in no interactive activities.

Alex and Victoria had different early lockdown experiences. Victoria had always home schooled her children, easing the transition. However, aware of her own health conditions, Victoria watched with concern as others passed her house without masks and ignored social distancing. Adding to her fears of the virus itself were fears for her children's future: "I learnt this weekend that if I catch the virus and die ... my kids would 'most likely be sent to their father' ... The man who'd hit my daughter anytime she spoke without permission ... If I die, my kids go to him? I'm horrified" (July 2020). For Victoria, COVID-19 presented new existential threats. Nonetheless, Victoria got on with her neighbours and as time progressed, they supported and helped one another. Alex's difficulties were more compressed, as early lockdown blended into her bullied daughter's withdrawal from school and even greater isolation set in. From the outset, Alex distrusted government and media messages and engaged with conspiracy theories. As time progressed, her posts became less extreme but her anxiety did not: "Sleepless night with anxiety. Tear streaming down my face this morning. This Corona madness needs to stop now. Stop the media's daily count and scaremongering" (November 2021). For Alex, lockdown meant being at home with an autistic daughter, with abundant anxiety arising from their circumstances and compounded by her understanding of the world. Both women struggled with daily costs, describing their difficulties through food. For Alex, it was watching her daughter's plate and finishing what little food she left, and the indignity of being reliant on a food bank: "I am aware of food banks. I walk to them and feel the humiliation knowing the father of my child is living in luxury as a businessman taking his pick from takeaway menus or eating out to help out. Not a penny for our child" (December 2020). Both women also associated their precarity with abuse. Financial security had meant physical and emotional danger; now they were physically safe, their finances were much more precarious. Victoria describes:

'I knew when I left my ex that I was making a choice between living in hell with him or living in relative poverty without him, I chose the latter cos at least my kids would be safe from abuse on benefits. But it's a shitty choice … Hunger or assault. A poor example of living, or the daily risk of death.' (March 2021)

Abuse remained a persistent companion for both. Alex's ex-partner refused to pay child maintenance, and she saw the Child Maintenance Service's failure to help as sustained abuse from an uncaring, patriarchal government. Victoria's memories of abuse were triggered by her experiences of the (controlling, dominant, and seemingly punitive) social security system: "Just thinking about it, about having to go to the job centre again and be approved the money needed to feed my kids for another month, makes me feel physically sick, dizzy and clammy. It's a very unhealthy environment for anyone, let alone abuse survivors" (May 2021). For Alex and Victoria, life before lockdown had been tough, but manageable. However, lockdown brought with it new challenges – new precarity, new fears of ill health, new reminders of old trauma – rooted in gendered inequalities, and greatly increasing their sense of vulnerability and exposure.

Implications of this work for policy

As qualitative, diary-based research, Covid Realities has been well positioned to capture rich insights into the daily lives and experiences of families on a low income as the pandemic has unfolded. These experiences point to one clear message: that the social security system is failing families. Moreover, the inadequacies within the system have been greatly exacerbated by the pandemic (Brewer and Gardiner, 2020; CPAG, 2020; Trades Union Congress [TUC], 2020). It is clear that we are not 'all in it together' (Nolan, 2021); rather, pre-existing social inequalities have been hardened by social security structures that force families into hard, swift decisions between debt and hunger, and that make it incredibly difficult to escape.

There have been some positives during the pandemic, as we also see in Chapters 6, 8, and 9. At a time when families found themselves in dire need of support, significant new steps were taken – an uplift of £20 UC for some, a pause in conditionality, and the suspension of the minimum income floor (for example Brewer and Handscombe, 2020: 7; Joseph

Rowntree Foundation, 2020). Social security administration processes coped effectively despite 2.3 million households initiating a UC claim in the first eight weeks of lockdown alone (Mackley, 2021 :3). Nonetheless, despite extensive budgeting and financial management strategies (see Brewer and Patrick, 2021), our families had nothing to spare. They had no surplus for emergencies, no buffer to keep the car going, no capacity to absorb the costs of utilities. The £20 uplift was barely noticed by our families, because provision still fell so far short of adequately covering the basics: food, clothing, and utilities. Contrastingly, its end was widely feared because it threatened harder times still.

Nor has the policy response adequately addressed the particular needs of families. Having children meant home schooling; home schooling added meals, heating, materials, and entertainment to family costs (Brewer and Patrick, 2021). The cost of school uniforms also represented a unique burden on families, compelling some to choose between heating, eating, or a new school blazer (Page et al, 2021). Lockdown – and home schooling – then added disproportionately to the stresses and strains of family life. Parents had no option but to become teachers, counsellors, and constant companions to children who were themselves enduring a generational event. The stress of doing this within small houses and flats, sometimes without access to outside space, was severe. Our participants were clear about the harmful impact on their mental health and about the causes of this: inadequate food, inadequate heating, inadequate clothing, inadequate housing, and an inability to prosper, thrive, or adequately feed their children left them struggling with low mood and persistent stress and anxiety – key themes also highlighted by Cameron et al in Chapter 6.

For the families who signed up to Covid Realities, life was hard before COVID-19 arrived. Years before the pandemic, Meg lost nearly everything when chronic disability and domestic abuse changed her life:

'Before I was swept into poverty due to circumstances beyond my control, I was in full-time employment in the NHS, I was married with children, I was buying my own home with my husband via a mortgage, I was studying for a degree and I was doing all of those things.'

Through hearing directly from parents and carers such as Meg, Covid Realities research has been able to reframe and challenge harmful, negative stereotypes about poverty and has highlighted just some of the myriad different circumstances by which people may find themselves experiencing poverty and accessing social security. Traditional accounts of stigma often foreground the passivity of those who are stigmatised, but people can and do challenge negative stereotypes if given the space to do so (Thoits, 2011).

At the heart of Covid Realities has been a belief that policies should be developed in partnership with people who have lived experience. Social security can – and we would argue should – have a protective impact. With adequate benefits, predictable payments, and robust processes the welfare system could be a tremendous resource for resilience – particularly at times of crisis. To this end, some policy recommendations are clear. Firstly, social security should enable a decent, basic standard of life that accounts for the significant additional needs of families with children. Secondly, this level of support should be available when claims are first initiated – processes that begin with a hard choice between indebtedness or starvation cannot be fit for purpose. Thirdly, this level of support should be available for all; that some support measures, such as the £20 uplift, was only applied to some benefits creates additional inequities within an already unjust system.

Through Covid Realities, parents and carers have communicated directly with politicians, the media, and the public, to generate greater understanding about poverty and social security, as well as what needs to change and why. In doing so, Covid Realities has also demonstrated the inadequacy of our current safety net for supporting families and provided a space for resistance. As we move forward through the pandemic, Covid Realities participants will continue to engage with policymakers and their stories will act as a living archive for researchers and the public, both now and in the future.

Notes

[1] This may be an overestimation – through the Big Ideas Groups we know of several non-White and asylum-seeking participants who did not provide any demographic information.

[2] Male partners were also very rarely mentioned by diarists who identified as partnered or married.

References

Bell, K. (2012) Poverty, social security and stigma. [Online]. Available at: https://cpag.org.uk/sites/default/files/CPAG-Povertyarticle-stigma-0213.pdf

Brewer, M. and Gardiner, L. (2020) Return to spender: findings on family incomes and spending from the Resolution Foundation's Coronavirus Survey. London: Resolution Foundation.

Brewer, M. and Handscombe, K. (2020) This time is different – Universal Credit's first recession: assessing the welfare system and its effect on living standards during the Coronavirus epidemic. London: Resolution Foundation.

Brewer, M. and Patrick, R. (2021) Pandemic pressures: why families on a low income are spending more during Covid-19. London: Resolution Foundation.

Brien, S., Emmerson, C., Tetlow, G. and Timmins, N. (2021) Social security advisory committee independent report. Jobs and benefits: the COVID-19 challenge. Available at: www.gov.uk/government/publications/jobs-and-benefits-the-covid-19-challenge/jobs-and-benefits-the-covid-19-challenge

Cameron, C. (2021) More please, for those with less: why we need to go further on the Universal Credit uplift. [Online]. Available at: https://blogs.lse.ac.uk/politicsandpolicy/covid-realities-uc/

Chant, S.H. (2007) Female household headship and the feminisation of poverty: facts, fictions and forward strategies. [Online]. Available at: http://eprints.lse.ac.uk/574/1/femaleHouseholdHeadship.pdf

Chant, S.H. (2008) The 'feminisation of poverty' and the 'feminisation of anti-poverty programmes'. Room for revision? *Journal of Development Studies*, 44(2), 165–97.

Child Poverty Action Group (CPAG) (2020) Mind the gaps – Briefing 8. Available at: https://cpag.org.uk/sites/default/files/files/policypost/CPAG-mind-the-gaps-briefing-26-Jun.pdf

Corrigan, P.W., Rafacz, J. and Rüsch, N. (2011) Examining a progressive model of self-stigma and its impact on people with serious mental illness. *Psychiatry Research*, 189(3), 339–43.

Department for Work and Pensions (DWP) (2021) Universal Credit statistics. 29 April 2013 to 14 January 2021. Available at: www.gov.uk/government/statistics/universal-credit-statistics-29-april2013-to-14-january-2021/universal-credit-statistics-29-april-2013-to-14-january2021

Education Endowment Foundation (2020) Impact of school closures on the attainment gap: rapid evidence assessment. London: EEF.

Hakitova, M., Skinner, C., Hiilamo, H. and Jokela, M. (2019) Child poverty, child maintenance and interactions with social assistance benefits among lone parent families. A comparative analysis. *Journal of Social Policy*, 49(1), 19–39.

Health England (2020) Beyond the data. Understanding the impact of COVID-19 on BAME groups. London: PHE.

Institute for Fiscal Studies (IFS) (2020a) COVID-19 and inequalities. London: IFS and Nuffield Foundation.

Institute for Fiscal Studies (IFS) and Nuffield Foundation (2020b) The idiosyncratic impact of an aggregate shock: the distributional consequences of COVID-19. London: IFS.

Joseph Rowntree Foundation (2020) Briefing: Autumn Budget – why we must keep the £20 social security lifeline. Available at: www.jrf.org.uk/report/autumn-budget-why-we-must-keep-20- social-security-lifeline

Judge, L. and Rahman, F. (2020) Lockdown living: housing quality across the generations. London: Resolution Foundation.

Lister, R. (2020) *Poverty*. Cambridge: Polity Press.

Mackley, A. (2021) Coronavirus: Universal Credit during the crisis. London: House of Commons Library. Available at: https://researchbriefings. files.parliament.uk/documents/CBP-8999/CBP-8999.pdf

Marmot, M., Allen, J., Boyce, T., Goldblatt, P. and Morrison, J. (2020) Health equity in England. The Marmot Review 10 years on. London: Institute for Health Equity.

Marmot, M., Allen, J., Goldblatt, P., Boyce, T., McNeish, D., Grady, M. and Geddes, I. (2010) Fair society, healthy lives: strategic review of health inequalities in England post 2010. Available at: www. instituteofhealthequity.org/resources-reports/fair-society-healthy-lives-the-marmot-reviewMental Health Foundation (2021) Mental health statistics: poverty. Available at: www.mentalhealth.org.uk/statistics/ mental-health-statistics-poverty

NatCen (2021) Society Watch 2021: Mental health, should we be worried? [Online]. Available at: www.natcen.ac.uk/media/2050456/Society-Watch-2021-Mental- Health-Should-We-Be-Worried.pdf

Nolan, R. (2021) 'We are all in this together!' Covid-19 and the lie of solidarity. *Irish Journal of Sociology*, 29(1), 102–06.

Norman, J. (2020) *Gender and COVID-19. The immediate impact the crisis is having on women*. London: LSE and online. Available at: http://eprints.lse. ac.uk/104638/1/politicsandpolicy_gender_and_covid_19.pdf

Office for National Statistics (2020) *Coronavirus (COVID-19) related deaths by occupation, England and Wales*. London: ONS and online. Available at: www.ons.gov.uk/peoplepopulationandcommunity/healthandsocialcare/ causesofdeath/datasets/coronaviru scovid19relateddeathsbyoccupationeng landandwales

Page, G., Power, M. and Patrick, R. (2021) Uniform mistakes: the costs of going back to school. [Online]. Available at: https://media.covidrealities. org/CovidRealities-UniformMistakes.pdf?v3

Patrick, R. and Lee, T. (2021) Advance to debt. Paying back benefit debt: what happens when deductions are made to benefit payments? Available at: https://media.covidrealities.org/COVID%20realities%20-%20Advance%20to%20debt%2022%20Dec.pdfPublic

Pybus, K., Wickham, S., Page, G., Power, M., Barr, B. and Patrick, R. (2021) 'How do I make something out of nothing?': Universal Credit, precarity and mental health. Covid Realities rapid response report. Available at: https://covidrealities.org/learnings/write-ups/ universal-credit-precarity-and-mental-health

Ridge, T. (2009) Living with poverty: a review of the literature on children's and families' experiences of poverty. Department for Work and Pensions Research Report No. 594. [Online]. Available at: www.bris.ac.uk/poverty/ downloads/keyofficialdocuments/Child%20Poverty%20lit%20review%20 DWP.pdf

Royal College of Psychiatrists (2021) Country in the grip of a mental health crisis with children worst affected, new analysis finds. Available at: www.rcpsych.ac.uk/news-and-features/latest- news/detail/2021/04/08/country-in-the-grip-of-a-mental-health-crisis-with- children-worst-affected-new-analysis-finds

Thoits, P. (2011) Resisting the stigma of mental illness. *Social Psychology Quarterly*, 74(1), 6–28.

The Trussell Trust (2019) Five weeks too long: why we need to end the wait for Universal Credit. [Online]. Available at: www.trusselltrust.org/wp-content/uploads/sites/2/2019/09/PolicyReport_Final_ForWeb.pdf

TUC (2020) Our social security net is failing during the COVID-19 crisis. Available at: www.tuc.org.uk/blogs/our-social-security-net-failing-during-covid-19-crisis

12

Living through a pandemic: researching families on a low income in Scotland – findings and research reflections

Beth Cloughton, Fiona McHardy, and Laura Robertson

Introduction

Get Heard Scotland[1] (GHS) is a programme led by The Poverty Alliance[2] and funded by the Scottish Government. GHS helps people on low incomes to have their voices heard on the policies and decisions that most impact their lives and communities. GHS aims to ensure that efforts to meet Scotland's child poverty reduction targets[3] are shaped by the participation and voices of households experiencing poverty and those working to tackle poverty within localities. The Poverty Alliance coordinates GHS based on the commitments made by the Scottish Government's Every child, every chance: child poverty delivery plan (2018–2022) (Scottish Government, 2018). The Scottish Government publishes annual reports on the progress of the delivery plan which the work of GHS has fed directly into.

This chapter examines the final stages of GHS, which focuses on low-income families' experiences of the pandemic. GHS captured some of the emerging impacts of COVID-19 on low-income families as well as on third sector and community organisations in the local authorities of Inverclyde and Renfrewshire.[4] Discussions with organisations delivering front line services across the local authorities were facilitated between August and October 2020 (The Poverty Alliance, 2020; 2021). Follow-on qualitative research was then conducted with families experiencing poverty between October 2020 and March 2021, with a focus on the family groups identified as key priority targets by the Scottish Government.[5]

The neighbouring local authorities of Inverclyde and Renfrewshire have differing levels of child poverty. Evidence from the Scottish Index of Multiple Deprivation (SIMD) indicates 45 per cent of data zones in Inverclyde are among the 20 per cent most deprived areas in Scotland (Scottish Government, 2020a). Renfrewshire has seen a fall in its levels of deprivation since 2016 (Scottish Government, 2020a), but wider analysis undertaken by Loughborough University in 2020, on behalf of the End

Child Poverty Coalition (2021), found rising levels of child poverty in Renfrewshire, with an additional 900 households now experiencing child poverty – a 3.8 per cent increase.

This chapter outlines findings of family experiences in Scotland,[6] on social security, mental health, and digital exclusion. As this research attests, the pandemic ushered in a host of new pressures over a condensed period of time, including: impacts on caring responsibilities, changing experiences in the workplace, and altered delivery of a range of voluntary and statutory support services. A clear message has emerged on the depth of challenges households have faced and the need for targeted and widespread measures to mitigate the impacts. Moving forward, there is a need to address underlying poverty and inequality and avoid people being locked into long-term poverty.

Methodological reflections

GHS was designed to gather rich insights into the daily realities of low-income family life. We thus adopted a qualitative approach which underwent a rapid re-design due to the constraints of COVID-19. Originally, the research engaged participants through a variety of in-person approaches – methods like focus groups and toolkits for a range of community groups – to co-deliver the aims of the inquiry themselves. While this became impossible, the restrictions presented new opportunities to develop digital capabilities in the research team, by expanding our repertoire to telephone and Zoom interviews and digital diaries. The restrictions also helped the research team to recognise different modalities of participation, ethics, and their relationship to low-income family life.

While the digitalisation of our research allowed a portal into the lives of people who were isolated because of lockdown, we recognised a new barrier to participation as a consequence of prevalent digital and data exclusion for those in Scotland living in poverty (Halliday, 2020).

Approach

GHS revolved around the core values of The Poverty Alliance: care and justice. These two principles are embedded in all our work which aims to combat poverty. Adhering to the principles of a feminist ethics of care (Hall, 2019) equipped us with a critical perspective on the intersecting and dynamic nature of poverty, which disproportionately affects particular groups of people. Justice is our second central value; experiences of social inequalities are often overlooked as critical insights with which to create just policy decisions. Considering this, we followed in the canon of disability studies – 'nothing about us without us' – making recommendations to the

Ending Child Poverty Delivery Plan for Scottish Government that are directly informed by what families have told us.

Our approach was neither discrete nor individualised in form; as a team and organisation we worked collaboratively so as not to repeat existing research, but also to draw upon on the skills of a range of stakeholders. GHS traversed the sectors of Government, local authorities, the third sector, and individuals with lived experiences: the landscape of this research therefore consists of multiple scales, sectors, experiences, and insights.

Methods

Our methods toolkit consisted of structured digital interviews, conducted via either Zoom or mobile phone, and digital diaries. The digital diaries were an enhanced version of the interview guide, to maintain consistency in the final stage of GHS responses. We allocated approximately 45 minutes for interviewing, although the duration exceeded this with almost every participant speaking to the potential therapeutic element within interviewing (Birch and Miller, 2010) at a time of heightened isolation: "I feel a bit relieved as well speaking about this, you know?" (Interview: single mother with two children). This finding, while beyond the remit of the primary research question, is critical in highlighting the importance of a flexible, sensitive research design which facilitates a safe space to express emotions, and the necessity for advocates of justice in positions of influence to listen.

For the Zoom-facilitated interviews, we noticed through reflective notes that there was a shared level of spatial exposure with both researcher and participant having 'real' backgrounds as opposed to augmented realities. This changing spatiality of research accentuated potentially unnoticed aspects within the interviewing process: the domestic space as the background where research takes place has the potential to bring with it vulnerability and exposure, as well as a shared intimacy.

Recruitment and safeguarding

The recognised prevalence of digital exclusion made GHS think creatively about how we could recruit a range of identities and experiences in order to avoid presenting a homogenous or stereotyped case. Our focus was on capturing experiences from the six priority groups for combatting child poverty, and so we worked with our developed networks throughout the two local authorities to ensure both wide participant-reach and a level of safeguarding. Working in this way meant we were able to widely disseminate the opportunity to participate and raise awareness of our continuing lived experience work of the Community Activist Advisory Group (CAAG).[7]

CAAG runs as a permanent participative structure at The Poverty Alliance and was highlighted as a continuation of involvement to avoid participants feeling like they were left in the research 'spaces' post-interview. Using existing organisational relationships was a way of contributing to a sustainable research participation culture.

A safe and ethical research practice was a fundamental concern throughout GHS. The pandemic exacerbated many already-existing problems and introduced novel issues, like home-schooling and additional caring responsibilities with reduced service provision. Alongside working with organisations who recommended participants, we also developed a 'chat pack' which was delivered by priority post to all participants. This contained a local authority-specific support document listing freephone numbers of over 30 services, a notebook, pens, teabags, and information about The Poverty Alliance to help demystify the 'who' behind the research.

Within the research team, staff underwent training in safeguarding and suicide awareness. Unfortunately, this training became immediately essential, with a higher rate of social care referrals made and safety protocols actioned, compared to previous projects. Not only that, but we were mindful of 'living at work' and the reduced movement of researchers between spaces where interviews take place and the domestic home. To address this, the team had weekly overview debriefs, and a culture of work-life balance was emphasised.

Analysis

Our analysis consisted of two iterative levels; the first was our primary community researcher thematically drawing out data using the software Dedoose. In line with the principles of qualitative inquiry, we thematically coded our data to highlight nuances and richness within the large data set. Our first round of analysis grouped over 1,000 pages of data into five broad, key themes and several minor, though noteworthy, topics (for example, urban green space). Once this initial round was completed, we organised six co-analysis sessions with participants who had consented to be contacted for future opportunities and were both able and wanted to participate. These co-analysis sessions formed the basis of a structured analytical conversation whereby participants went through the key themes and presented recommendations to what was highlighted. In this way, we adopted a model of co-production for analysing the data and for generating recommendations from the preliminary findings.

Findings and para-data[8]

The data gathered from how we remunerate participants who have shared their experiences (in ways that do not affect access to benefits) resulted in vouchers, either emailed or posted, of each participant's choosing. A large majority decided on supermarkets, which we saw as a reflection of the high levels of food insecurity in areas with high deprivation.

A temporal dimension of the para-data was in the 'ending' of the research. Concluding research is a complex terrain, especially in a short-term, digitally conducted design. However, without proper consideration, people who tend to be over-consulted, over-promised, and underwhelmed by conclusive actions (for example, those living in low-income households), means attention must be paid to how we expand the scope of involvement beyond the discrete conversation.

Looking inwards, reflective notes highlighted the importance of an empathetic, supportive work culture; the position of researcher is often sidelined in considerations around secondary or vicarious trauma (Pascoe Leahy, 2021) as is the impact of home-working on those conducting research. Reflective diary entries from our research team noted that the interview exists both prior to and beyond the actual interviewing conversation itself. In explicitly acknowledging the messy, emotional journey of conducting research, we demystify the actual process of 'doing' research itself that more accurately reflects the affective nature of research more than the sanitised, linear article form.

Challenges

Like many researchers during the pandemic, there were a plethora of challenges to think through, some of which did not have neat conclusions. Of note was increased vulnerabilities and risk: it was difficult to assess risk over a single phone call and some emails or texts. There was an increase in the amount of care referrals the research team made, due to our limited ability to assess risk and participants' contexts, and wanting to ensure everyone was accessing appropriate care, coupled with the increased vulnerabilities exacerbated by the pandemic. In addition, there were personal challenges to conducting research; care had to be taken to protect researchers who were also struggling with pandemic life (see also Introduction and Chapter 14).

Additionally, we found representation a challenge (an issue prevalent in much work with marginalised groups). Our work only captures a partial depiction of who we spoke with (see also Chapter 11). Therefore, we must reflect upon how participation is political, especially in the age of digital. It also challenges the use of the terms 'hidden' or 'hard to reach' communities, by placing responsibility on those in positions of power to ensure research is accessible (see Chapters 11, 13, and 14). We recognise, however, the precarity and often short-term and competitive nature of funding streams that do not necessarily facilitate access to marginalised communities. We welcome further attention to this issue underlying research projects.

Families' experiences of social security during the pandemic

Since social security powers were devolved to Scotland in 2016, a range of new benefits have been introduced for low-income families. The underpinning principles of the new social security system in Scotland were outlined in the *Social Security Charter* as 'dignity, fairness and respect' (Scottish Government, 2019). For families, new benefits include the Best Start Grant (three one-off payments for children under the age of five introduced from 2018) and the Scottish Child Payment (a weekly payment of £10 for each child under the age of six introduced in early 2021, that increased to £20 a week from April 2022). However, Universal Credit (UC) and Jobseeker's Allowance (JSA), the key working-age benefits in the UK, continue to be delivered by the Department for Work and Pensions.

The experiences of the families we spoke to add to the substantial evidence base that UC does not provide an adequate level of income for families and propels claimants into debt (Maddison, 2020; Patrick and Simpson with UC:Us, 2020). Families frequently told us that the money they received through UC was not enough to get them through the month. The impacts of UC deductions in particular make managing family budgets difficult (see also Chapters 3 and 11).

While families welcomed the £20 a week uplift to UC that was introduced in April 2020, many parents reported that this was quickly consumed by increased costs of bills and food during the pandemic. For families on low incomes, finances have become increasingly stretched due to the additional threat of unemployment, furlough, and the extra costs of staying at home (Save the Children, 2021). Anxiety over how families would manage budgets when the uplift ends (September 2021 at the time of writing) was common. Parents were also worried about how they would explain to their children that they had less money to be able to do things as a family: "it's been a lifesaver to just have an extra £20 come in. And it's sad to think that £20 changes ... changes your life, but it really does" (Interview: single mother with one child). Families frequently spoke of the inadequacy of UC, with many sharing their experiences of having to access emergency funds. Reflecting variable policies across nations, the Scottish Welfare Fund (SWF) was introduced by the Scottish Government in 2013. In contrast to England, where the local welfare assistance fund is not ring-fenced and support is no longer available through grants in many local authorities (Whitham, 2018), the SWF provides immediate financial support through crisis grants. During the height of the pandemic, the Scottish Government added an additional £22 million to the SWF as well as introducing a Self-Isolation Support Grant of £500. Several of the families interviewed as part of GHS had applied to the SWF. However, mirroring findings from the Menu for Change project (MacLeod, 2019) which examined food insecurity in Scotland, we found that applicants to the SWF were being limited to a maximum of three applications in a 12-month period, despite regulations allowing local authorities to use their discretion to allow more than three awards in *exceptional circumstances* (Scottish Government, 2021): "They do have the Welfare Fund but getting that is like trying to get blood oot [out] of a stone" (Interview: single dad with two children). Limited access to state support is concerning, particularly as many of the families we spoke to had to rely on family and friends for access to adequate financial support; this was also clear in Chapters 1 and 8 in particular. Feelings of embarrassment and anxiety were evident across interviewees' accounts in relation to access to financial support.

The introduction of the Scottish Child Payment has been a key policy development in terms of both tackling child poverty and social security reform in Scotland. From February 2021, eligible families have received £10 a week for each child under six, which rose to £20 a week in April 2022, with the Scottish Government committing to roll out the payment to families with children under the age of 16 by the end of 2022 (Sinclair, 2021). In GHS research, families who had started receiving this payment spoke of the benefits of the extra income on their financial circumstances and welcomed its extension to children under 16: "Obviously shopping-wise, as soon as I was receiving that money, then I was just going out and buying more shopping so that there was more stuff in for them" (Single mother with three children). At the time of writing, modelling by the Fraser of Allander Institute and the Joseph Rowntree Foundation has shown that the Scottish Child Payment would need to be raised to £20 a week for the Scottish Government to meet their 2024 and 2030 child poverty targets (Scottish Poverty and Inequality Commission, 2021). While the Scottish National Party has committed to doubling the Scottish Child Payment by the end of this parliamentary term (2026), a coalition of 120 anti-poverty organisations have called for an urgent doubling of the payment, with concerns that the end of the UC uplift will further propel families into poverty (Davidson, 2021).

Families' experiences of mental health

The pandemic and resulting lockdown measures in March 2020 brought significant life changes to families both across the UK and beyond. The World Health Organization predicted the pandemic quarantine and the related disruption to households' routines, activities, and livelihoods would result in increased levels of loneliness, depression, harmful alcohol and drug use, and self-harm or suicidal behaviour (World Health Organization [WHO], 2020). Similarly, within our study, families reported loneliness, depression, and anxiety within their household (see also Chapters 1, 3, 5, 6, 7, 8, 9, 10, and 11).

The nature of the crisis resulted in changes to households at very short notice, and families had little opportunity to prepare or adapt to the forthcoming challenges they would face. Families had to navigate several simultaneous challenges including the risk of contracting COVID-19 or dealing with infection alongside the rewriting of their everyday lives because of the restrictions. The psychosocial impacts of the pandemic cannot yet be fully understood; however, pre-existing socio-economic inequalities have been exacerbated and intensified in this new context, as we see across this collection (British Academy, 2021). The impact of the pandemic on mental health and wellbeing has been unprecedented with the full effects still unknown and service provision likely to be permanently changed (Tarrant et al, 2021). Alongside this, there has been an intensification of pre-existing mental health conditions and new mental health impacts for all, including children and young people (see also Chapter 5).

Evidence from the Get Heard research suggests that the experience of mental ill-health has been common among families experiencing poverty both pre- and during the pandemic. The rapid pace of change following the first lockdown and the waves of restrictions that followed limited participants' feelings of control over their daily lives and brought about a loss of daily structure and routine. This was interwoven with a range of new expectations for parents and caregivers emerging from lockdown measures: increased caring responsibilities, facilitating home schooling, online delivery of further education, and changes within employment including personal risks of exposure to COVID-19. The unexpected nature of the pandemic left households unprepared and confused. This confusion was experienced across families, including by children and young people: "Naebody knew this was gonna happen. So the fact that there's nothing in place makes you wonder, why is there nothing in place? But at the same time, you're like, well, naebody ever knew this was gonna happen, so don't – it's like 50/50" (Interview: single father of two children). Household experiences were circumstantial and shaped by a complex variety of access to resources including support networks, access to formal support, and pandemic impacts on their individual circumstances; for example, family size, pre-existing health conditions, and disabilities. Lockdown measures resulted in reduced or no social contact with family and friends, limited ability to engage in everyday activities for children, and in some cases, confinement to a house that did not meet adequate housing standards. A key challenge for families was the loss of childcare and family support by relatives resulting in isolation (see also Chapters 1 and 6).

As mental health impacts increased, support services to assist with mental health were in flux and had to pivot rapidly to a digital offer, as well as telephone models of support (see also Chapter 9). The options for support were often restricted to the home space rather than an in-person therapeutic space. This pivot, however, resulted in unintended barriers for low-income families, such as childcare, time and freedom to talk confidentiality, as well as digital access barriers. 'Invisible' barriers such as stigma around disclosing mental ill health were also discussed. The loss of respite care imposed particular pressures on families where disabilities or health conditions were present:

> 'All his support just boomf, went away and we have been left from social work, from his respite, literally everything went. We've had no support from any of them. We tried getting him back into a school provision and we were told no. We tried to get him extra support through social work, we were told, "Sorry, can't do anything."' (Interview: partnered mother with two children)

Families also discussed the 'compounding' of mental ill health across the household, including among children and young people who experienced increased stress with loss of daily routines and interactions. This combined with losing both informal and formal support. Households saw the loss of protective buffers such as family support networks which were pivotal in avoiding isolation and stress. Households discussed worries specific to the pandemic for those shielding or for those with experience of contracting COVID-19 directly and long COVID. There were the big 'unknowns' such as the changing labour market and impacts on the economy long term as well as wider structural service changes. In combination, these created a perfect storm for worsening mental health. Alongside the broader impact of poverty, there was a clear relationship between feelings of shame and the precariousness of living on a low income which intensified during this time. This resulted from feelings of being unable to adequately meet daily needs within households. For those in the study who had complex mental health needs, lockdown exacerbated previous traumas caused by domestic abuse (also seen clearly in Chapter 11), childhood sexual abuse, addiction and bereavement, and other complex experiences. The lockdown also resulted in problematic disruptions or delays to ongoing support and treatment.

The impacts of digital exclusion on families

Research by Carnegie UK and UNICEF UK (2021) states that digital inclusion is dependent on five components: a suitable device, a strong connection, skills and support, a safe online environment, and sustainability of access. In Scotland, it was estimated that 18 per cent of households in lower-income brackets did not have any internet access at all in 2019 (Scottish Government, 2020b). In the months after the beginning of the pandemic in March 2020, the Scottish Government responded by providing funding towards technology for at-risk, digitally excluded individuals and school children.

Many of the families we spoke to did not have access to suitable devices, experienced low-quality internet, or struggled to afford internet access. Additionally, (in)capacity to pay for electricity to charge phones/devices – as well as data – made accessing support more difficult. Several parents only had internet access via their phone. These key issues presented more intensely for those in larger families or in circumstances where parents were working irregular hours. As noted earlier, digital exclusion therefore impacted on families' ability to access support and services and to stay in contact with family, friends, and the local community during the pandemic (see, for example, Chapter 7). Regular internet costs were often described as a pressure on family budgets with families having to prioritise essentials such as bills and food and not having enough left over to pay for phones/ internet:

'I'm only topping up my phone enough to have a couple o' minutes in it. If I need to phone the midwife, I've got access to phone the midwife ... I would rather not have internet, not have a phone, not have stuff that I need, just so she [daughter] can have a good day.' (Interview: single mother with one child)

Despite valuing the additional £20 a week available through UC, challenges around claiming it and applying for jobs online was an apparent issue. Parents claiming UC are expected to look for work when their child is over three. With the continued closure or part closure of public libraries, several parents shared concerns around meeting strict UC conditionality requirements, including completing their online journal and applying for jobs, as also seen in Chapter 9: "And I can't be looking for certain, for work on my phone in the ... writing application with my phone so, yes, I have problems, 'cause I don't have it. But my internet also is not good enough to sustain my son and myself" (Interview: single mother with one child). In relation to accessing online support services during the pandemic, families' experiences were mixed. Some had had positive experiences of local organisations adapting and providing online parent support groups, for example. Being able to connect with other parents online reduced feelings of isolation for some parents. Wanting places where parents and children could go to access the internet in the community was frequently raised during interviews: "The libraries cannae [can't] obviously open because o' this, but having somewhere where people can go and set up a wee camera and talk to their family and stuff, that would be good" (Interview: single father with two children).

Conclusions and recommendations

Research implications

The pandemic shifted the methodological approach of GHS and while we were nevertheless ambitious, we recognise the limits of this work. For example, this research was situated in a Scottish urban central belt. Recognising the topography of Scotland, we suggest there is a need for further work in rural settings including island communities and coastal towns.

Research that involves the whole family is also required to combat the marginalisation of the voices of children and young people within low-income families, especially during the past year. There are core questions around issues such as school closures and the educational attainment gap. We need targeted solutions which draw on the voices of children and young people. Alongside this is the need to consider the intersections of ethnicity and experiences of the pandemic (see for example Chapter 5).

Methodologically, there will have been limitations in the reach of research methods used by research teams not just in Get Heard but by other studies undertaken during the pandemic. Further analysis exploring the impacts of the pandemic should explore interactions and impacts in terms of place and different households for example. Those in more precarious forms of housing and navigating experiences of trauma have likely gone unheard as well as those who were brought into poverty for the first time and navigating life on a low income.

Policy implications

It is clear the pandemic has altered the context for households living on low incomes in measurable and immeasurable ways. There are key lessons for communities, services, and policymakers that need to be accepted if we are to 'build back better'. The targets set out in Scotland around tackling child poverty will be under significant pressure as we navigate the recovery context. The pandemic has demonstrated that we can re-design systems and support when the context demands it. Therefore, it is critical that we consider both positive and negative impacts from the pandemic as we plan for the future.

GHS has identified several key policy asks for the UK and Scottish Governments. Families' experiences of struggling to make ends meet on UC, as well as facing barriers to accessing support through the SWF, are illustrative of a precarious social security net. New benefits introduced in Scotland for families living on low incomes provide reasons to be positive; however, to lift families out of poverty there must be a rise in the current level of the Scottish Child Payment. There is also a need to monitor and research take-up of new benefits in Scotland to ensure that eligible families are accessing the benefits they are entitled to.

Supporting families with their mental health should also be a priority as we move out of the pandemic. Families in our research called for targeted and tailored support for both parents and caregivers as well as for children and young people. Support needs to be cognisant of the new challenges and issues households have encountered during the pandemic and delivered in ways that meet households' needs. Addressing the diverse range of issues in terms of the mental health of low-income households will require nuanced and targeted policy and practice responses. The relationship between poverty and mental health prior to the pandemic illustrated an increased risk of experiencing mental ill health and mental ill health being both a cause and consequence of poverty (Elliot, 2016). The pandemic is adding new layers to this relationship in terms of needs and responses and the scale of the challenges that lie ahead.

The acceleration of the usage of digital technologies during the pandemic has not been experienced equally across Scotland and the UK. Tackling the issues of digital exclusion requires a multi-pronged approach and thinking both at scale on digital infrastructure and service design as well as at a household and community level on the facilitation of digital access and supporting people with their digital needs (see also Chapters 9 and 10).

Crucially, as we move out of the pandemic, there is a need for a fresh focus on voices of lived experience and ensuring our work is collective so that we genuinely create systems that work for all. In Scotland, Get Heard provides the opportunity for low-income families to have a voice in the decisions that affect them. With rising levels of child poverty as a result of the pandemic, now more than ever we must engage with people with experience of poverty to identify the steps that we must take to loosen the grip of poverty on our communities.

Notes

[1] More information about Get Heard Scotland can be found at: www.povertyalliance.org/get-involved/get-heard-scotland/

[2] More information about The Poverty Alliance can be found at: https://www.povertyalliance.org/

[3] More information about Scotland's child poverty reduction targets can be found at: www.parliament.scot/bills-and-laws/bills/child-poverty-scotland-bill

[4] These are the two local authority areas that GHS concentrated on in the final stage.

[5] The six priority family groups include: lone-parent families; a household where someone is disabled; families with three or more children; minority ethnic families; families with a child under one year old; and families where the mother is under 25 years of age (Scottish Government, 2018).

[6] The chapter in this book by Scullion et al (Chapter 4) will look at 'support beyond the family' in England, offering a counterpoint to GHS Scottish policy focus.

[7] More information on the CAAG can be found here: www.povertyalliance.org/get-involved/join-our-community-action-group/

[8] Para-data, or meta-data refers to data about the process of collection; it is data about data.

References

Birch, M. and Miller, T. (2010) Inviting intimacy: the interview as therapeutic opportunity. *International Journal of Social Research Methodology*, 3(3), 189–202.

British Academy (2021) The COVID decade: understanding the long-term societal impacts of COVID-19. London: The British Academy.

Carnegie Trust and UNICEF UK (2021) Closing the digital divide for good: an end to the digital exclusion of children and young people in the UK. Carnegie UK Trust and UNICEF UK.

Davidson, G. (2021) Nicola Sturgeon urged 'do the right thing' on child poverty. *The Scotsman*. 18 August.

Elliott, I. (2016) Poverty and mental health: A review to inform the Joseph Rowntree Foundation's anti-poverty strategy. London: Mental Health Foundation.

End Child Poverty Coalition (2021) Child poverty in your area 2014/15–2019/20. [Online]. Available at: www.endchildpoverty.org.uk/local-child-poverty-data-2014-15-2019-20/

Hall, S.M. (2019) *Everyday Life in Austerity. Family, Friends and Intimate Relations*. London: Palgrave Macmillan Studies in Family and Intimate Life.

Halliday, A. (2020) Digital exclusion in Scotland. [Online]. Available at: www.inspiringscotland.org.uk/wp-content/uploads/2020/06/Digital-Exclusion-in-Scotland-final-full-report-1.pdf

MacLeod, M. (2019) Found wanting: understanding journeys into and out of food insecurity: a longitudinal study. Glasgow: Oxfam.

Maddison, F. (2020) A lifeline for our children: strengthening the social security system for families with children during the pandemic. York: Joseph Rowntree Foundation.

Pascoe Leahy, C. (2021) The afterlife of interviews: explicit ethics and subtle ethics in sensitive or distressing qualitative research. *Qualitative Research*. Doi: 10.1177/14687941211012924.

Patrick, R., Simpson, M. and UC:Us (2020) Universal Credit could be a lifeline in Northern Ireland, but it must be designed with people who use it. York: Joseph Rowntree Foundation.

The Poverty Alliance (2020) Briefing – GHS in Renfrewshire: voices from the third sector. Glasgow: The Poverty Alliance.

The Poverty Alliance (2021) Briefing – GHS in Inverclyde: an overview of initial discussions. Glasgow: The Poverty Alliance.

Save the Children (2021) 'Dropped into a cave': how families with young children experienced lockdown. Scotland: Save the Children.

Scottish Government (2018) Every child, every chance: tackling child poverty delivery plan 2018–2022. Edinburgh: Scottish Government.

Scottish Government (2019) Social security Scotland: our charter. Edinburgh: Scottish Government.

Scottish Government (2020a) Scottish Index of Multiple Deprivation 2020. Edinburgh: Scottish Government. [Online]. Available at: www.gov.scot/news/scottish-index-of-multiple-deprivation-2020

Scottish Government (2020b) Scottish Household Survey 2019: annual report. Edinburgh: Scottish Government.

Scottish Government (2021) Scottish welfare fund statutory guidance update March 2021. Edinburgh: Scottish Government.

Scottish Poverty and Inequality Commission (2021) Child poverty delivery plan progress 2020–2021: scrutiny by the Poverty and Inequality Commission. Glasgow: Scottish Poverty and Inequality Commission.

Sinclair, S. (2021) Policies and processes for tackling poverty, in J.H. McKendrick, J. Dickie, F. McHardy, A. O'Hagan, S. Sinclair and M.C. Treanor (eds) *Poverty in Scotland 2021: Towards a 2030 Without Poverty*. London: CPAG, pp 122–31.

Tarrant, A., Way, W. and Ladlow, L. (2021) Supporting at a distance: the challenges and opportunities of supporting young fathers through the COVID-19 pandemic. Briefing Paper 3. University of Lincoln. https://followingyoungfathersfurther.org/asset/working-papers/

Whitham, G. (2018) The decline of crisis support in England. Manchester: Greater Manchester Poverty Action.

World Health Organization (2020) Mental health and COVID-19. [Online]. Available at: www.euro.who.int/en/health-topics/health-emergencies/coronavirus-covid-19/publications-and-technical-guidance/mental-health-and-covid-19

13

The Commission on Social Security and participatory research during the pandemic: new context, abiding challenges

Rosa Morris, Ellen Morrison, Michael Orton, and Kate Summers[1]

In this chapter we examine a project called the Commission on Social Security, led by Experts by Experience (hereafter, 'the Commission'). The aim of the project is to produce a White Paper-style document on social security, setting out policy proposals for a better benefits system. The project takes a ground-breaking approach with all the Commissioners being people with lived experience of the social security system, that is, current or recent benefit claimants (referred to as 'Experts by Experience', the term having been decided on by the people with lived experience who became involved in the project).

The innovative nature of the project means practice and process have become a major source of learning and the key question examined in this chapter is whether, and how, the pandemic posed new challenges to the Commission's deeply participatory ways of working. We begin by discussing the background to the Commission project and then presents key findings, outlining policy proposals before then giving detailed consideration to issues around practice and process. Key themes include: a tension between urgency to act versus long-term planning; the realities of inclusion and accessibility; and challenges around capacity building. We then turn to methodological reflections. This includes the observation that while COVID-19 has largely been heralded as creating unprecedented problems requiring new approaches, the Commission project illustrates that in some ways it is rather the case that the pandemic has highlighted or exacerbated challenges that already existed.

The pandemic has also, to some extent, opened up more opportunities around inclusion and accessibility and how adjustments to conventional ways of working can enable more people to be involved or contribute. What is striking is that because accessibility has always been central to the work of the Commission, much of those adjustments were ones the Commission already had in place. In addition, the move away from more conventional ways of working, made necessary by the pandemic, allowed some people to be more involved than they would have been if more traditional ways of working had continued. With the Commission project we see that COVID-19 has thrown challenges of successfully conducting participatory work into sharper relief, but also find that outcomes are highly dependent on the level to which those challenges had been addressed – or not – pre-pandemic. Thus, this chapter complements others in this book concerned with participatory research, in particular, Chapters 11, 12, and 14.

Introduction

While there is a considerable history to the formation of the Commission project, two motivations are of particular importance here: the need for new and solutions-focused approaches to anti-poverty; and people with lived experience having a central role in policy development. These themes have been discussed previously (Orton, 2019) and are exemplified in Beresford's (2017) argument that there is currently a 'well-rehearsed conversation' in which researchers who produce ever more evidence about problems that are only too well known seem to think that by telling the government how much damage its policies are doing it will stop imposing them; or if they show the public how bad things are then 'something will have to change'. Instead, Beresford (2017) contends that what is needed is to 'support people in poverty to develop their own ideas and solutions for change instead of asking them how awful things are'. There is a rich and growing literature on what in broad terms can be referred to as co-production, but which encompasses a range of approaches to the involvement of people with lived experience in policy development (see for example, Chapter 14; Bergold and Thomas, 2012; McIntosh and Wright, 2019; Patrick, 2019; Beresford, 2021; Beresford et al, 2021a; Williams et al, 2021).

The Commission project began with the broad aim of Experts by Experience having a central role in developing solutions by producing a White Paper-style document on the future of social security policy. In 2018, funding was awarded by Trust for London for such a project to be developed through a partnership between an academic researcher and two Experts by Experience from user-led groups. The funding application envisaged an advisory board made up of Experts by Experience and professionals, and an Experts by Experience-led working group. But initial discussions led to immediate questioning of this approach in terms of whether it provided a meaningful way of involving Experts by Experience. The result was a very significant shift in approach.

In short, it was agreed that to make the work truly led by people with lived experience a project inception group should be formed, with members comprising Experts by Experience. This inception group was formed through the networks of the original two Experts by Experience. In accordance with the funding for the project, the inception group had two non-negotiables: the project must produce a White Paper-style document on social security, and people with lived experience must be at the centre of decision making. But what model the project should use and how to proceed were for the inception group to decide.

The group decided that a Commission of Inquiry model should be used for the project. It was also decided that all Commissioners would be Experts by Experience, and there would be a secretariat/support team of 'professionals'. In total 16 Experts by Experience became Commissioners via a wide range of claimant/user-led groups and Deaf and Disabled People's Organisations. They brought with them a diverse range of experience of different elements of the social security system, and diversity in terms of age, ethnicity, gender, and other identity dimensions. The secretariat consisted of two academic researchers, one independent researcher, and a representative of the funder.

In the interests of transparency, the authors of this chapter are an Expert by Experience who acted as Co-chair of the Commission and three members of the secretariat. The ground-breaking nature of the Commission's approach means that the practice and process of the project have become a major source of learning. This chapter is based on the authors' (auto-)ethnographic reflections on the participatory methods used in the Commission project, findings from which will now be discussed.

Findings: urgency, inclusion, and capacity building

Before considering issues around practice and process, policy proposals made by the project will be briefly outlined. In February 2020, just ahead of the onset of COVID-19, the Commission set out a number of initial policy proposals. These took the form of key headline ideas as a basis for further work, rather than a comprehensive new scheme. However, the pandemic then dramatically changed the socio-economic context, including debates about social security (see Morris et al, 2020; Simpson, 2020; Machin, 2021; Summers et al, 2021). In summer/autumn 2020, the Commission launched a revised set of draft proposals and commenced a major public consultation on them. The draft proposals include: a Guaranteed Decent Income equivalent to the Joseph Rowntree Foundation's Minimum Income Standard; a completely new approach to disability benefits using the social model of disability; Child Benefit to be increased to £50 per child per week; and a range of supporting points around housing costs, childcare, and so on. The final set of proposals will be published in late 2021.

Another key project output which should be noted is a set of five concise principles to underpin social security, which Commissioners agreed in 2019 (available at the Commission's website www.commissiononsocialsecurity. org/). The five principles are as follows:

- Make sure everyone has enough money to live – and support extra costs for example to do with disability and children.
- Treat everyone with dignity, respect, and trust, and the belief that people should be able to choose for themselves.
- Be a public service with rights and entitlements.
- Be clear, simple, user-friendly and accessible to all, involving people who have actual experience of the issues, including from all impairment groups, in creating and running the system as a whole.
- Include access to free advice and support. Make sure people can access support to speak up, be heard, or make a complaint.

Their underpinning nature meant the principles remained relevant to the changed circumstances of the pandemic and were not revised when COVID-19 hit. The principles are discussed in detail elsewhere (Orton et al, 2021) so will not be considered further here. Instead, this chapter reflects on issues relating to practice and process that were highlighted and often exacerbated by the pandemic. These reflections in turn provide lessons for conducting participatory work. We begin with the urgency to act versus long-term planning.

The urgency to act versus long-term planning

The onset of the pandemic demonstrated how unfit for purpose the current social security system is and the need for urgent action (Garnham, 2020). The Government responded with some immediate measures such as the £20 uplift to Universal Credit; and the suspension of conditionality, sanctions, the minimum income floor, and face-to-face assessments, which all made immediate and substantial effects on people's lives and demonstrated that rapid, reasonably extensive change was possible. This subsequently led to civil society campaigns for the uplift to be extended to legacy benefits, and then to be made permanent (see, for example, Covid Realities, 2021). Some third sector organisations began another campaign for the rate of Child Benefit to be increased and Marcus Rashford's work on free school meals serves as a further example of an initiative pursuing urgent action (Hansard HC Deb, 2021). These actions all constitute important steps that could achieve positive material outcomes for millions of households.

However, such measures do not represent a transformation of the Government's approach to social security. They were pragmatic changes to cope with the overnight shutdown of much of the labour market and are likely to have been reversed by the time this chapter is published.[2] Nevertheless, they do present opportunities for raising awareness of the inadequacy of levels of benefit payments and provide a potential platform for gaining broader support for more fundamental reform.

A tension between the urgency to campaign for immediate improvements versus long-term planning was a dynamic that has run through the Commission project and was evident pre-pandemic. Within the project, this was in evidence as the need to act quickly to make improvements to the benefits system alongside the time-consuming nature of the Commission's work in seeking to develop a holistic and transformative set of proposals. Experts by Experience often expressed anger or frustration with current problems with social security benefits. Self-evidently, people were drawing on their own experience of the social security system including wider and often very personal issues such as racial discrimination while navigating the system as a person of colour; challenges of daily living when a disabled person's impairment is not adequately recognised; or stigma faced as a full-time carer. Discussion was not therefore at an abstract or purely technical level, but rooted in people's personal biographies, including experiences of trauma and struggle. Wanting to be heard has also been a recurring theme. The form that the 'professional' endeavour of the Commission to produce policy recommendations took can therefore not be separated from the personal experiences of Commissioners and how this fundamentally shaped their approaches to the task at hand.

In practice what this meant was on occasions one or more Commissioners explicitly took the position that discussions were taking too long, and felt that the Commission should be moving more quickly to pursuing action. At the same time, however, Commissioners emphasised the need to consult widely on proposals and produce a coherent, convincing proposed plan of action. There was sometimes reluctance to force decisions to be made without issues being talked through and discussed in detail among Commissioners, and time allowed for reflection and engagement with wider networks and groups. This undercurrent of tension between recognising that the Commission's way of working required time and long-term thinking, with the urgency to act, characterised the group's ongoing work.

The point to make is that while from an academic view, thinking in terms of short-term amelioration and long-term transformation seems a reasonable analytical approach, for the Commission's Experts by Experience the starting point is grounded in the realities of how badly the current system is failing. Change therefore needs to be both urgent *and* transformative, it is not an either/or choice. One Commissioner emphasised this strain in February 2020 when telling the group that they needed to focus on the fact that "this is real people's lives": the pressure to get things right, but to get things right quickly, was keenly felt. This in part reflects the solutions-focused approach of the Commission project. Working towards proposals for an improved future system has proved positive in framing work as generative. This avoids centring difficulties (unless Commissioners want to), or mining and exploiting traumas within the research process. We would suggest that the Commission project teaches us that while COVID-19 created a moment where the need for urgent, ambitious policy responses became more widely recognised, that need – and the scale and immediacy of the challenge – was one about which the Experts by Experience were already acutely aware and grappling with.

The realities of inclusion and accessibility

Another effect of COVID-19 has been on inclusion and accessibility. Lockdown meant the cessation of face-to-face meetings and events. Online interactions became the norm, and awareness of digital exclusion then grew (for example Baker et al, 2020). At an individual level, people had to shield; live in small bubbles or complete isolation; home school and adapt to a wide array of new arrangements. Getting by day-to-day became a challenge for many.

These factors also affected the Commission project, in which inclusion and accessibility had been established as key requirements at the very first meeting of the project inception group and continued to be regularly emphasised. Pre-pandemic Commission meetings were held monthly, in-person, and with arrangements made to enable accessibility, for example by booking taxis to enable travel, and having British Sign Language interpreters and Personal Assistants available. It was also possible for Commissioners who could not attend a meeting in person to join or contribute in whatever way worked best for them, with people joining meetings by Zoom long before the pandemic made Zoom use widespread. Supported pre-meeting preparation time was another approach that developed, enabling Commissioners who wished to do so to talk through the agenda and consider any points they would like to make in advance of the meeting proper.

A commitment to inclusion and accessibility extends to the Commission's outward-facing work. Commissioners have been consistent in wanting to ensure a wide range of voices are included in the Commission's work and that outputs from the project are widely communicated. In 2019, a public Call for Solutions was issued, encouraging people to submit ideas and suggestions to the Commission for how the benefits system can be improved. Reflecting the concern to make the process as accessible as possible and to include groups invariably excluded by the practices of similar initiatives, a number of steps were taken. For example, the Call for Solutions document was produced in Easy Read (a method of presenting written information to make it easier to understand for people who have difficulty reading). Commissioners decided all documentation should be Easy Read by default rather than seeing it as an add-on. When the Call for Solutions went live, the bespoke website also used Easy Read and included British Sign Language videos with subtitles and audio so there were multiple ways to access the questions being posed. Accessible ways to respond to the Call were offered. Even more than this, a legislative theatre event and poetry day were held, providing means for contributions to the Call for Solutions to be expressed in ways beyond standard written submissions.

COVID-19 meant an end to in-person Commission meetings and events such as the legislative theatre. Individual Commissioners were affected by the factors mentioned earlier such as shielding and lack of access to online tools for meeting. Wider consultation was also problematic both in terms of practical issues around not being able to hold in-person events but also many groups ceasing activities or having to concentrate on key priorities and emergency responses to the pandemic. However, the Commission project was able to adapt and continue, largely due to the recurring theme we raise in this chapter, that is, that many issues highlighted by COVID-19 were already evident in some form and required action, including in relation to accessibility and inclusion. While most Commissioners attended pre-pandemic Commission meetings in-person, meetings were in fact conducted using what are now being referred to as hybrid or blended means. As previously mentioned, the Commission was using Zoom in 2019, well before COVID-19, as a way to facilitate the involvement of Commissioners when for health or other reasons they were unable to attend in person. Ensuring accessibility meant that pre-COVID-19, Commissioners would sometimes have one-to-one sessions or telephone calls, for example to go through documents or talk about particular policy topics. Physical and mental ill health meant several Commissioners took periods out from involvement in the Commission project, and flexible ways of working developed to keep people in touch and to catch up when it was possible for them to re-engage. All of this experience meant it was possible to adapt to the circumstances of the pandemic using some Zoom sessions, but primarily tailoring engagement to what worked for each Commissioner and their individual circumstances and access requirements as had previously been done, with COVID-19 providing further impetus to do so.

Working in such ways enabled progress to continue, for example in developing and agreeing the revised draft policy proposals discussed earlier, and launching the public consultation online where Commissioners made contributions either live or through pre-recorded film and audio. Online events were used for the public consultation and worked well. Furthermore, awareness of digital exclusion meant that some funding was given to a number of grassroots groups to undertake consultation within their own communities in ways appropriate to local circumstances, especially in relation to conditions created by the pandemic. This process of *enabling* rather than *doing* was a result of the need to respond to the impact of COVID-19 and has been an important learning point. But the major challenges posed by the pandemic were successfully met and project activity continued, largely because inclusion and accessibility were already identified and acted upon as key issues within the Commission.

Challenges around capacity building

A further effect of COVID-19 in relation to the Commission project has been on capacity building for Commissioners. Commissioners brought with them to the project their experience and a wide variety of expertise. There was no expectation that Commissioners needed to do more than contribute their experience and expertise, but it was implicit that capacity building would be part of the project. This manifested in a number of ways. For example, in relation to responses to the 'Call for Solutions', a session was run for Commissioners on qualitative approaches to analysing data. Just before the pandemic, training was held on engagement with the media for Commissioners who were interested (see also Chapters 11 and 14). At an individual level, some Commissioners were supported in speaking at external events and one person undertook personal development to chair meetings.

COVID-19 brought an end to such activity and no formal capacity building has taken place since the onset of the pandemic. On reflection, we can see that pre-pandemic, opportunities for capacity building did arise and were seized, but did not happen as part of a formal, intentional programme of work. The key point is that pre-pandemic, capacity building was implicit within the project rather than an explicit aim. The approach tended to be somewhat reactive and ad hoc rather than there being a clear, explicit strategy. The disadvantage of this was that capacity building often slipped to the bottom of agendas as priority focused on successfully ensuring the project met its aim of producing policy proposals.

While COVID-19 did have an impact on capacity building, arguably the greater problem was with issues evident pre-pandemic and to which insufficient attention had been given. If the project had been as developed in terms of capacity building as it was in relation to inclusion and accessibility, the pandemic would have required adaptation, but the tools would have been in place to allow more capacity building to continue to take place.

Methodological reflections

Reflecting on the aforementioned points returns us to a key concept raised at the start of the chapter: co-production. Beresford et al (2021b) argue that in the light of COVID-19, there is a need to consider the relative strengths and weaknesses of approaches typically taken in modern politics and public policy and to consider alternatives that could better serve us in the future, with co-production key among these alternative approaches. We note, for example, that disabled people with vast experience of social isolation could have made valuable contributions to 'shielding' policies but typically were not invited to contribute to decision-making processes. The same applies to mental health service users/survivors and mental health organisations, who had developed their own strategies to deal with the consequences of isolation long before the onset of the pandemic.

More broadly, Beresford et al (2021b: 14) contend that those who are already familiar with the concept of co-production and believe in the value of working in this way are facing significant challenges. Due to its collaborative and inclusive aims, co-production usually relies on bringing people together, but the pandemic has meant being faced with the challenge of 'co-producing at a distance' which, while seen by some as providing opportunities, is seen by other practitioners as a rather contradictory notion.

In terms of the Commission on Social Security project, however, there is a different concluding point to make. It is self-evident that COVID-19 created a new and hugely changed context and has had myriad effects on the Commission project. But in terms of the challenges created for practice and process, it is not so much the case that the pandemic *of itself* created these, but rather highlighted or exacerbated issues that already existed and which the Commission's ways of working were already tackling. Across the key themes we identify in this chapter: a tension between urgency to act versus long-term planning; the realities of inclusion and accessibility; and challenges around capacity building, the key insight is that challenges were clearly evident pre-pandemic. How well they were responded to after the onset of COVID-19 was more to do with how far they had already been addressed rather than simply to do with the new circumstances being faced.

The concluding point to make, therefore, is that while COVID-19 has largely been seen as creating new problems which have demanded new approaches, deeply participatory ways of working – as sought in the Commission on Social Security project – faced challenges pre-pandemic. These challenges may have been thrown into sharper relief by the changed context, but they are not necessarily of themselves new. The pandemic has illustrated the inadequacies of the current social security system, opening up opportunities for campaigning for change. However, the premise of the Commission's work is that the transformative change which is required cannot take place without Experts by Experience being fully involved in the process of policy development. Thus, participatory research and co-production approaches faced challenges pre-pandemic, during the pandemic, and will continue to do so post-pandemic. The lessons learnt during the pandemic will help to further develop participatory research methods and approaches to co-production which are so necessary to creating a social security system which truly works for those who experience it. Context of course matters when pursuing participatory ways of working, but the challenges faced by those committed to such approaches are abiding, and something we must remain vigilant of both through and beyond the pandemic.

Notes

[1]   In the spirit of co-production and rejection of hierarchy, we have simply listed the authors of this chapter alphabetically.

[2]   In July 2021 the government did indeed announce the £20 uplift would end; a 'Keep the Lifeline' campaign continued to challenge this decision.

References

Baker, C., Hutton, G., Christie, L. and Wright, S. (2020) COVID-19 and the digital divide. *Rapid Response Post*, UK Parliament. 17 December. Available at: https://post.parliament.uk/covid-19-and-the-digital-divide/

Beresford, P. (2017) Endless reports on rising poverty do little to change government policy – there's another way. *The Conversation*. 11 December. Available at: https://theconversation.com/endless-reports-on-rising-poverty-do-little-to-change-government-policy-theres-another-way-88740

Beresford, P. (2021) *Participatory Ideology: From Exclusion to Involvement*. Bristol: Policy Press.

Beresford, P., Farr, M., Hickey, G., Kaur, M., Ocloo, J., Tembo, D. and Williams, O. (eds) (2021a) *COVID-19 and Co-production in Health and Social Care Research, Volume 1: The Challenges and Necessity of Co-production Policy, and Practice*. Bristol: Policy Press.

Beresford, P., Farr, M., Hickey, G., Kaur, M., Ocloo, J., Tembo, D. and Williams, O. (2021b) Introduction to Volume 1, in P. Beresford, M. Farr, G. Hickey, M. Kaur, J. Ocloo, D. Tembo and O. Williams (eds) *COVID-19 and Co-production in Health and Social Care Research, Volume 1: The Challenges and Necessity of Co-production Policy, and Practice*. Bristol: Policy Press.

Bergold, J. and Thomas, S. (2012) Participatory research methods: a methodological approach in motion. *Forum: Qualitative Social Research*, 13(1).

Covid Realities (2021) Statement on £20 uplift. Available at: https://covidrealities.org/learnings/write-ups/statement-on-20-pounds-uplift

Garnham, A. (2020) After the pandemic: COVID-19 and social security reform. *IPPR Progressive Review*, 27(1), 8–17.

Hansard HC Deb. (2021) Volume 696, columns 2–25. 24 May 2021. [Online]. Available at: www.parliament.uk/

Machin, R. (2021) COVID-19 and the temporary transformation of the UK social security system. *Critical Social Policy*. DOI: 10.1177/0261018320986793.

McIntosh, I. and Wright, S. (2019) Exploring what the notion of lived experience might offer for social policy analysis. *Journal of Social Policy*, 48(3), 449–67.

Morris, R., Orton, M. and Summers, K. (2020) Social security responses to Covid-19: the case for £50 Child Benefit. *Discover Society*, 15 April.

Orton, M. (2019) Challenges for anti-poverty action: developing approaches that are solutions focused, participative and collaborative. *Journal of Poverty and Social Justice* 27(1), 131–6.

Orton, M., Summers, K. and Morris, R. (2021) Guiding principles for social security policy: outcomes from a bottom-up approach. *Social Policy and Administration*. DOI: 10.1111/spol.12782

Patrick, R. (2019) Unsettling the anti-welfare common-sense: the potential in participatory research with people living in poverty. *Journal of Social Policy*, 49(2), 251–70.

Simpson, M. (2020) The social security response to COVID-19: read the small print. *Discover Society*, 2 April. Available at: https://archive. discoversociety.org/2020/04/02/the-social-security-response-to-covid-19-read-the-small-print/

Summers, K., Scullion, L., Baumberg Geiger, B., Robertshaw, D., Edmiston, D., Gibbons, A., Karagiannaki, E., de Vries, R. and Ingold, J. (2021) Claimants' experiences of the social security system during the first wave of COVID-19. *Welfare at a Social Distance*. Project report. Available at: www. distantwelfare.co.uk/winter-report

Williams, O., Tembo, D., Ocloo, J., Kaur, M., Hickey, G., Farr, M. and Beresford, P. (eds) (2021) *COVID-19 and Co-production in Health and Social Care Research, Volume 2: Volume 2: Co-production Methods and Working Together at a Distance*. Bristol: Policy Press.

14

UC:Us now? Reflections from participatory research with Universal Credit claimants during COVID-19

Ruth Patrick, Ciara Fitzpatrick, Mark Simpson, and Jamie Redman with UC:Us Members

Introduction

UC:Us is a group of people in receipt of Universal Credit (UC) in Northern Ireland. The group came together through a participatory study to document experiences of UC in the unique Northern Ireland context and develop claimant-led proposals for improvements to policy and processes. UC:Us and the researchers supporting the group entered 2020 with exciting plans for our work together. We planned to cement and build on our co-produced research by sharing our findings with politicians and policymakers across the UK, pressing for change to address some of the negative aspects of receiving UC we had identified, and to develop the first-ever co-produced, accessible guide to the benefit. The arrival of the COVID-19 pandemic changed everything, virtually overnight. Our personal and professional lives were upended as we suddenly had to cope with lockdowns, home schooling, and massive shifts in where and how we and our participants worked. We all had to adjust quickly to a new and often terrifying context.

The economic fallout from COVID-19 and the initial March 2020 lockdown brought a massive spike in new UC claims across the UK. Northern Ireland was no exception: March and April 2020 saw the number of new claims increase from an average of 7,000 per month to 35,440 and 20,560 respectively (Department for Communities [DfC], 2020). Against this context, the tasks we had originally set ourselves felt as pressing as ever.

To that end, we sought to pivot our activities online, swapping face-to-face meetings for evening Zoom sessions, finding ways to adapt our approach to a new virtual working world while continuing to research ethically – balancing the competing demands of paid employment, and for many (researchers and participants alike) parenting in a crisis. In this chapter, co-written by members of the research team and participants, we share participants' own accounts of life on a low income and on UC during COVID-19. We also reflect on the methodological learnings from our virtual, participatory work together, focusing on ethical challenges within participatory research. In the concluding section, we set out key implications for policy, research, and participatory practice. The writing by participants was facilitated through a series of workshops with a specialist facilitator, Rebecca Sharp, in summer 2021.

The UC:Us approach: participatory, co-produced research, utilising arts-based approaches

The UC:Us project started life as a participatory study to explore experiences of UC in Northern Ireland, funded by the Joseph Rowntree Foundation. This initial study, from 2019 to 2020, involved the establishment of an 'expert by experience panel' of UC claimants. This approach inspired in part by the Scottish Government's social security experience panels, a unique experiment in the co-design of social security policy and practice as a partnership between government and people with experience of the UK system (see Scottish Government, nd). Our panel convened in a series of participatory workshops to document and share experiences of the benefit and develop recommendations for change. The workshops, which took place in Belfast, provided a space to meet, share experiences, develop recommendations for change, and to offer peer support.

A total of 17 people participated in one or more UC:Us workshops between June 2019 and January 2020, with attendance averaging around eight claimants per workshop. Workshops employed arts-based tools to create an informal and inclusive space to share experiences and collaborate. Icebreakers were used to break down barriers and set up an atmosphere of informality. Opportunities to create individual hand-drawn 'UC journeys' allowed participants to reflect on and creatively articulate their experiences on the benefit, whether or not they felt comfortable expressing these orally. Initially, the researchers targeted claimants in Belfast, but participation has gradually widened – enabled in part by virtual ways of working during the pandemic – to include rural Northern Ireland. At present, there are eight regularly active members of UC:Us, with additional participants dipping in and out. UC:Us members have a range of personal circumstances including parenting and caring responsibilities, experiences of paid employment and volunteering, and additional health needs. The project is underpinned by an ethics of care and reciprocity and formally received ethical approval from the University of York.

Participants have been involved in key decisions across the study, including deciding what format arts-based outputs should take. The decision was taken to create an illustrated leaflet, which led to collaboration with a graphic designer, Dan Farley, and an illustrator, Hannah Miller. Participants worked with Dan and Hannah to develop the illustrations used in the leaflet and took key decisions on both substantive and stylistic content. Figure 14.1 shows an illustration developed by Hannah with Deirdre. The image reflects Deirdre's description of the five-week wait for a first UC payment as having a domino effect, with its negative impact on multiple areas of her life still being felt many months later.

Findings were published in a report and illustrated leaflet (see Patrick and Simpson with UC:Us, 2020; UC:Us, 2020). They were also shared directly with politicians through a round-table event at which participants attended and spoke.

Following the conclusion of the initial project in summer 2020, we secured ESRC funding to continue our efforts to influence social security policy and processes – and to advocate a more participatory approach within government. We have met with key Northern Ireland policymakers (including senior officials and Assembly members) as well as Westminster

Figure 14.1: The domino effect of the five-week wait

politicians and Welsh stakeholders. We have also been developing a participant-led guide to Universal Credit. The researchers have submitted evidence to Parliamentary inquiries around the design and implementation of Universal Credit. UC:Us members have become prominent experts and spokespeople on Universal Credit in Northern Ireland (see, for example, BBC Radio Ulster, 2020; Jones, 2020; Smyth, 2020; BBC, 2021; Sandhu, 2021).

Main findings

The narrative accounts shared here are of three UC:Us members, Caroline, Deirdre, and Joanna. In what follows, Caroline, Deirdre, and Joanna reflect on their experiences of living on a low income during the pandemic and the wider engagement work they have done as members of UC:Us. In doing so, they reveal some of the hurdles they have faced in their personal lives and the empowering potential that participatory activity can offer for both participants and researchers seeking to use social research as a vehicle for positive change.

Living on a low income during the COVID-19 pandemic

Caroline

I joined UC:Us around September 2020 after signing onto UC in the middle of the COVID-19 pandemic. I had lost my job and needed help with my rent, which I couldn't get through Working Tax Credits (WTC). I didn't have much awareness of UC and how it worked, though I received some great advice via advocates on Twitter. They were able to advise me on how to access discretionary support through the contingency fund so I wouldn't be waiting for six weeks with no income. As a single mum with a growing pre-teenager, there was no way I'd last six weeks on top of trying to keep my rent up-to-date. I never had debts and had always lived within my means before I lost my job.

Living on a low income is the norm as a single mum. Finding a job that fits around my child is difficult, but I managed to get by when I was self-employed on WTC. There was stability in the level of support I received for the year, so I could plan and manage my regular household bills and even managed to put a few pounds aside for the bigger bills such as oil heating. With UC there is no stability, as the support changes monthly. I never know what I'm getting until two days beforehand. I discovered that accessing dental and optician support wasn't as simple on UC either – you have to apply for everything separately, and the rates for eligibility are much lower on UC than WTC. Even the maximum income for accessing free school meals (FSM) is over £2,000 less on UC.

UC is already a lower level of support than WTC and it comes with additional risks. I look at peers on WTC earning more than me and getting all this with ease, while I worry about going over the threshold and having the rug pulled out from under me.

Deirdre

I worked four jobs to get myself through university. I did a PGCE, got a job, and I had a career. I was loving life and the world was my oyster. Then a baby came along. I assumed my boyfriend would stick with me to support me raising his child. I woke up to a note and he was gone. I didn't choose to be a single mother. I was in England, with a permanent post, but I was adrift with few friends. I went back to Belfast assuming I'd walk into a job, but there were very few teaching posts available. I became homeless and fell into the benefit trap. I was one of the first to go on UC. Some people think it's a choice to go on benefits, but it isn't. Being on UC isn't easy and it was even more difficult during COVID-19. When I was working in England I'd put food in the local Asda food bank crates – little did I know I'd be availing of that service years later.

I had to wait over eight weeks for money when I signed up for UC. The debt nearly broke me financially and emotionally. No one informed me about the contingency fund, I was told I had to borrow. Immediately I was catapulted into severe debt. I was at the end of a five-year family court battle, already struggling to hold it together. In my eyes, rather than building me up, the UC system tried to destroy my mental health. I call it 'the domino effect', where debt dominos into adult poverty, then child poverty; and adult mental health dominos into child mental health issues. It's a vicious circle made worse through COVID-19. It's demeaning and demoralising.

I would have been lost during COVID-19 if it wasn't for the generosity of the local food bank. To this day I have no idea who put my name forward but I was unbelievably grateful for this support. Times were hard, I was lonely, fed up, without internet, at a loss, and hardly leaving the house as my son can't stand crowds. I was chosen as part of an eight-week hot meal scheme, offered by the chef from *Game of Thrones*. Every Wednesday my kids and I each received a hot meal. It was such a relief and a blessing to get hot food delivered straight to your door. But if UC provided enough liveable income there genuinely would be no need for food aid.

Joanna

I was already on UC before the pandemic. Having worked all my life, at the start of 2017 I found myself redundant. My mother was suffering with dementia and I became her carer. Sadly, I lost her at the beginning of 2018. I became ill too, as I'd neglected myself while looking after my mother.

After a few months on Employment and Support Allowance (ESA), I got a job on a return-to-work scheme at a benefits advice centre. At the end of the placement I was asked if I would like to stay on and train voluntarily to be a benefits advisor. I took the offer with both hands, as I saw the good work the girls there did, hoping to one day get a permanent job. I enjoyed helping people, letting them know when they were entitled to more benefits that could maybe dig them out of the hole they were in. And I understood more than the clients were aware because I too was in receipt of UC.

When COVID-19 hit, I had just moved in with my daughter and her family, as I was due to start renovations on my house. I also had a Saturday job in a café that I was saving money from, to decorate my house when I moved back in. COVID-19 meant that my training stopped, with no chance of getting a job using my new skills. The café job stopped almost overnight – so there was no more money to save.

I had moved into a family home. Instead of only having myself to feed, there were four of us. My son-in-law was working from home, so more electric was used. More oil used for heat and although I was only a guest, I took on the worries of this. My daughter had been in a temporary position and had lost the opportunity of this going permanent after COVID-19 hit. She was pregnant at the time and missed out on receiving maternity payment by one day when her contract came to an end. On top of the money worries, my daughter had previously lost two babies, so the fear of losing another one or catching COVID-19 put pressure on the whole house.

The country shut down. The work on my house still didn't start. I knew my family were struggling and I felt like a burden on them. I was trying to do my bit for my family, but living on £70 a week I couldn't afford to do it – all my savings for my decorating disappeared very quickly. I found I was spending more and more time in my room.

I don't know if I'd have felt differently if I'd been living alone, in my own house, if I would have coped financially or emotionally. One thing I do know is that the pandemic has been the hardest time of our lives.

Being a part of UC:Us

Caroline

Being part of UC:Us has given me the freedom to express my fears and concerns for the future; how I feel the system could better support families and households to live healthy lives. Our desires are modest – all most of us want is to be able to put food on the table, keep a roof over our children's heads, have heating and other services that so many take for granted. Internet access and a decent working phone are two examples, which can be costly but are needed to apply for UC.

I feel empowered listening to the shared experiences of the UC:Us participants. It is a central focus of the project to show our experiences to policymakers, while enabling those who are under-confident or who wish to remain anonymous to still have their voices heard.

With the right policies, every home and household could live with a decent level of support. It could be time to take seriously the discussion around Universal Basic Income where every person receives a living income, and the social stigma and insecurity faced by so many would be removed.

Deirdre

The stories of real people need to be heard, especially since the impact of COVID-19. The removal of the £20 uplift is causing me concern, as it was a much-needed increase. My hopes are for a social security system that genuinely recognises and addresses the experiences of real people.

Joanna

We decided to name our group UC:Us because we felt the government, politicians, and the staff in the benefits offices didn't see us as human. We talked about strategies to change this. We cried at each other's stories, comforted each other, tried to give advice. Most of all, we felt that we could work to make a real difference. We hoped other people wouldn't have to suffer the despair we felt, living on UC.

Mark and Ruth set up a meeting for UC:Us to talk about our experiences with politicians and policymakers from the DfC. First, the politicians. We shared our stories. They listened, asked how they could help and what changes they could make. I felt empowered. It felt like if we had their backing, we could give people back their feeling of self-worth.

Next, the policymakers. They believed that UC was the benefit of the future, that £317 a month was enough to live on. They believed that the contingency fund was readily available to everyone who needed it and that the staff in benefits offices were informing claimants about it. They believed that people on UC should be grateful for the pittance they received. They believed that staff treated people with respect, empathy, and an understanding that we do want to work again. I left that second meeting feeling deflated.

Since COVID-19, the UC:Us group has kept in contact through Zoom. We're still fighting, still pushing to be heard, no less determined – and I know I've made friends for life.

Hardship intensified: experiences of UC in the pandemic

Caroline's, Deirdre's, and Joanna's reflections all indicate that living on Universal Credit during the pandemic was marked by greater financial instability and additional difficulty in meeting essential needs. Saliently, Joanna reveals how added financial difficulties can trigger a range of other negative outcomes, such as additional strain on family relationships and mental health decline (cf Pybus et al, 2021). The accounts also reveal that, for some low-income families, household spending increased substantially during the pandemic (cf Brewer and Patrick, 2021). Consequently, these reflections reinforce an emerging evidence base suggesting that issues of benefit (in)adequacy remain pertinent (Summers et al, 2021). This persists in spite of key policy changes that have been implemented to ameliorate the effects of the pandemic, such as the temporary £20 uplift to Universal Credit and WTC payments, as several chapters in this collection also show (see Chapters 2, 3, 4, 10, and 11).

While the pandemic placed additional financial pressures on Caroline, Deirdre, and Joanna, many pre-pandemic pressures were also present in their accounts. Most notable was their endurance of the stigma that typically accompanies benefit receipt and poverty (Whelan, 2021). As their reflections attest, experiences of stigma have been central in shaping the objectives of UC:Us and their continued engagement with powerful stakeholders. They are determined to ensure claimants are recognised as human beings with a set of needs, demands, and interests. They are determined to erase long-standing ignorance around the behaviour and values of people living on a low income. They are determined that people on a low income should be involved in the design and implementation of policies that have very real, and often very severe, impacts on their lives.

Methodological reflections: navigating virtual participatory research during a pandemic

COVID-19 dramatically shifted the way UC:Us works, bringing many challenges as well as some opportunities (Bennett and Brunner, 2022). Generally, it has increased the effort and innovation required from the researchers to encourage continued engagement and participation in the project. From the outset, the work has been underpinned by an ethic of care and reciprocity, which is itself informed by a feminist research praxis (Thomson and Holland, 2010; Oakley, 2016: 197). The researchers have striven to create spaces to work together that are as non-hierarchical as possible, and to invest time and energies in acts of care and reciprocity. This approach brings its own challenges, exacerbated by the unavoidable changes prompted by the pandemic (Gaventa and Cornwall, 2008).

In the initial phase, the researchers and UC:Us met in person, monthly. It was a social event, where participants could catch up over lunch, share their experiences, and gain invaluable peer support. When COVID-19 hit, we had to adapt to a new online world. Meetings moved to Zoom, which about a quarter of participants found problematic. One disengaged with the project entirely, while others said they would re-engage if opportunities to meet face-to-face returned. We re-allocated funding for travel-related expenses to purchase equipment and contribute towards internet costs for continuing participants. Seven participants received IT equipment, while ten were provided with broadband expenses. Considerable time was spent familiarising each individual with the functionality of both the hardware and Zoom. One participant, who had no broadband contract, reported feeling nervous about the prospect of making an additional financial commitment: "I'm just struggling with my reception and I am worried about signing a Wi-Fi contract as I'm worried about making the wrong decision as I am not very technical." The researchers have continuously sought alternative ways to engage digitally excluded participants. We continued to telephone, to keep them updated on ongoing work, and to offer digital support. In one case, this strategy paid off, as a long-absent participant finally managed to join a Zoom meeting with his son's help. The participant acknowledged the value of re-engaging with those who were going through similar experiences to him for some peer support at a difficult time (see Goldstraw et al, 2021). We tried to keep one participant updated via phone, but he eventually changed his telephone number and we lost contact. Another participant sporadically joined WhatsApp conversations but did not join Zoom sessions. The restrictions associated with working online made it difficult to expand the group, but we did manage to recruit one new participant, Caroline, who is digitally fluent and has consistently contributed. Although Caroline did report frequent connectivity issues; a challenge she persistently endures as someone who resides in a rural area of Northern Ireland.

One attraction of the initial project for many participants was particularly difficult to recreate in a virtual setting: the opportunity for informal conversation and peer-to-peer support. The researchers allocated the last half an hour of each meeting to an informal catch-up, but genuine informality proved elusive on Zoom. The platform is more geared towards individual contributions and it quickly becomes difficult if participants attempt to talk over each other. Consequently, researchers had to facilitate the 'informal' chat, to try and mitigate people's voices getting lost.

It was always clear that different participants had different motives for being involved with UC:Us. For some, the work was directed squarely at affecting policy change, which is a common motivation for participatory engagement in poverty research (Bennett and Roberts, 2004): "We need to win [the Minister for Communities] over to make things happen. To change what's wrong with UC." For others, UC:Us was primarily an opportunity for peer support and connection. As a research team, it has been important for us to acknowledge and work with these different and sometimes diverging drivers of engagement or 'competing ethical communities', while recognising that the shift online has been hardest for those who are most driven to engage for peer-support reasons (Dougherty and Atkinson, 2006). Attempts to provide space for the group to continue to serve this less formal purpose ultimately brought about the greatest 'ethically important moment' the research team has faced to date (Guillemin and Gillam, 2004).

A WhatsApp group set up at an early stage of the project initially served as a useful, accessible way to share meeting dates and details, communicate opportunities for media engagement, and general management of the project (Jailobaev et al, 2021). With face-to-face contact ruled out by COVID-19, the group became an extremely active space for informal conversation and peer-to-peer support. Researchers and participants interacted on an almost daily basis and often outside conventional 'work hours'. The role of the researchers, as project facilitators, became distorted in this space. The researchers simultaneously played the role of equal participants in informal conversation and of signposters to advice services and additional support (Smith et al, 2010). Communication was instant, with no opportunity to review whether a message contained anything another member of the group might find offensive. No one had envisaged the WhatsApp group evolving in this way and consequently the role of the researchers in this grey area had never been defined. Was it a conversation between equal adults who had voluntarily joined the group, or did its link with the research project imply a responsibility on the part of the researchers to act as moderators, with some kind of disciplinary role in the last resort? When exchanges occurred late at night, the researchers' ability to respond rapidly was in any case limited.

Following a particularly heated exchange which spilled out of the WhatsApp group (involving other public agencies), and having sought advice from the university ethics committee, the researchers ultimately left the WhatsApp group, designated clear communication routes between participants and themselves (including named points of contact), and limited exchanges to working hours. This re-established a clear division between researchers and participants. Researchers were also advised by the ethics committee to initiate a 'cooling-off period' for those participants who had been in dispute and to reaffirm the commitment from all participants that communication would be respectful and maintain confidentiality. This process was difficult, sensitive, and time-intensive to navigate. This kind of use of WhatsApp as a communication tool during the pandemic was completely new territory for the researchers and for the ethics committee. Every action required careful consideration and implementation. While this initially impacted on the dynamic of the group, time and space for reflection has supported healing and a recalibration of relationships between participants. This episode reinforces the inherent messiness of participatory research processes. By nature, these seek to blur hard dividing lines between researcher and participant, and to minimise power differentials. However, there are risks associated with moving too far into a contested and unclear space; which is arguably what happened when researchers and participants were all active online (Guillemin and Gillam, 2004; Dougherty and Atkinson, 2006; Smith et al, 2010; Bennett and Brunner, 2022).

Despite this messiness, and these challenges, UC:Us did remain productive as we navigated the move online. As noted earlier, UC:Us members have engaged with elected representatives, policymakers, and other stakeholders in Northern Ireland, Wales, and at UK level. Moving online meant these events became more accessible for participants, particularly those with caring responsibilities, as travel was not required.

Will you ever see us? The UC:Us approach and implications for the future

The research on UC was designed from the outset to produce a set of participant-led recommendations for social security policy and practice, whether in Northern Ireland or across the UK, that would improve claimant experiences of the benefit. An obvious 'ask' emerging from the work, then, is the implementation of a set of six measures that UC:Us members believe could reshape UC in line with the group's vision for 'a social security system that treats everyone with dignity and respect as valued members of society'. The recommendations are:

- pay UC at a level that enables people to meet their living costs, including housing;
- end the five-week wait for a first UC payment;
- stop UC triggering debt;
- make the process of initiating and managing a UC claim more user-friendly;
- ensure that the staff delivering UC is well trained, and that recipients have access to independent advice;
- protect, enhance, and raise awareness of the protections available to UC claimants in Northern Ireland.

(Patrick and Simpson with UC:Us, 2020)

The research also points to an underlying need for more fundamental change to how social security is conceptualised, designed, and evaluated, in Northern Ireland and beyond.

The Northern Ireland Assembly has received a Ministerial commitment to 'look at co-design' of social security (Hargey, 2020) – however, at the time of writing this remains an aspiration. The COVID-19 pandemic may provide a partial explanation – as discussed, UC:Us have found that remote working makes collaboration more challenging. Yet the group has also found that remote collaboration can be facilitated in most cases, and has made considerable strides towards the co-production of a claimant's guide to Universal Credit with advice sector partners. A genuine commitment to co-production, whether by a researcher, funder, or policymaker, means a commitment to devoting the necessary time and money to the project.

There are particular opportunities for co-production in Northern Ireland, given that it is the only UK country where social security is fully devolved. Co-production in Northern Ireland thus has the potential to bring fresh ideas that the UK Government could subsequently adopt, as well as empowering claimants to share their experience and opinions (see Somerville, 2019), thus creating a stronger sense that social security is *their* service. Our conclusions about both the value and challenges of co-production are, of course, as valid for other parts of the UK as they are for Northern Ireland.

References

BBC (2021) Covid and hardship. BBC. 16 February. Available at: www. bbc.co.uk/programmes/m000sgm6

BBC Radio Ulster (2020) Evening extra. BBC. 14 August. Available at: www.bbc.co.uk/programmes/m000ln4d

Bennett, F. and Roberts, M. (2004) Participatory approaches to research on poverty. Joseph Rowntree Foundation. Available at: www.jrf.org.uk/report/participatory-approaches-research-poverty

Bennett, H. and Brunner, R. (2022) Nurturing the buffer zone: conducting collaborative action research in contemporary contexts. *Qualitative Research*, 22(1), 74–92.

Brewer, M. and Patrick, R. (2021) Pandemic pressures: why families on a low income are spending more during Covid-19. Resolution Foundation Briefing. Available at: www.resolutionfoundation.org/publications/pandemic-pressures/

Department for Communities (DfC) (2020) Universal Credit statistics – May 2020. Department for Communities. Available at: www.communities-ni.gov.uk/articles/universal-credit-statistics

Dougherty D.S. and Atkinson, J. (2006) Competing ethical communities and a researcher's dilemma: the case of a sexual harasser. *Qualitative Inquiry*, 12(2), 292–315.

Gaventa, J. and Cornwall, A. (2008) Power and knowledge, in P. Reason and H. Bradbury (eds) *The SAGE Handbook of Action Research* (2nd edition). London: SAGE.

Goldstraw, K., Herrington, T., Croft, T., Murrinas, D., Gratton, N. and Skelton, D. (2021) *Socially Distanced Activism: Voices of Lived Experience of Poverty During COVID-19*. Bristol: Policy Press.

Guillemin, M. and Gillam, L. (2004) Ethics, reflexivity, and 'ethically important moments' in research. *Qualitative Inquiry*, 10(2), 261–80.

Hargey, D. (2020) Response to AQO 29/17–22. NIA deb. 125(5), 42. 3 February.

Jailobaev, T., Jailobaeva, K., Baialieva, M., Baialieva, G. and Asilbekova, G. (2021) WhatsApp groups in social research: new opportunities for fieldwork communication and management. *Bulletin of Sociological Methodology*, 149(1), 60–82.

Jones, R.W. (2020) Universal Credit mum living without heating and cooker fighting for £20 lifeline. *Mirror*. 11 December. Available at: www.mirror.co.uk/news/uk-news/mum-plunged-debt-universal-credit-23149331

Oakley, A. (2016) Interviewing women again: power, time and the gift. *Sociology*, 50(1), 195–213.

Patrick, R. and Simpson, M. with UC:Us (2020) Universal Credit could be a lifeline in Northern Ireland, but it must be designed with people who use it. York: Joseph Rowntree Foundation.

Pybus, K., Wickham, S., Page, G., Power, M., Barr, B. and Patrick, R. (2021) 'How do I make something out of nothing?': Universal Credit, precarity and mental health. Covid Realities Rapid-Response Report. Available at: https://covidrealities.org/learnings/write-ups/universal-credit-precarity-and-mental-health

Sandhu, S. (2021) Universal Credit increase: 'I feel sick at the thought of losing the £20-a-week uplift in 6 months'. *iNews*. 3 March. Available at: https://inews.co.uk/news/politics/budget/universal-credit-increase-20-pound-a-week-uplift-end-after-6-months-2021-budget-896706

Scottish Government (nd) Social Security Experience Panels: publications. Edinburgh: Scottish Government. Available at: www.gov.scot/collections/social-security-experience-panels-publications/

Smith, L., Bratini, L., Chambers, D.A., Jensen, R.V. and Romero, L. (2010) Between idealism and reality: meeting the challenges of participatory action research. *Action Research*, 8(4), 407–25.

Smyth, C. (2020) Universal Credit: hundreds of tenants in debt due to admin error. *BBC News NI*. 15 August. Available at: www.bbc.co.uk/news/uk-northern-ireland-53785836

Somerville, S.A. (2019) SP Social Security Committee. Column 3. 31 January.

Summers, K., Scullion, L., Baumberg Geiger, B., Robertshaw, D., Edmiston, D., Gibbons, A., Karagiannaki, E., de Vries, R. and Ingold, J. (2021) Claimants' experiences of the social security system during the first wave of COVID-19. Project report. Welfare at a (Social) Distance.

Thomson, R. and Holland, J. (2010) Hindsight, foresight and insight: the challenges of longitudinal qualitative research. *International Journal of Social Research Methodology*, 6(3), 233–44.

UC:Us (2020) Our Policy changes: time to listen and learn. Available at: www.ucus.org.uk/recommendations. Belfast: UC:Us.

Whelan, J. (2021) *Welfare, Deservingness and the Logic of Poverty: Who Deserves?*. Newcastle: Cambridge Scholars Publishing.

Conclusion

*Rosalie Warnock, Kayleigh Garthwaite, Ruth Patrick,
Maddy Power, and Anna Tarrant*

Introduction

What all the chapters in this collection emphasise is that while the COVID-19 pandemic has been unprecedented, its impacts have been so severe because poverty, insecurity, and financial hardship were already factors of life for many families on a low income even before the first lockdown in the UK in March 2020. Not only has the COVID-19 pandemic exacerbated existing inequalities, but without radical, targeted policy intervention, families on a low income are likely to feel the heightened repercussions of the pandemic for years to come. As the chapters in this collection illustrate, people find themselves trapped in protracted states of precarious, low-paid, and temporary employment, reliant on inadequate social security payments for some or all of their income, and with spiralling debts. Yet despite rapidly changing national socio-economic conditions that are making adequately paid employment ever more challenging to secure, low-income families continue to be held responsible for their own poverty. Consequently, the complexities of the labour market and structure of the social security system operate to keep families in poverty rather than lifting them out of it as they should. The chapters here provide evidence that, despite central and devolved Governments implementing short-term measures to bolster some aspects of social security during the pandemic, the financial, practical, emotional, and social consequences of COVID-19 for low-income families have been acute.

In this brief concluding chapter, we draw out three key overarching themes across the chapters, with accompanying policy recommendations. Then, we reflect on the benefits of collaborative research on low-income family life, before finally offering suggestions for how this way of working could continue well beyond the pandemic, and why this matters.

Theme one: financial and employment precarity

An overriding finding across many of the chapters (see Chapters 1, 3, 5, 6, 9, and 12) was that pre-existing financial insecurity made dealing with the COVID-19 pandemic harder for many families, especially for those already living on low incomes (Hill and Webber, 2021). This was particularly the case for those with unstable, temporary, or otherwise precarious employment. Notably, our evidence for this comes both from longitudinal (pre-pandemic and post-March 2020) and rapid response projects, and is evidenced by quantitative, qualitative, and mixed methods research findings. Prior to the pandemic, fluctuations in earned income resulted in (sometimes wildly) inconsistent Universal Credit (UC) payments which made consistent household budgeting virtually impossible (for example, Griffiths et al, Chapter 3). The chapters also illustrate a variety of experiences of employment during the COVID-19 pandemic for families on a low income. Tarrant et al (Chapter 9) note that fathers with older children were more likely to be in stable employment than those with young children. While lower furlough or self-employment replacement pay, redundancy, and a loss of casual employment has made life even harder for some, Griffiths et al (Chapter 3) report that furlough actually provided welcome stability for others. As Chapters 2, 4, 7, and 9 all show, single parents have been more deeply affected by the pandemic. As discussed in Chapters 7 and 8, many single parents and primary carers in dual-parent households (both often women) shared fears that being long-term furloughed put them at greater risk of redundancy – which became a reality for some participants. Consequently, some were forced to give up paid employment, often with serious ramifications for their household finances. For some single parents in particular, changes to their own earnings have been accompanied by changes to their ex-partner's pandemic employment. Clery et al (Chapter 8) argue that for some this has had knock-on effects on child maintenance payments and therefore household finances.

Understandably, as seen in Chapters 1, 3, 4, 5, 7, 8, 9, 10, 11, and 12, financial precarity both pre- and during the COVID-19 pandemic has been, and continues to be, a cause of considerable anxiety and stress for both adults and children (Reeves et al, 2020; Pybus et al, 2021; Tarrant and Reader, 2021). Redundancy and a lack of employment opportunities, inadequate and conditional social security benefits, coupled with rising household costs and costs of living because of home working and learning (as shown by Chapters 2, 3, 8, 12, and 14), added to the stress and anxiety experienced by families on a low income during the pandemic. Chapters 2, 3, 6, 7, and 12, in particular, illustrate how this was heightened by difficulty obtaining or paying for resources that their children needed to access online learning, including Wi-Fi and technological devices. The result was digital exclusion. As discussed in Chapters 4, 12, and 14, this was also the case for adults without the skills, technology, or connectivity to access digital UC applications. As Chapters 9 and 10 show, in these situations, local services have been essential in enabling individuals and families to access technology and make online applications, in cases where the state has not provided this support. The wider impact of the social security system response will be explored below in Theme two.

Theme two: social security changes

As Chapters 3, 13, and 14 make clear, social security provision has proven inadequate to meet the rising costs incurred by families as a result of the pandemic (see also Brewer and Patrick, 2021). Crucially, there has been a distinct lack of policy responses targeted specifically at families on a low income, despite the multiple challenges they have faced. The household cap and two-child limit, implemented as austerity measures, have remained firmly in place. While the £20 uplift to UC has been welcome, Chapters 3, 4, 11, and 12 highlight how this has not always (or even often) made a decisive difference to the everyday hardship experienced by families with dependent children living in poverty. This is also because the uplift was not extended to households already at the UC cap, or to those still claiming legacy benefits. Therefore, as food and utility bills have risen (due to panic buying, food shortages, and the effects of Brexit), few have received financial support that adequately meets these additional costs of living (Brewer and Patrick, 2021). Two thirds of the chapters in this collection (Chapters 1, 3, 4, 6, 7, 9, 11, 12, and 14) therefore report that low-income families have relied on food banks and other sources of charitable provision during the pandemic; some using them for the first time, and others, using them more often than usual.

This is particularly the case for families who appear to have fallen through the net. Dickerson et al (Chapter 5) and Cameron at al. (Chapter 6) highlight how strict eligibility criteria restricted access to the Self-Employment Income Support Scheme (SEISS) and furlough pay for some. Tarrant et al (Chapter 9) further show how COVID-19 job losses have been particularly steep among young adults (and so too for young parents). However, as Webber and Hill (Chapter 1) and Robertshaw et al (Chapter 2) raise, young adults were also the most likely to be unaware of their rights to benefits and/or worried that claiming benefits would affect their own parents' income where they were living at home.

Theme three: (altered) support networks

Nearly all chapters reported on how the COVID-19 pandemic had altered formal and informal support networks and approaches. As Tarrant et al (Chapter 9) and Scullion et al (Chapter 10) illustrate, in many places, formal support services were initially scaled down and/or moved online to accommodate new social distancing measures, or sometimes disappeared completely. These two chapters remind us how crucial formal and community support networks are to low-income families managing work and caring responsibilities. The absence of familial support was keenly felt by many during the early stages of the pandemic, as lockdown isolated households from each other and restricted such family interdependencies (see, for example, Cameron et al, Chapter 6). Yet Chapters 1, 2, 4, 6, 8, 9, and 12 show that while family support networks may have become *harder* to access during the pandemic, they nevertheless remained an essential coping strategy for many. It is also important to recognise that not everyone has a familial network to draw on. Chapters 9 and 10 illustrate how formal support services – albeit in different guises under social distancing – remained vital for many who did not have strong kinship support during the pandemic (for example, some veterans and some young fathers who did not live with their children or own parents).

As discussed in Chapters 3, 4, 9, 10, 11, and 14, associated with this are the particular strains that the pandemic has put on relationships between both cohabiting partners and ex-partners as they try to balance work, money, and childcare. Comparing coupled and single parents, Griffiths et al (Chapter 3) show how fitting paid work around childcare and home-schooling has been increasingly difficult for most, but particularly so for single parents and cohabiting parents trying to balance shift work around each other. As Chapters 1, 6, 7, 8, and 11 emphasise, such difficulties – apparent pre-March 2020 but exacerbated by lockdown – also highlight the lack of flexible employment opportunities for those with childcare responsibilities. It is also important to acknowledge the gendered impacts of the pandemic here (see Chapters 1, 3, 7, 8, and 9) wherein the burden of childcare and wider caring responsibilities often fell disproportionately on mothers. This has only worsened since March 2020 as people's social worlds shrank further at the height of the pandemic (Clery et al, 2020; Local Government Association, 2020). Chapters 6, 7, 8, and 11 all discuss the particular difficulties faced by single parents who shouldered the burden of the pandemic alone. All chapters explain how the introduction of support bubbles helped to ease this sense of isolation, with an especially positive impact on single parents' mental health and wellbeing.

Policy recommendations

Each of the 14 chapters in this collection make their own detailed policy recommendations. Here, however, we offer a number of overarching recommendations which speak to the concerns raised in individual chapters. These centre around employment, social security, and increasing provision for support services.

Employment

Our collective findings illustrate the need for access to secure, well-paid employment opportunities – and more of them (see for example Cameron et al, Chapter 6; Tarrant et al, Chapter 9). The proliferation of temporary and zero-hours contracts, coupled with a national minimum wage well below the Minimum Income Standard (Davis et al, 2021) is forcing more families on low incomes into in-work poverty, exacerbating financial insecurity through fluctuating and unpredictable household incomes, and creating money-related anxiety and stress (see for example Scullion et al, Chapter 4). As we continue to grapple with the longer-term effects of the COVID-19 pandemic, Reader and Andersen (Chapter 7) call for specialist employment support to help those who have lost skills or confidence while furloughed, and/or who have been made redundant or have experienced long-term unemployment. Flexible working and the right to disconnect, as championed by the Labour Party in June 2021 (BBC, 2021) could better facilitate parents with caring responsibilities – and particularly single parents – to access high-quality, well-paid employment opportunities that match their skill set. As Chapters 3, 7, 8, and 9 argue, coupled with this is the need for more high-quality, flexible, accessible, and affordable childcare options, and shared parental leave entitlements that are available to all, regardless of employment status and gender of the parent.

Social security

Central and devolved Government initiatives during the COVID-19 pandemic have shown what effective social security support could look like – and we strongly urge that this learning is heeded going forwards. As nearly all chapters have shown, while a lifeline for many, COVID-19 social security measures (including the £20 uplift, furlough scheme, Self-Employment Income Support Scheme, and one-off Working Tax Credit bonus) did not reach enough people or go far enough. Additionally, there was a complete lack of policies directly targeted at supporting families with children living on a low income. Chapters 4, 5, and 7 call for specific policy measures to support families with children which respond to family size. Our collective evidence suggests that in the short term, the £20 uplift should be brought back (it ceased in September 2021) and extended to (those currently at the benefit cap and those still receiving legacy benefits), and the five-week wait, the benefit cap, and the two-child limit should all be scrapped. A real-terms increase to the level of Child Benefit is long overdue and should not be subject to the problems associated with means testing that can undermine Universal Credit. Longer-term, policy interventions must be designed to respond holistically and flexibly to family circumstances, recognising the complexity of interacting factors affecting families on a low income (for example, job security, housing security, health, and childcare needs) (see, for example, the discussion by Webber and Hill, Chapter 1). As Cloughton et al (Chapter 12) and Webber and Hill (Chapter 1) emphasise, this includes recognising and addressing the links between low income, financial insecurity, and mental ill health for both adults and children living in poverty.

Increasing provision for support services

The chapters in this collection clearly demonstrate the vital role of formal and informal support networks, on which families on a low income are often reliant to survive. There is a real need to commit to longer-term funding of non-kinship forms of formal (and) community support, alongside adequate social security provision. As Tarrant et al (Chapter 9) and Scullion et al (Chapter 10) emphasise, this is particularly important for those who may not have well-established kinship support networks. The availability of support also continues to be a 'postcode lottery', meaning access is currently determined by where someone lives. This is unlikely to be challenged by the shift of services to becoming 'digital by default', although attempts to address digital exclusion remain pertinent. There is a need to upskill and 'kit out' families on a low income to ensure they have the necessary digital literacy and infrastructure (technological devices and Wi-Fi) to access online social security portals (for example UC), online service delivery (for example counsellors or support workers), and for children to access online (see, for example, Tarrant et al, 2021). Finally, we must continue to reflect critically and unpack the Government's purported intention to 'build back better'; asking ourselves 'what is the policy direction we want to see?' – and calling for evidence-based change where we think it could be better. To truly build back better, we need to listen to and engage with the expertise that comes from – and can only come from – lived experience.

COVID-19 collaborations: working together to research family life on a low income

The findings set out in this book would not be so powerful if it were not for the fact that they are based on the experiences of over 4,000 families living on a low income across the UK. Our projects collectively combine mixed methods, including qualitative, quantitative, longitudinal, and rapid response investigations of the impacts of the COVID-19 pandemic as it has unfolded. They span three of the four devolved nations (England, Scotland, and Northern Ireland), enabling comparison of national social security contexts and COVID-19 responses, highlighting variation in experiences across the UK. Most importantly, this collection has only been possible because of the collective and collaborative work of the 14 projects, who came together at a time of international, national (and for many, personal) crisis. The projects were united by shared questions about the impacts of this particular historical moment and its implications for low-income families. We conclude with a brief reflection on the strengths of this collaborative approach, how it has enhanced our understanding of low-income family life during the COVID-19 pandemic, and offer suggestions to encourage future researchers to engage in collaborative work in the future.

Ultimately, the COVID-19 pandemic has encouraged us to make long overdue changes in academic practice and significantly change the way we work as social researchers. Working together has enabled a broader and richer understanding of the experiences of families living on a low income during the pandemic. Collaborating during the pandemic has meant that we are able to draw on each other's networks, knowledge, and skills to communicate our findings effectively and meaningfully and to a broader audience than we might have been able to individually. Flexibility, understanding, and regular communication have been key to ensuring the most meaningful collaborative approach possible. Our work has been achieved through developing a collaborative framework from the outset, exploring and forefronting the ethics of collaboration, and taking time to establish effective research relationships, while creating space for reflection and iteration of the collaborative approach. The solidarity and sense of community offered through the collective has been particularly welcomed by all as we navigated the difficulties brought about in the new social conditions produced by the pandemic. Working online has facilitated more frequent meetings, across a broader geographical reach, than if we were working together in person (Hacker et al, 2020).

There have been challenges in adopting this way of working – collaborating with various research teams both inside and outside of academia requires a serious amount of planning, consideration, negotiation, and above all, time. Important questions have arisen over data ownership, claims to intellectual property, outputs, and key messaging, all of which needed to be carefully considered on an ongoing basis. Deciding on the 'right' time to synthesise findings and agree on policy recommendations was also difficult and, following several discussions at our SIG meetings, emerged organically as we responded to parliamentary calls for evidence, and gave joint presentations. Being responsive to policy interests in this way enabled the identification of key themes and policy-relevant recommendations. Synthesis is both time- and resource-intensive (Davidson et al, 2019), as Urrieta and Noblit (2018: viii) capture effectively in their discussion of the challenges of synthesising findings across several research teams:

> Our colleagues went to work, and work it was, as synthesis is not all revelation. Rather it takes a dogged determination to search out all that can be found, to create decision rules about what to keep and what to set aside, to refine and reconceptualize what one is in fact addressing

and what one is not, to read deeply and repeatedly, and then try to figure out what all the studies say as a group, and ultimately what one as a researcher thinks they say about the area of focus ... Work, work, work. For all of us, though, all this work was worth it.

Going forward – and especially important in a post-pandemic context – we encourage researchers to seek opportunities to collaborate more, funders to support this work, and to create spaces to do so. The academy often prioritises and rewards competition and individual success. These ways of working are especially ill-suited to poverty research, which should be more firmly orientated towards substantive policy improvement and improved knowledge bases, drawing upon participant-led expertise rooted in lived experience, rather than being contingent on individual career development.

Finally, working collaboratively has had significant advantages in terms of communicating messages from a strong combined evidence base. In sharing our collaborative efforts with both the wider research community, as well as with practitioners, professionals, and those in positions of power, we hope to emphasise the possibilities, challenges, and ultimately importance of prioritising meaningful collaboration in researching poverty – especially important as we move towards a post-pandemic context in the UK.

References

BBC (2021) Give people the right to switch off after work – Labour. Available at: www.bbc.co.uk/news/uk-politics-57529702

Brewer, M. and Patrick, R. (2021, 11 January) Pandemic pressures: why families on a low income are spending more during COVID-19. Resolution Foundation. Available at: www.resolutionfoundation.org/app/uploads/2021/01/Pandemic-pressures.pdf

Clery, E., Dewar, L. and Papoutsaki, D. (2020) Caring without sharing: single parents' journey through the COVID-19 crisis. Interim Report. Gingerbread in partnership with the Institute for Employment Studies. 12 November. Available at: www.gingerbread.org.uk/wp-content/uploads/2020/11/Gingerbread-Caringwithoutsharing-v3.pdf

Davidson, E., Edwards, R., Jamieson, L. and Weller, S. (2019) Big data, qualitative style: a breadth-and-depth method for working with large amounts of secondary qualitative data. *Quality and Quantity*, 53(1), 363–76.

Davis, A., Hirsch, D., Padley, M., and Shepherd, C. (2021) A Minimum Income Standard for the United Kingdom in 2021. *Joseph Rowntree Foundation*. Available at: https://www.jrf.org.uk/file/58716/download?token=uXENQWP4&filetype=full-report

Hacker, J., vom Brocke, J., Handali, J., Otto, M. and Schneider, J. (2020) Virtually in this together: how web-conferencing systems enabled a new virtual togetherness during the COVID-19 crisis. *European Journal of Information Systems*, 29(5), 563–84.

Hill, K. and Webber, R. (2021) Staying afloat in a crisis: families on low incomes in the pandemic. Joseph Rowntree Foundation. Available at: www.jrf.org.uk/report/staying-afloat-crisis-families-low-incomes-pandemic

Local Government Association (2020) Loneliness, social isolation and COVID-19. 21 December. Available at: https://local.gov.uk/publications/loneliness-social-isolation-and-covid-19

Pybus, K., Wickham, S., Page, G., Power, M., Barr, B. and Patrick, R. (2021) 'How do I make something out of nothing?': Universal Credit, precarity and mental health. Available at: https://covidrealities.org/learnings/write-ups/universal-credit-precarity-and-mental-health

Reeves, A., Fransham, M., Stewart, K. and Patrick, R. (2020) Did the introduction of the benefit cap in Britain harm mental health? A natural experiment approach. LSE Centre for Analysis of Social Exclusion. CASE/221. Available at: https://sticerd.lse.ac.uk/dps/case/cp/casepaper221.pdf

Tarrant, A. and Reader, M. (2021) Mental health and the pandemic: why it is inaccurate to say fathers were largely unaffected. LSE British Politics and Policy blog. 18 August. Available at: https://blogs.lse.ac.uk/politicsandpolicy/parents-mental-health-covid19/

Tarrant, A., Ladlow, L. and Way, L. (2021) University of Lincoln – Written Evidence (YUN0013) Youth Unemployment Committee Inquiry. Available at: https://committees.parliament.uk/writtenevidence/35464/pdf/

Urrieta Jr, L. and Noblit, G.W. (eds) (2018) *Cultural Constructions of Identity: Meta-Ethnography and Theory*. Oxford: Oxford University Press.

Afterword

It's a strange sensation reading about yourself. It's even stranger reading about yourself in a category you'd rather not be in. But the strangest thing, by far, is reading about yourself through the eyes of people like you.

We get used to how life on a low income is seen on political and popular levels. It's a perception twisted into such negative stereotypes and anti-welfare rhetoric, that the outside observer is left completely desensitised. How we are viewed is so often how we are treated. With every interaction with the social security system, every fight to feed and clothe our families, we are reminded of our 'failure' and our 'choice', systematically gaslit by the very structure intended to help us. We live with a description of our life that bears little resemblance to living it.

People make assumptions. People distance themselves from experiences they are afraid of. People are influenced by dominant philosophies that become embedded in politics, the media, and popular culture. And sometimes it takes a moment, a defining point in our collective history, for the truth to break through. For the smoke and mirrors to shift, a crack appearing – a foothold in the fight for change.

Now is that time, in the quiet after.

Research over the last 18 months showed very quickly that low-income families are one of the groups most impacted by the pandemic, and confidently predicts that the effects of COVID-19 will continue to exacerbate inequalities for the long term. It's safe to assume that the aftershocks of the pandemic will not only hit families on a low income harder, but make it more difficult for them to recover, with the precarity aggravated by the pandemic leaving them far less able to weather future challenges, such as those brought about by Brexit (for example, the fuel panic, gas price increases) and political decisions (for example, the loss of the £20 uplift, and increased National Insurance tax).

The research shared here is a first step, a new way of working collaboratively and inclusively, both among research teams and across institutions, fully integrated with the voices of lived experience. Working together, research can keep highlighting the new and ongoing inequalities brought about by the pandemic. It can gain a greater understanding of how the current social security system needs changing, and can provide practical changes and simple, actionable improvements to policy. Collaborative research can become a platform for more fundamental reform.

As conversations with those of us using the social security system confirms, policies and systems not grounded in research are usually flawed and unhelpful, and at their worst ... harmful, inaccessible, and discriminatory.

Research can offer policymakers holistic interventions and focused solutions, which challenge their own assumptions and privilege. Research can address the gap between rhetoric and reality, it can shine a spotlight on the inequalities and reveal that we're clearly not 'all in this together', and prevent families on low incomes from being ignored. Targeted policy intervention is vital to inform and reduce the long-term repercussions of COVID-19 on low-income families.

It is the double-bind of the most marginalised in our society – that their position makes it so very hard to challenge the prejudice that keeps them there. So many of us who find ourselves depending on a system in which we have no agency, urgently want to offer solutions so that things might get better for ourselves and for others.

Educational institutions, research bodies, and action groups have power, and access. But they don't need to speak for us. Instead, they can share their power – build a bridge that uplifts and supports the human faces and voices with the lived experience of the realities of poverty.

In sharing its power, research can amplify marginalised voices. It can strive to represent all the intersectional identities and varied circumstances faced by families on low incomes. And it can empower the traditionally disempowered.

Including people with direct experience in research, not only as data sources, but also as collaborators, is the only way to uncover a holistic picture of families and their circumstances living on a low income. It gives an invaluable insider perspective that is unattainable for most researchers held back by their own – most likely compassionate – assumptions and preconceptions. If we want to create a social security system that truly works for the people who experience it, it is paramount to listen to their voices.

People with direct experience bring a deeper and richer understanding to research. They add the humanity and the story to black-and-white data.

Sharing the power and welcoming people with lived experience to the conversation, where they are not only listened to but are elevated to the position of expert, can only benefit the joint goals of informing policy and deepening the understanding of poverty.

COVID-19 will live on as a defining moment in our history. So much of it will be remembered with regret and despair, at the mistakes that were made, and the lives it cost. But there will be the research, that sought to change policy, that fought for a fairer system. And most importantly, there will be the voices, the real-life stories of living through a pandemic despite all the odds.

Cat Fortey, participant in Covid Realities, October 2021

Index

References to figures and photographs appear in *italic* type;
those in **bold** type refer to tables. References to endnotes show
both the page number and the note number (54n6).

A

accessibility 198–200
alcohol misuse 152
Alternative Payment Arrangement
    (APA) 62
Armed Force Bill (2012) 150
Armitage, R. 37
arts-based research 205–7
Atkinson, J. 213, 214
austerity 4–5, 15

B

Banks, J. 113
basic needs 113
BBC 114, 222
Beggs Weber, J. 135
benefit cap 169, 220
    families with children 46, 54n6
    larger families on low income 107,
        111–12, 113, 114, 116, 117–18
    lone parents 132
Benefit Changes and Large Families
    research project 107
benefit claims **95–6**
benefit fraud 47–8
Bennett, F. 30, 56, 211, 212, 214
Benzeval, M. 107, 108
Beresford, P. 194, 200, 201
Best Start Grant 184
Bingham, D.D. 82
Birch, M. 181
Blanden, J. 113
Boardman, B. 66
Borderline Personality Disorder 65, 68
Born in Bradford COVID-19 research
    programme 73–85
    findings 76–82
    methods reflection 82–3
    policy and practice implications 83–5
    timelines **75**
Bradshaw, J. 46, 106
Braun, V. 82
Brawner, J. 83
Brewer, M. 6, 15, 20, 45, 47, 54, 113,
    167, 173, 174, 220
Brien, S. 166
British Academy 186
British Medical Journal (BMJ) 1
Brunner, R. 211, 214

budgeting 166–8
Burgess, A. 137
Burrell, S. 1

C

Cameron, C. 91, 98
capacity building 200
Caplovitz, D. 66
Caraher, K. 32
care, feminist ethics of 180
Carer's Allowance 49
Caring without Sharing research
    project 122–33
    case study 129–30
    findings 123–9
    policy implications 130–3
Carnegie UK 187
cash benefits for children 46–7
Centre for Social Justice 150
Cheetham, M. 34
Cheng, Z. 37
Child Benefit 26, 49, 54, 168
    conditionality 46
    need to increase 195, 196, 222
    value 5, 44
child poverty xix, 5, 15, 46
    larger families on low income 106
    London case study 88, 89
    Scotland 179–80, 185
Child Poverty Action Group (CPAG) xx,
    2, 5, 6, 23, 125, 165
childcare 8, 221, 222
    larger families on low income 109
    lone parents 20, 132
    young fathers 139–40, 146
    see also Caring without Sharing
        research project
children
    cash benefits 46–7
    disability 5
    mental health 79–81, 82, 84
    physical activity 81–2
Citizens Advice 37
Clery, E. 129, 221
co-production 194, 200–1
collaboration 1, 223–5
    see also co-production; Covid Realities
        research project; participatory research
Collard, S. 103, 104
Cominetti, N. 111

Commission on Social Security 193–202
  findings 195–200
  methodological reflections 200–2
Community Activist Advisory Group
  (CAAG) 181–2
community participation 140–1
community support 143–5
comorbidity 152
conditionality 154, 156–7, 159
Cooper, K. 47, 106
Coram Family and Childcare Trust 132
Corlett, A. 15
Cornwall, A. 211
Coronavirus Job Retention Scheme 20,
  32–3, 40n6
cost of living *see* living costs
Cover, R. 37
"*Covid-19 and families on low income:
  Researching together*" collective 2–4
COVID-19 government response **75**
Covid Realities research project xx, 2–4,
  149, 157, 165–6, 223–5
Crossley, T.F. 108, 109
Cundy, J. 146
Curchin, K. 30, 149, 152, 153, 154, 159

D

Dale, A. 103
Daly, M. 157
Davidson, E. 224
Davidson, G. 185
Davies, L. 141
Davies, S. 66
Davis, A. 222
debt repayments 168–9
Department for Communities
  (DfC) 204, 210
Department of Work and Pensions (DWP)
  benefit cap 118
  positive experiences with 154
  poverty 15, 46
  Universal Credit (UC) 21, 31–2, 51, 64,
    132, 165
depression 63, 78, 85n2, 125, 151, 170
Dermott, E. 137
Dickerson, J. 76, 78, 83
Dickson-Swift, V. 40
digital exclusion 34, 219, 223
  Commission on Social Security 198, 199
  Following Young Fathers Further
    (FYFF) 145
  Get Heard Scotland (GHS) 181,
    187–8, 190
  UC:Us 212
digitalisation 33–4, 36
disability 5, 166, 200–1
disability studies 180
Discretionary Housing Payment 65
domestic abuse 170–1, 173, 174

Dougherty, D.S. 213, 214
Duncan, S. 135
Dwyer, P. 30, 56, 57, 154, 156, 159

E

East End *see* London case study
Easy Read 198
"Eat Out to Help Out" 169
Edmiston, D. 30, 34
Education Endowment Foundation 165
Edwards, Z. 15, 21, 23
Ekpanyaskul, C. 38
electricity 21, 48, 65–6, 78, 188
employer flexibility 125–6
employment 18–20, 26, 221–2
  larger families on low income 108–12
  Tower Hamlets and Newham 88–9,
    93–4, 103
employment precarity 6, 18, 20, 218–19
  low income families 109
  young fathers 139–40
  see also job insecurity
employment security 77
Employment Support Allowance
  (ESA) 40–1n6, 152, 153, 156, 158,
    166, 209
employment support schemes 132
English Government COVID-19
  response **75**
Eshragi, A. 37
ethnic diversity 73, 76
  Tower Hamlets and Newham **90**, **91**
  see also Pakistani heritage families
European Commission 103
Experts by Experience 194, 195, 197, 198,
  201, 205
Exploring Universal Credit in Salford
  project 56–68
  experiences during COVID-19 64–8
  policy implications 68
  pre-COVID-19 experiences 58–64
  project overview and method 57–8
  research participants **59–60**

F

families 149–50
families on low income 5–8, 220, 227
  Born in Bradford COVID-19 research
    programme 76–8
  Get Heard Scotland (GHS) 179–90
    analysis 182–3
    families' experiences of social
      security 184–8
    methodological reflections 180–2
    policy implications 189–90
    research implications 189
  larger families 106–18
    basic needs 113
    case study 115–17

definition 118n3
employment 108–12
implications 117–18
mental health 113–15
methodological approach 107
participatory research 165–75
  case study 171–3
  implications for policy 173–5
  key themes 166–71
role of financial circumstances 15–27
  case studies 23–5
  financial situation over four
    interviews 19
  key findings 17–23
  research method 16–17
  see also London case study
family circumstances 152
family support 220–1
  Get Heard Scotland (GHS) 186, 187
  London case study 103
  lone parents 130
  military veterans 157, 159
  Salford case study 66–7
  young fathers 140–1
fathers 219
  see also Following Young Fathers Further
    (FYFF)
Fawcett Society 125
Fear, N.T. 152
feminist ethics of care 180
fieldwork 1, 3
  social and temporal disruption 36–40
financial adequacy 61–2, 65
financial circumstances 15–27
  case studies 23–5
  financial situation over four
    interviews 19
  key findings 17–23
  research method 16–17
financial insecurity 76–8, 83, 85n1
financial instability 211
financial precarity 5–6, 218–19
financial stability 65–6
flexible working 131, 146, 222
Flowerdew, J. 57
Following Young Fathers Further
    (FYFF) 135–46
  formal support services 141–3
  case study 143–5
  implications for policy and
    practice 145–6
  trajectories of young fathers 137–41
food banks xix, 6, 17, 48, 168, 172–3, 220
  larger families on low income 113
  London case study 97
  Salford case study 56, 62
  UC:Us 208
food costs 21–2, 113
food insecurity 6, 77

London case study 92, 97
food shortages 6
formal support 7, 22–3, 27, 220, 223
  Borderline Personality Disorder 68
  mental health 186–7
  military veterans 149
  Universal Credit (UC) claimants 34–6
  young fathers 136, 141–5
Fossey, M. 150
Fraley, D. 206
free school meals 21–2, 116, 196, 207
free-text responses 82–3
furlough 219, 220
  Born in Bradford COVID-19 research
    programme 77
  by family type 112
  larger families on low income 109, 111–12
  young fathers 139, 144
furlough recipients 38
furlough scheme 20, 32–3, 83, 108

G

Gardiner, L. 173
Garnham, A. 5, 6, 196
Gaventa, J. 211
Geiger, B.B. 31, 32
gender 6, 67, 221
General Health Questionnaire
    (GHQ-12) 114, 115
Get Heard Scotland (GHS) 179–90
  analysis 182–3
  families' experiences of social
    security 184–8
  methodological reflections 180–2
  policy implications 189–90
  research implications 189
Gibbons, A. 56
Gibson, L.Y. 83
Gillam, L. 213, 214
Gingerbread 126
Goldman, R. 137
Griffiths, R. 7, 44, 57
Guillemin, M. 213, 214

H

Hacker, J. 224
Hadley, A. 135
Hakitova, M. 171
Hall, S.-M. 136
Halliday, A. 180
Halpin, S. 67
Hamnett, C. 4
Handscomb, K. 45, 54
Hansard HC Deb. 196
Hargey, D. 215
health 62–4
  see also mental health; physical health
health problems 98
health support 22–3

heating 62, 167, 170, 174, 207, 210
Hickman, P. 17
high-income families *see* London case
  study 114, 115
Hill, J. 106
Hill, K. 5, 16, 21, 22, 23, 26, 218
Hills, J. 47, 117
Hirsch, D. 15, 118
Holland, J. 211
Holt-Lunstad, J. 37
home schooling 6, 21, 37, 39–40, 165,
  174, 221
  Bradford case study 80
  by family type *111*
  larger families on low income 109
  Salford case study 66, 67
  see also remote learning
home working 109, *110*, 126–8, 131
  see also remote working
Hood, A. 44
household costs 113
household income 91, **92**
housing 97–8, *99*–**100**
Howlett, M. 1, 38
Hynes, C. 150

I

illness *see* health problems; mental health;
  physical health
in-work poverty 5, 15, 62, 222
inclusion 198–200
income 89, 98
income insecurity 22
income stability 18–20, 26
inequalities 4–5
iNews 114
informal support 8, 22, 26, 220–1, 223
  London case study 98, 103–4
  lone parents 130
  mental health 187
  military veterans 149, 157–9, 159–60
  Salford case study 64, 65, 66–7
  Universal Credit (UC) claimants 34–6
  young fathers 136, 140–1
  see also family support; peer support
Ingold, J. 33
Innes, D. 5
Institute for Fiscal Studies (IFS) 46–7, 165
internet access 187–8
  see also digital exclusion
Inverclyde 179
Iversen, A.C. 152

J

Jahoda, M. 37
Jailobaev, T. 213
Jensen, T. 4, 117
job insecurity 22, 128–9, 144
  see also employment precarity

job security 26
  see also employment
Jobseeker's Allowance 184
Johnson, B. 1, 7
Johnson, S. 150
Jones, E. 152
Jones, K. 56
Joseph Rowntree Foundation (JRF) 4, 5,
  15, 16, 185, 205
Joyce, R. 47
Judge, L. 165
justice 180

K

Kelly, G. 157
key workers 109, *110*

L

labour market 5
Labour Party 222
larger families on low income 106–18
  basic needs 113
  case study 115–17
  definition 118n3
  employment 108–12
  implications 117–18
  mental health 113–15
  methodological approach 107
Lau Clayton, C. 138
Lees, T. 7
legacy benefits 21, 38, 40–1n6
life expectancy 88
living costs 6, 21–2, 220
  see also food costs
lockdown
  Bradford case study 84
  costs 167
  and family support 220–1
  larger families on low income 114
  London case study 89
  low income families 169–70, 174
  and mental health 186
  single parents 124, 125
  social and temporal disruption 36, 37
  and support networks 35
  young fathers 137–8, 146
Lockyer, B. 79, 82, 83
London case study 88–104
  characteristics of Tower Hamlets and
    Newham 88–9
  ethnic diversity **90, 91**
  families 89–91
  findings 91–103
  policy implications 103–4
  survey participants 91
lone parents (single parents) 23, 24, 172,
  219, 221, 222
  Caring without Sharing research
    project 122–33

case study 129–30
  findings 123–9
  policy implications 130–3
child maintenance payments 171
childcare 20
  London case study 98, 101
  Salford case study 62–3
  UC:Us 207–8
long-term planning v. urgent action 196–8
low income families 5–8, 220, 227
  Born in Bradford COVID-19 research
    programme 76–8
  Get Heard Scotland (GHS) 179–90
    analysis 182–3
    families' experiences of social
      security 184–8
    methodological reflections 180–2
    policy implications 189–90
    research implications 189
  larger families 106–18
    basic needs 113
    case study 115–17
    definition 118n3
    employment 108–12
    implications 117–18
    mental health 113–15
    methodological approach 107
  participatory research 165–75
    case study 171–3
    implications for policy 173–5
    key themes 166–71
  role of financial circumstances 15–27
    case studies 23–5
    financial situation over four
      interviews 19
    key findings 17–23
    research method 16–17
    see also London case study

M

MacDonald, R. 139
Mackley, A. 174
MacLeod, M. 184
Maddison, F. 184
Main, G. 46
Marin, L. 37
Markham, A.N. 3
Marmot, M. 73, 82, 83, 103, 165, 170
Marra, A. 39
McDowell, L. 139
McEachan, R.R. 74
McEachern, M. 56
McLeod, J. 17
McNeil, C. 4, 5, 15
Meers, J. 30
mental health 49
  Born in Bradford COVID-19 research
    programme 78–81, 82, 83–4
  Commission on Social Security 199

Get Heard Scotland (GHS) 185–7,
  190
  impact of home working on 38
  impact of lockdown on 50
  larger families on low income 113–15,
    117
  low income families 170–1
  military veterans 149, 150, 151–2,
    154, 155–6
  Salford case study 63, 65, 67–8
  single parents 125
  support services 22–3
mental health service users/survivors 201
Middleton, S. 17
military veterans 149–60
  experiences of COVID-19 benefits
    system 153–7
  peer support 157–9
  policy implications 159–60
  project background and methods 150–2
Millar, J. 20, 30, 56
Miller, H. 206
Miller, T. 137, 181
Mitchell, W.J.T. 37
Murphy, D. 152

N

NatCen 170
National Health Service (NHS) 22–3
national minimum wage (NMW) xx
Neale, B. 17, 25, 26, 57, 135, 136, 137,
  141, 146
Nellums, L. 37
"New-Style" benefits claimants 38, 41n6
Newham
  benefit claims **96**
  characteristics 88–9
  employment **94**
  ethnic diversity **90, 91**
  families in 89–91
  findings 91–103
  food bank use **97**
  household income **92**
  housing **100**
  policy implications 103–4
  relationship quality **100**
  survey participants 91
Noblit, G.W. 224–5
Nolan, R. 165, 173
Norman, J. 165
North East Young Dads and Lads
  (NEYDL) 143–5
Northern Ireland
  UC:Us 204–15
    implications for the future 211–14
    main findings 207–11
    methodological reflections 211–14
    research approach 205–7
Northern Ireland Assembly 215

O

Oakley, A. 211
Office for Budget Responsibility xix
Office for National Statistics
    (ONS) 126, 165
Office for Veterans' Affairs (OVA)
    150
Ofsted 132
Organisation for Economic Co-operation
    and Development (OECD) 103
Orton, M. 194, 196

P

Padungtod, C. 38
Page, G. 6, 174
Pakistani heritage families 76–7
Pakistani heritage mothers 78
Pakistani heritage parents 81
Paremoer, L. 1
part-time work 54, 108, 112, 130,
    131
participatory research
  Commission on Social Security
    193–202
    findings 195–200
    methodological reflections 200–2
  low income families 165–75
    case study 171–3
    implications for the future 173–5
    key themes 166–71
  UC:Us 204–15
    implications for the future 214–15
    main findings 207–11
    methodological reflections 211–14
    research approach 205–7
Pascoe Leahy, C. 183
Patrick, R. 6, 7, 15, 30, 57, 113, 167, 174,
    184, 214, 220
peer support 157–9, 159–60, 213
Personal Independence Payment
    (PIP) 152, 153
personal tax allowance xx
physical activity 81–2
physical health 22–3, 38, 66, 67, 199
physical impairment 150
Pierce, M. 74
policy recommendations 221–3
poverty 4, 5, 106, 167–8, 169, 171
  see also child poverty
Poverty Alliance 179
poverty premium 66
Power, K. 67
Power, M. 1, 6, 7
precarity 5–6, 146
  see also employment precarity;
    financial precarity
Public Health England (PHE) 165
Pybus, K. 171, 219

R

Rahman, F. 165
Rashford, M. 196
Reader, M. 219
Reeves, A. 219
relationship circumstances 152
relationship quality **100**
remote learning 138
  see also home schooling
remote working 142, 145
  see also home working
Renfrewshire 179, 180
research approaches 1, 3–4
  social and temporal disruption
    36–40
Resolution Foundation 47
Reuter, E. 32
Richmond upon Thames 89
Roberts, E. 150
Roberts, M. 212
Royal College of Psychiatrists 170
Ruxton, S. 1

S

safeguarding 181–2
salaries 89
  see also income
Salford case study 56–68
  experiences during COVID-19 64–8
  policy implications 68
  pre-COVID-19 experiences 58–64
  project overview and method 57–8
  research participants **59–60**
Salford City Partnership 56
Sanctions, Support and Leavers project
    (SSSL)
  background, methods and
    participants 150–2
  experiences of COVID-19 benefits
    system 153–7
  peer support 157–9
  policy implications 159–60
Save the Children 184
Scholz, F. 33
schools 141
Scotland
  Get Heard Scotland (GHS) 179–90
    analysis 182–3
    families' experiences of social
      security 184–8
    methodological reflections 180–2
    policy implications 189–90
    research implications 189
  social security experience panels 205
Scottish Child Payment 184, 185
Scottish Index of Multiple Deprivation
    (SIMD) 179
Scottish Welfare Fund (SWF) 184–5

Scullion, L. 30, 56, 57, 149, 152, 153, 154, 159
self-employment 32, 38, 77, 83, 207
Self-Employment Income Support Scheme (SEISS) 40n6, 101–2, 220
Self-Isolation Support Grant 184
Shelter 44
Simpson, M. 184, 214
single parents see lone parents (single parents)
Sivasubramanian, R. 82
Smith, L. 214
Smith, N. 17
social disruption 36–40
social distancing 35, 36, 37, 113–14
social isolation 36–7, 67–8, 127, 157, 200–1
social media 167
social security 222–3
  access to 30–40
    findings 31–4
    formal and informal support 34–6
    research method 36–40
  Commission on Social Security 193–202
    findings 195–200
    methodological reflections 200–2
  Get Heard Scotland (GHS) 184–8, 189
  London case study 92
  low income families 168–9, 175
  military veterans 149–60
    experiences of COVID-19 benefits system 153–7
    peer support 157–9
    policy implications 159–60
    project background and methods 150–2
  see also Child Benefit; Employment Support Allowance (ESA); Job seeker's Allowance; Universal Credit (UC); Working Taxy Credit (WTC)
social security changes/reforms 6–7, 30, 220
Social Security (Coronavirus) (Further Measures) Regulations 2020 154
social security cuts 106
social security experience panels 205
social security spending xix
social security support 21, 26–7
social security system 6, 136, 171, 173
social support 136
Stewart, K. 106
stigma
  full-time carers 197
  mental health 187
  poverty 168, 169, 174
  Universal Credit (UC) 32, 210, 211
  young fathers 135
Stone, J. 15
suicide 63–4

Summers, K. 7, 30, 32, 34, 58, 61, 68, 211
Sunak, R. 45
support bubbles 125, 221
support networks 7–8, 22–3, 26, 27, 220–1, 223
  London case study 98–101, 103–4
  mental health 186–7
  military veterans 149
  Salford case study 66–7
  young fathers 136, 146
  see also community support; family support; formal support; informal support; peer support
Sweden 136
synthesis 224–5

T
Tarrant, A. 7, 137, 138, 146, 186
television 167
temporal disruption 36–40
Thoits, P. 174
Thomas, M. 150
Thompson, R. 17
Thomson, R. 211
Timewise 129, 131
Tower Hamlets
  benefit claims 95
  characteristics 88–9
  employment 93
  ethnic diversity 90, 91
  families in 89–91
  findings 91–103
  food bank use 97
  household income 92
  housing 99
  policy implications 103–4
  relationship quality 100
  survey participants 91
Trades Union Congress (TUC) 173
Trussell Trust 6, 168
Trust for London 88, 89, 194
Tucker, J. 46
two-child limit 46–7, 48, 220
  larger families on low income 107, 112, 113, 114, 115, 117, 118
  Salford case study 62
Tyler, I. 4, 117

U
UC:Us 204–15
  implications for the future 214–15
  main findings 207–11
  methodological reflections 211–14
  research approach 205–7
Understanding Society survey 107, 113
unemployment 128–9, 130–1
  see also employment
UNICIF UK 187

Universal Credit (UC) 4–5, 44–54, 219,
    220, 222
£20 uplift xx, 7, 21, 26–7, 45–6, 47,
    49–50, 64, 65–6, 169, 171, 174, 196
application process 31–4
case studies 47–53
cash benefits for children 46–7
and childcare costs 132
debt deductions 168–9
and digital exclusion 188
Exploring Universal Credit in Salford
    project 56–68
    experiences during COVID-19 64–8
    policy implications 68
    pre-COVID-19 experiences 58–64
    project overview and method 57–8
    research participants **59–60**
formal and informal support 34–6
larger families on low income 112
London case study 92
military veterans 152, 153, 156
number of claimants 165
payment levels 166
Scotland 184
single parents 130
UC:Us 204–15
    implications for the future 214–15
    main findings 207–11
    methodological reflections 211–14
    research approach 205–7
urgent action v. long-term planning 196–8
Urrieta Jr, L. 224–5

V

Van Voorhees, E.E. 152

W

Warren, J. 150

Waters, T. 44, 47
Waugh, P. 7
Webber, R. 5, 16, 23, 218
Welfare at a (Social) Distance 30–40
    findings 31–4
    formal and informal support 34–6
    research method 36–40
welfare reforms 4–5
    see also social security changes/reforms
wellbeing 62–4, 67, 186
Wenham, C. 1
WhatsApp 84, 212, 213
Whelan, J. 211
Whiteford, P. 20
Whitham, G. 184
Williams, S.N. 27
work coaches 132, 154–5, 156, 159
Work and Pensions Committee
    (WPC) 32, 153
work stability 18–20
    see also employment
working hours 108–9, 111–12, 117,
    125–6
    see also flexible working; part-time work
Working Tax Credit (WTC) 45, 46, 64,
    92, 169, 207–8
World Health Organization (WHO) 185
Wright, S. 30, 56, 57, 156, 159

X

Xu, X. 113

Y

Young, D. 30, 34
young adults 20, 21, 220
young fathers see Following Young Fathers
    Further (FYFF)
younger workers 108